Immigration and Race Relations

Immigration and Race Relations

Sociological Theory and John Rex

Edited by
Tahir Abbas
Frank Reeves

I.B. TAURIS
LONDON · NEW YORK

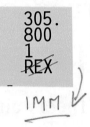
Published in 2007 by I.B.Tauris & Co Ltd
6 Salem Road, London W2 4BU
175 Fifth Avenue, New York NY 10010
www.ibtauris.com

In the United States of America and Canada distributed by
Palgrave Macmillan a division of St. Martin's Press
175 Fifth Avenue, New York NY 10010

ISBN : 978 1 84511 383 4

A full CIP record for this book is available from the British Library
A full CIP record for this book is available from the Library of Congress

Library of Congress Catalog Card Number : available

Printed and bound in India by Replika Press Pvt Ltd, camera-ready
copy edited and supplied by the authors

Contents

List of Contributors   vii

Acknowledgements   ix

Introduction   xi

Part I   John Rex's Life, Ideas and Contribution to Sociology

1   The Place of Theory: John Rex's Contribution to the
    Sociological Study of Ethnicity and 'Race'   3
    RICHARD JENKINS

2   John Rex: Some Reflections   13
    KAMPTA KARRAN

3   Race, Class and Ethnicity: A Mexican Perspective on the
    Sociology of John Rex   31
    LAURA VELASCO AND OSCAR CONTRERAS

Part II   Key Problems in Sociological Theory: Exploring the
               Implications of John Rex's Neo-Weberianism

4   The Place of Values in the Study of Ethnicity and 'Race':
    Reflections on the Contribution of John Rex   47
    MARTIN BULMER

5 The Long March with a Key Problem: Can Explanation and
Understanding Be Linked? 61
MARGARET S. ARCHER

Part III Commemorating John Rex's Contribution to Social
Policy: Immigration and Racial Inequality

6 Child Deprivation: Minorities Ten Years On 79
ROBERT MOORE

7 The Politicisation of Immigration 99
TOMAS HAMMAR

8 'Race Relations': The Problem with the Wrong Name 111
STEPHEN STEINBERG

Part IV Race Relations in the City: Revisiting John Rex's Local
Studies of Race Relations in Birmingham

9 Sparkbrook, Housing Classes & the Market Situation: Forty
Years On 121
TAHIR ABBAS

10 Exposing the Urban Systems Driving Ethnic Integration and
Conflict: Our Debt to John Rex 135
FRANK REEVES

11 Race and Education in Birmingham: Then and Now 159
SALLY TOMLINSON

Notes 175

References 179

Index 191

Contributors

Tahir Abbas. Reader in Sociology and Director of the Centre for the Study of Ethnicity and Culture, University of Birmingham.

Margaret S. Archer. Professor of Sociology, University of Warwick.

Martin Bulmer. Professor of Sociology, Department of Sociology, University of Surrey.

Oscar Contreras. Professor-Researcher, Industrial Relations Program, El Colegio de Sonora, Hermosillo, Sonora, Mexico.

Tomas Hammar. Professor Emeritus, Centre for Research in International Migration and Ethnic Relations (CEIFO), University of Stockholm.

Richard Jenkins. Professor of Sociology and Head of Department, University of Sheffield.

Kampta Karran. Postgraduate Research Fellow, University of Warwick.

Robert Moore. Professor Emeritus, University of Liverpool.

Frank Reeves. Director of Race Equality West Midlands and Visiting Professor at the Centre for the Study of Ethnicity and Culture, University of Birmingham.

Stephen Steinberg. Professor of Urban Studies at Queens College and Graduate Centre, City University of New York.

Sally Tomlinson. Professor Emeritus, University of Oxford.

Laura Velasco. Professor-Researcher, Department of Cultural Studies, El Colegio de la Frontera Norte, Tijuana, Baja California, Mexico.

Acknowledgements

We would like thank John Rex for initially inspiring us to prepare this *festschrift*, celebrating over fifty years of his professional life as a sociologist. We have both benefited from being taught by or working closely with this eminent figure, and we believed it important to provide a useful reminder to the world of sociology the immense contribution John Rex has made and continues to make to the discipline and to the field of 'race', ethnicity and multiculturalism.

We are especially thankful to the contributors who provided chapters worthy of this collection, and their patience in the witnessing the publication come to fruition.

We would also like to thank Liz Friend-Smith, Steven (Musa) Woodward Furber and Nicola Denny for helping to make real the opportunity to publish this volume.

T A and F W R
Birmingham, UK
23 March 2007

Introduction

FRANK REEVES AND TAHIR ABBAS

This important collection honours the achievements of John Rex, undoubt-edly one of the most distinguished living sociologists in the world. Part I deals with the life and work of John Rex. First, Richard Jenkins provides a warm and readable appreciation of John Rex's theoretical contribution to the sociological study of ethnicity and race relations, by extracting and analysing key positions and arguments from his major published works, particularly *Key Problems of Sociological Theory*, *Social Conflict*, and *Race, Community and Conflict*. Richard remarks that if *Key Problems* was the first British social theory, then *Race, Community and Conflict* was among the first properly-theorised works of empirical sociology in Britain. Far from anodyne in its approach, the chapter tackles the strengths, limitations and weaknesses of Rex's theories, reviewing the criticisms of his Weberian con-cept of social class and its role in relation to ethnic collectivity as well as the accusations that his work supported the status quo by downplaying or ignoring the importance of racism and the exercise of power by majority groups. Richard makes its very clear that a central plan of Rex's sociology is the role given to social conflict. Rex sees conflict, diversity and competi-tive politics as a fundamental ingredient of normal social life, not so much disrupting it, as helping to provide collectivities with their character and shape. Points of conflict reveal the uneven distribution of power and the vulnerability of society to challenge 'from below'.

Kampta Karran's chapter consists of a verbatim interview with John himself, first persuading him to recall his upbringing and politicisation in South Africa in the period immediately after the Second Word War and then to explain his move to England. In England, he joined the extra-mural department at the University of Leeds, teaching sociology, social history and philosophy to working-class people and arranging meetings for some of the future African leaders. Later, while at Leeds, he wrote his first book, *Key Problems of Sociological Theory* and an important article for the *British Journal of Sociology* on the plural society in sociological theory. In 1962, John moved to Birmingham and began to study its inner city race relations, culminating in Rex and Moore's seminal work, *Race, Community and Conflict*. Kampta, being from Guyana, questions John very closely as to whether at that time or later he had detected any emergent conflict between the Asian and black Caribbean communities of Birmingham, an interesting and prescient line of questioning given the subsequent inter-ethnic conflict in Autumn 2005 in Birmingham Lozells. The discussion then switches to what Kampta calls the racialisation versus race relations dilemma. John makes it very clear that he regards conflict as being material conflict about jobs, housing, etc., rationalised as racist by the powerful, and that he was amazed when Robert Miles suggested that he (John) believed the presenting problems should be conceptualised in terms of 'race'. Kampta asks John about the efforts of conceiving the relations he describes as 'ethnic' rather than 'racial': does it make it more difficult to deal with racism? John agrees that while some solutions do relate to cultural difference, conflictual situations are generally about oppression and exploitation, and what is important is to recognise the conflictual nature of the relationship and its underlying reasons.

Kampta asks John where his Marxism stops and Weberianism begins. Is it true that he has attempted to straddle the two? John points out that their political sociology shares much in common in that it is about conflict, but while Marxian economics was based on the labour theory of value and the undeniable crisis of capitalism, Weber subscribed to the marginalist theory of value and the continuity of struggles over economic, political and other interests. John's account of class conflict does involve dropping some Marxist assumptions and adopting a Weberianised form of Marx, but what John is most concerned about is a sociology based on conflict. Kampta tempts John with the question of whether there is, in fact, as Rexian model of society. John responds spontaneously that one feature of his world picture is that it is deeply pessimistic, whether applied to the first world, second world, or third world, he supports his claim to pessimism with a resume of these societies' intractable problems, ranging from inequalities continuing to exist under capitalism, including drug addition to the AIDS crisis. At this stage, Kampta cleverly interjects a further question highlighting John's perceived optimism: how can you reconcile your views on multicultural society and plural society with your optimism? John is triggered into providing a wonderfully-condensed account of Furnivall's and M G Smith's theories of the plural society. He then returns to where the chapter began, South Africa, his country of birth, to argue that this was possibility the paradigm case of a plural society. For John, a plural society differs from the ideal multicultural society in which cultural diversity is coupled with a state of equality of opportunity, as encapsulated in Roy Jenkin's memorably statement of the 1960s. Without equality, a multicultural society becomes a plural society, both in Europe and Britain, it is not possible to campaign for the ideal of a democratic multicultural society. Kampta immediately demands to know the difference between a multicultural and antiracist society. John provides the example of French society where it is held desirable to abandon cultural difference so that all can be treated equally. Personally, he is opposed to an egalitarian society which shows contempt for people's separate cultures, as well as to a multicultural society which doesn't recognise the importance of equality of treatment for every individual.

As with Kampta's chapter, Laura Velasco and Oscar Contreras transcribe the content of a series of interviews they held with John at the University of Warwick, but first they situate John's contribution to sociology and its considerable influence in the context of the development of Mexican sociology in the 1970s and 1980s. Their original contribution to this book contains a section entitled, 'From colonisers to colonised: South Africa and the encounter with sociology', which described John's early years at Rhodes University in South Africa and his politicisation in opposing white supremacy until, when teaching in what was then Southern Rhodesia in 1949, he was declared an undesirable and forced to leave. A similar account of John's early life as a student in South Africa can be found in Kampta's chapter. Other sections of Laura and Oscar's account of their conversations with John are subtitled, 'England: experiences with class and race' and 'colonisation of England: migration, race and ethnicity', the first dealing with his experiences with the labour, anti-colonial, anti-apartheid and peace movements in England and the second with his contribution to the theorisation of the sociology of race and ethnic relations. Throughout the interviews, Laura and Oscar focus on John's unique input to the academic debates of the age and highlight, in particular, his interest in and impact on the Latin American intellectual landscape.

Part II deals with some of intellectual implications of John Rex's neo-Weberianism, and two chapters from eminent sociologists explore this concern in detail. Drawing on John Rex's seminar book, *Key Problems in Sociological Theory*, Martin Bulmer examines the role of values in the study of ethnicity and race. He discusses the ways in which social theorists such as Max Weber, Heinrich Rickert, Karl Mannheim and Gunnar Myrdal have tackled the issue of value, going on to explore its application to the field of ethnicity and race relations. He provides notable examples from Myrdal's famous study, *An American Dilemma: the Negro Problem and Modern Democracy* (1944) and his own experience as editor of *Ethnic and Racial Studies*, when he proposed to publish special issues on ethnic relations in Israel. Rex's *Key Problems* argues that problems are selected according to their 'relevance for value', but that socialists are not expected to make value choices but they might expose more sharply the value choices facing social actors. Max Weber expected the sociologists to produce explanations which were both adequate at the level of meaning and causally adequate. Rex believes that sociological objectivity is achieved by making value assumptions explicit and clearly relating them to the structures of power. Martin concludes that John Rex's approach to the place of values in sociological inquiry as been stimulating and has pointed sociologists to be attentive to issues which otherwise might conveniently have been ignored.

Acknowledging her early debt to John Rex in introducing her to the sociology of Max Weber, Margaret Archer uses her chapter to explore the relationship between explanation and understanding concepts which have so often been juxtaposed dualistically and irreconcilably in sociological theory. Far from excluding one another, the objectivity of social structure and the subjectivity of human agency are both needed to provide any adequate account of human beings' interaction with the social or physical world. She argues that the link between structure and agency lies in a process of 'mediation'. Human agents respond to structures by subjectively conceiving courses of action which become 'projects' when intentionally embarked upon. The uniquely human element of subjectivity which has been neglected in sociological theory is reflexivity: human beings' abilities deliberate in an anticipatory manner about perceived social constraints and enablements. Reflexivity is the answer to how 'the causal power of social forms is meditated through human agency'. It can be conceived as a kind of 'internal conversation' deliberating on the impact of the social form and determining our response to it. This internal conversation is the missing link in the account of interplay between structure and agency, thus transforming separately-told stories about explanation and understanding into a single account. Thus, structural and cultural properties objectively shape the situations confronting human agents, fashioning their subjective concerns. Then through a process of reflexive deliberation, the agents subjec-

tively determine their practical projects in relation to their objective cir-
cumstance. As Margaret so eloquently puts it, 'our subjectivity is dynamic,
it is not psychologically static, nor is it psychologically reducible, because
we modify our own goals in terms of their contextual possibility, as we see
it'. Both John and Margaret have always acknowledged their debt to Max
Weber. Their enthusiasm for the great master was matched by their deep
puzzlement of the issue of autonomy of will and the determination of cause,
postulated originally by Kant. Here, Margaret continues to wrestle with the
old dilemma, somehow sliding between its norms, and providing suitable
homage both to John Rex and Max Weber.

Part III of the book explores the nature of John Rex's contribution to
social policy. Nearly forty ears after Rex and Moore's collaborative author-
ship of *Race, Community and Conflict*, Robert Moore, the other half of the
partnership, examines the statistics of social deprivation among children
from different ethnic backgrounds, highlighting the importance of factors
such as the number of adults in employment in the household and the type
and quality of the accommodation they occupy, in determining the rank
order of the deprivation. Comparing data from the 1991 and 2001 Censes
as it is possible to do so, Robert divides his sample of children into those
living in 'poor England' (the 21 local districts with the highest indices of
material and social deprivation) and the remainder of England. Unsurprisingly, ethnic minority children are over-represented in the local authorities
comprising poor England, where they form 37 per cent of the child population, compared with 10 per cent in the remainder of England. Between
1991 and 2001, children from all ethnic groups have become less deprived,
but significant differences between the groups remain, with 10 per cent of
white British, 14 per cent of white Irish and 16 per cent of other white, but
22 per cent of Pakistani, 24 per cent of Black Caribbean and 39 per cent of
Bangladeshis in the high deprivation category. By way of contrast, only 7
per of Indian children fall into this category.

Returning once more to the issue of housing and occupation featured
so notably in the Sparkbrook study, Moore explores the relationship between child deprivation and different ethnic groups' choice of housing and
position in the occupational structures, showing them to be closely related.
By way of example, in poor England, 45 per cent of white British children
live in detached or semi-detached houses, but only 24 per cent of black
Caribbean children, who are three times more likely than whites to live in
flats. Robert concludes that while fewer children are experiencing the high
levels of deprivation of 1991, the rank order of ethnic deprivation has altered only very slightly, with only Indian children's circumstances improving more than most. The characteristics of their deprivation, their domes-

tic circumstances and location continue to different Asian, black and white children from one another.

Thomas Hammar acknowledges the debt of the multidisciplinary study of international migration and ethnic relations to the vision and pioneering work of John Rex. Thomas's chapter consists of a short history of the politics of immigration in Western Europe and particularly in Britain and Scandinavia. He describes how governments had for many years treated international migration as an apolitical administrative matter and it had only been in recent years that the issue had become party political. There was still, however, a large gap between public policy on immigration control and public opinion about immigration, with the voting public consistently sceptical or hostile to continued immigration. Hammar discusses the problems of managing migration and the conspicuous failure of governments to implement restrictive immigration control policies in demonstrably effective ways. Although control policies have become more ambitious and more restrictive, they have still failed to stem unwanted immigration flows, more often just re-channelling the flows and creating further opportunities for people smugglers. Less restrictive politics might better serve national demographic and economic interests. While there is clearly public support for draconian immigration control, which has been effectively tapped by populist parties, this restrictive constraint can be countered by a liberal one, stressing the need to obscure fundamental human rights such as the right to asylum, liberty and security, respect for private and family life, and the freedom from discrimination.

Stephen Steinberg's article stresses the importance of clearly identifying the nature of the problem of 'race relations'. He argues that since the pioneers in the study of sociology and 'race', such as Robert Park in the 1930s, identified the concerns in relation to this experience, sociology has been witnessing a moderating of the approach to the study of what are effectively racially oppressed groups in societies. There is a 'benign language' for a 'malignant problem', where the term 'racial oppression' more accurately captures the dilemmas faced by structurally disadvantaged groups. Often, in current reporting on the problems facing racialised ethnic minorities, the nature, magnitude and seriousness of the problem is underemphasised. In more recent times, there has been a distinctive move towards socio-psychological understandings in relation to minority experiences rather than structures per se. In effect, racial oppression is a function of structures. It is not always about individuals, but the workings of society per se; not attitudes, but power. Programmes of action that stem from programmes of research and public policy thinking focus on reducing prejudice, but about empowering ethnic minorities is conspicuously absent.

Furthermore, there are problems with the terms 'prejudice' and 'discrimination', too. It leads to the erroneous conclusions that culture and practices are the essential problem rather the structures or workings of society per se: the causes are structural according to Steinberg. Instead of 'discrimination' in employment, for example, which perhaps suggests marginal degrees of concern, the term 'occupational apartheid' is preferred, and, in addition, distillation between the concepts of 'Individual racism' and 'institutional racism', as originally espoused by Stokely Carmichael and Charles Hamilton's, *Black Power* (1967). It is conceptually misconstrued to reduce social facts down to individual predispositions. For Steinberg, his is a problem not just with the term 'race relations', but with the entire paradigm associated with it. Steinberg's analysis suggests that John Rex's focus on structural constraints precisely focuses on these paradigmatic interests.

Part IV of the book relates to the study of the city of Birmingham, at the time of John Rex's two important works in this field, to the current period, and one in which sees the city undergoing tremendous changes to the economic, political, social and cultural landscape. Tahir Abbas analyses the theory of housing classes in the context of Sparkbrook, Birmingham, forty years on. With the advent of immigrant groups from beyond that of former New Commonwealth countries, these new arrivals, often Muslim in origin, find themselves subservient to a restrictive housing policy and prejudice from private landlords and gatekeepers, many of whom are of Pakistani origin, having experienced a similar set of problems four decades previously. Tahir suggests that the theory of housing classes is a powerful analytical concept but not without its criticisms. The current experience in Sparkbrook indicates that clustering of housing by certain ethnic and religious minority are being reproduced, reconfigured and re-conceptualised in the light of different Muslim minority groups being attracted to existing established Muslim ethnic enclave economies and social spaces. Frank Reeves provides a valuable insight into the nature of urban sociological dynamics pertaining to inter- and intra-ethnic group relations. With the city of Birmingham in sharp focus, Frank provides a detailed historical analysis of the nature of ethnic relations in an urban context, carefully determining the various ways in which the sociology of John Rex helps to inform a considered perspective. Frank argues that 'without a better understanding of the city systems determining its race relations, effective intervention to influence their peaceful development is unlikely'. John Rex started this type of sociological study, and its importance cannot be underestimated for theory, policy and practice.

More than twenty-five years ago, Rex and Tomlinson published *Colonial Immigrants in a British City*, a study of ethnic competition for the key social resources of employment, housing, education and other services, in the Handsworth area of Birmingham. Sally Tomlinson, John Rex's co-author, revises the important topic of the ethnic allocation of the city's educational resources in the 1970s and assesses how the situation has changed at the start of the twenty-first century. She attempts to answer the question of how far the children and grandchildren of those she and John interviewed in the 1970s have benefited from equal opportunity policy initiatives in Birmingham's schools and colleges, and how far their educational achievements have allowed them access to higher qualifications and employment and provided them with the social and economic security their parents desired for them. While in her view provision for minorities has certainly changed for the better, and the improvements in educational attainment in Birmingham has been significantly greater than the country as a whole, there are still considerable differences between groups in educational outcome, a situation unlikely to be remedies by the government's current educational initiatives. Rex and Tomlinson's forecast that classifications between ethnic minorities would become more pronounced appears to have occurred. The odds are still stacked against many young people achieving attempting to secure employment or mobility through education. While the incorporation of minorities as equal citizens in Britain and Birmingham depends on factors other than education, Sally concludes that the potential for disadvantage and new forms of educational exclusion remains.

Part I

John Rex's Life, Ideas and Contribution to Sociology

1

The Place of Theory: John Rex's Contribution to the Sociological Study of Ethnicity and 'Race'

RICHARD JENKINS

O N 5 MARCH 2005, John Rex was eighty, an age at which a lifetime's work may begin to be seen for what it is. As someone who was given his first job by John, and who has learned much from him,[1] it is my great pleasure to accept the editors' invitation to write something to mark this occasion. However, the commission poses a question: what *kind* of 'something' should I write? There would be no point in duplicating the tributes in his richly-deserved *festschrift* (Martins 1993). Nor is there space for the kind of detailed critical exploration of his work that an active career of fifty years, and a large bibliography, warrants.

Instead, I will attempt something more personal and more pointed: to identify what I think is John Rex's enduring contribution to sociology, and the sociology of ethnicity and 'race' in particular, and to assess its continuing value at the beginning of the twenty-first century. Running through this discussion is the claim that, viewed from where we are today, John Rex appears to be one of a very small number of genuinely influential voices in twentieth-century British sociology, who has made particularly compelling contributions to the development of sociological theory and the emergence of a genuinely sociological account of 'race' and ethnicity.[2] That his contribution in this respect may, at the moment, not be as widely acknowledged as it deserves, and the reasons why that might be so, I will leave others to ponder.

South African by origin, John Rex was an undergraduate at Rhodes University, Grahamstown, and spent a brief period in Southern Rhodesia before coming to Britain in 1948, where he began teaching in the Extra-Mural Department at Hull University, then based on Teesside. From there, he took a Ph.D in Sociology at the University of Leeds, under the supervision of the philosopher Stephen Toulmin, and held successive university appointments in sociology at the Universities of Leeds, Birmingham, Durham, Warwick, Aston and Warwick again; he effectively founded the sociology departments at Durham and Warwick. He was Director of the SSRC Research Unit on Ethnic Relations, which became the ESRC Centre for Research on Ethnic Relations, from 1979 to 1984. Long retired, he is still academically active, particularly on the international scene.

There is, of course, more to life than work, and it is worth briefly mentioning John Rex's involvement in politics here because, whatever else, his sociology has always been intensely political, and his interest in 'race' has always been more than academic. He was active in the South African National Union of Students, and during the 1950s was for a time, I believe, a Labour candidate in a North Yorkshire constituency. During the 1950s, and in more metropolitan circles, he was also a member of that network of left intellectuals that included Robin Blackburn and Stuart Hall, out of which came *New Left Review*. His political voice is one of the threads that binds together his career's work.

Looking at that work, it seems to me that several closely inter-related aspects of John Rex's sociology are of enduring significance and value and already look set to outlive the critical cultural studies approaches that generated the most robust criticisms of his work, during the 1980s (e.g., Gilroy 1980; Lawrence 1982). In short order, these are: first, the need to build a solid ontology of 'the social' as a basis on which to do sociology, second, the central place of conflict at the heart of human social life and, hence, of sociological analysis, and, third, the need for empirical research to be informed by theory and – perhaps even more important – for theorising to be grounded in real word concerns and systematic evidence.

For John Rex, theory is not a self-referential intellectual domain – in other words, it is not mainly about theorists and what they say – but, rather, it is a conceptual lens through which to observe the realities of human existence in groups. This doesn't, however, mean we should abandon our awareness of our intellectual genealogy: Rex's work is a lively testament to the foundational importance of the work of Marx, Weber, Durkheim, and Simmel, and the intellectual departure that their development of systematic social theory encouraged and allowed.

Understanding the social

The key text here remains the most important thing John Rex has written. *Key Problems of Sociological Theory* was published in 1961, when British sociology was still dominated by the political arithmetic tradition exemplified by David Glass at the LSE – which, in passing, may explain why much of Rex's argument in this text engages with social anthropology – and international social theory by functionalism in one version or another. As can be gauged from many of the contribution to his *festschrift*, it is difficult for subsequent generations to imagine the importance and impact of this one book. Although probably little read today, it is still full of lessons and challenges.

Offering a riposte to descriptive value-driven empiricism, on the one hand, and the natural science delusions of positivism, on the other, the return to first principles in *Key Problems* was arguably the first distinctively British sociological contribution to general social theory. For generations of students it was their introduction to 'the action frame of reference', and it paved the way for the theorising of the discipline in Britain during the late 1960s and into the 1970s. Like most theorists since the 1930s – and there are only a *very* few exceptions to this rule, and probably none of them British – his work is more synthesis than voyage of discovery, but this does not detract from its significance.

Rex's ontological starting point, which is also, necessarily, a methodological injunction, betrays his most important theoretical debts, to Weber and Simmel, in that the individual – in theoretical terms the 'hypothetical individual' – is the basis of any understanding of the wider social world. Each individual exists in a social environment composed of the expectations and expected actions of other significant individuals, and it is these that are the social determinants of behaviour. The subject matter of sociology is the observed behaviour of individuals and the 'participant theories' about each other's behaviour that they hold and develop (to be distinguished from the theories of sociologists, which are in principle subject to systematic testing).

Sociology must distinguish between the social and other factors that influence behaviour; in order to do so 'the social' must be adequately defined in terms of observable realities. Although 'interaction' and 'social relations', the elementary build of collectivity, are theoretically complex, they need to be empirically grounded. Thus interaction involves more than one party, some intersubjective understanding by the parties of what everyone is doing, and some expectation on all parts of what to expect from the others. For a social relation to exist, there must, in addition, be sufficient shared interests and/or values to create the possibility of mutual approval (all of which imply a degree of organised continuity). The empirical data of sociological research consists of verifiable statements about all of these aspects of behaviour and the behaviour itself.

Although he is a methodological individualist, Rex differs from the more radical 'rational actor' individualism of Banton, for example, in acknowledging the importance of the non-rational and the difficulty of incorporating it into sociological analysis (1961: 92, 178). He is also clear, unlike many methodological individualists, about the empirical reality and theoretical importance of collectivities. Groups, communities and societies – the consistently important collectivities with which sociology concerns itself – emerge, as institutionalised patterns, out of social relations. These too are complex theoretical concepts and should not be taken for granted, the theorising needs to be made explicit. Of particular importance in this respect is the need to go beyond everyday interaction and social relations between individuals if we are to understand the enduring reality of collectivities. 'Other sustaining activities' – such as institutionalised systems of production and exchange and education – are persistent aspects of collective life that cannot be reduced to the interactional give and take of the moment. Socialisation is particularly important in Rex's view (1961: 56–7) as a necessary precondition of the consistent meaningful intersubjectivity that informs both interaction and social relations. These considerations mean that he is also clear about the importance of large-scale studies at a national – or even international – level of abstraction.

Whether tacitly or explicitly, the basic ontology outlined in *Key Problems* has informed John Rex's approach to sociology throughout his career: his social world is made up of individuals, interaction and established relations between individuals, and socially meaningful collectivities and institutions. As he has made clear over and over again in various theorisations of ethnicity and 'race' – my scare quotes, not his – in *Race Relations in Sociological Theory* (1970; 1983), *Race and Ethnicity* (1986) and *Ethnic Minorities in the Modern Nation State* (1996), ethnic groups are *real* collectivities, as are the states which are the institutional arenas within which he has been sociologically interested in them.

'Races', however, are not real collectivities. This does not mean, however, that in his view it is illegitimate to talk about 'race relations'. Quite the reverse in fact: relations between ethnic groups and their individual members are often heavily influenced by participant theories, whether formal or informal, about 'races', and exploitative and discriminatory systems of production and exchange and education are often organised in terms of the same local models. These are 'race relations' situations and racism is one of their defining realities (Rex 1983: 116–61).

However, recognising perhaps that continuing to talk about 'race relations' might contribute to legitimising the notion of 'race', and in the context of a Europe in which disadvantaged minorities are often not racialised, Rex's more recent work (e.g., 1991, 1996) has focused on ethnicity and culture, and the nature of and prospects for cultural pluralism. Here we come to what may be his intellectual and political Achille's heel. A career long emphasis in his own research on ethnic minorities, combined with a gradual shift to an emphasis on culture and ethnic mobilisation, can be misinterpreted crudely as downplaying or ignoring the importance of racism, the exercise of power, and majorities; this was the basis for accusations that his work supported the *status quo* and 'blamed the victim' (e.g., Bourne and Sivanandan 1980; Gilroy 1980; Lawrence 1982). While it's possible to understood the source of these critiques, the thrust of Rex's theoretical work – as opposed to the relative emphases on minority and immigrant populations in his substantive research (Rex and Moore 1967; Rex and Tomlinson 1979) – points in another direction: away from stability and social integration and towards a recognition of the complexity of conflict and its necessary place at the heart of the social world.

Understanding conflict

An important part of the argument of *Key Problems* (pp. 53–54, 115–155) was concerned with the place of conflict within sociological theorising. In the context of the time, Rex was writing against Parsonian functionalism, with its excessive emphasis on normative systemic integration, and its revision by theorists such as Lewis Coser and Max Gluckman, who, while recognising the ubiquity of conflict, argued that it could best be regarded as integrative in that it contributed to the overall maintenance of social equilibrium (this latter an argument that resonated subsequently in the work of theorists of 'cultural reproduction' such as Bourdieu and Bowles and Gintis).

Drawing on Marx, and to a lesser degree Weber and Simmel, Rex offered two significant corrections to these views. First, addressing Parsons, he argued that 'perfect conflict' and 'perfect co-operation' were, at best, ideal types and that real social situations were somewhere on a continuum between these poles and necessarily involved both conflict and co-operation. Conflicts of interest and of values are only to be expected. In other words, conflict, far from being a disruption of normal life, is a fundamental part of normal life: social integration is not the norm. Second, addressing Coser and Gluckman, Rex is clear that conflict may be disruptive of existing social arrangements, and often is. To summarise his argument in 1961, Rex suggested that rather than *being* organised around value consensus, it was in fact points of conflict that provided collectivities with their 'shape' and character. These points of conflict usually tended to produce plural societies and unequal power balances, always vulnerable to challenge 'from below'. This is a model of the social world in which conflict, diversity and competitive politics are the routine state of affairs.

It is a model that Rex elaborated in further detail twenty years later in what is his least acknowledged important theoretical work (perhaps because it was published in an introductory textbook series). *Social Conflict* (1981) is a masterpiece of concise argumentation that manages to avoid talking down to its intended readership while being appropriately accessible. Starting from a viewpoint grounded in methodological individualism and a Weberian model of social action Rex aims to provide a coherent sociological perspective on conflict that includes, at one end of the spectrum, dyadic relationships between individuals and, at the other, conflict between collectivities, with states as the defining type. Whereas Parsons defined the core focus of sociology as 'the problem of order', Rex insists that, in fact, this is more realistically and helpfully understood as the 'problem of conflict'. Furthermore, where Parsons treats a degree of normative and cognitive consensus as axiomatic and the ultimate guarantor of order, Rex argues that it is conflicts of ideology and values and of 'rational' interests that characterise relationships between individuals and collectivities. What's more, the affective, psychological dimension of conflict is also important (and certainly more important than sociology at that time was able to acknowledge). Stable social arrangements, whether small or large scale, are always the outcome – however uneasy – of the balance of forces and powers that are in conflict at a particular place and time.

So far so good; and interesting and useful, too. For the purposes of this discussion, however, two aspects of Rex's approach to conflict require more attention. First, in *Key Problems* and *Social Conflict*, he consistently accords pre-eminence to class as the most important, indeed definitive, source of collective conflict in modern societies. This materialist approach is not based on a Marxian model of class, in which the propertied and the property-less confront each other in the labour market, the crucible of class consciousness and conflict, but, rather in a Weberian understanding of class as an emergent structure of collective identification that derives from the operation of various competitive markets, which is in close and complex, but not necessarily mutually reinforcing, relationships to status distinctions and politics.

In *Social Conflict*, he explicitly describes class as superceding ancient primordial ties of ethnicity and the compulsory associations of nationhood, as a consequence of the development of capitalism and the bourgeois political revolutions that were attendant upon that development. Immigrant workers, in this model, may become an underclass. His use of Northern Ireland as an example gives a good flavour of his thinking on this point: the primary fact of the Northern Irish situation is, apparently, 'the exploitation and oppression of the Catholic working class by a bourgeoisie with foreign ties' (1981: 118). Despite his immediate modification of the crudity of this analysis, it's reductionist and, even *if* it were correct – and I'd have to say that it's not – it's an over-simplification.

Reductionism aside, however, viewed from today's vantage point this perspective isn't persuasive anyway (although it should perhaps be remembered that the 1980s resonated to many confident assertions of the demise of nationalism, not least from Hobsbawm and Gellner). Ethnicity is not definitively primordial, any more than national identity and nationalism are always compulsory. Neither shows signs of withering away in the face of class. Nor is class any longer the self-evident core source of collective identification and conflict within modern nation states that sociology once took it to be (which isn't to subscribe to a current, no less erroneous, view, that class doesn't matter any more). In his earlier writings, and particularly in his empirical study of Handsworth, Birmingham (Rex and Tomlinson 1979), this lead to a situation in which Rex was vulnerable to criticism from the same set of critics – to whom I have already referred – but from two different directions. On the one hand, in emphasising class he wasn't allowing 'race', and particularly racism, sufficient autonomy as the major source of systematic disadvantage and oppression, while, on the other, in talking about 'race relations' he was focussing upon black people at the expense of looking at the structures of white domination. Heads they won, tails Rex lost. Addressing his discussion of the potential emergence of an ethnic underclass, these two strands converged in the accusation that he was, in some senses, writing black people out of society and the possibility of political action and blaming the victims.

While not all of these criticisms are borne out by an open-minded reading of what Rex actually said – and even the most plausible require some qualification – it is nonetheless possible to appreciate where they were coming from. The theoretical and substantive emphasis on class relations was an attempt to understand the realities of a new situation within an earlier theoretical framework that was not appropriate. In his recent writings on ethnic mobilisation and the possible futures for multi-culturalism (Rex 1991,

1996), we find a more nuanced and less reductionist approach to these issues. There are a number of aspects to this. For example, ethnic and immigrant groups are seen either as 'quasi-classes' or as status groups in their own right, or indeed both. Class conflict and class-based affiliations – in the labour movement for example – are no longer seen as fundamental or the most appropriate arena for collective action. The importance of ethnic differentiation within the 'black' or 'immigrant' population is acknowledged, with all that this entails for political mobilisation and integration.

Even within this more flexible approach, however, John Rex still appears to see the market, and class relations, as historically corrosive of ethnic attachments. In the pursuit of their own interests people apparently 'grow up' out of the 'cocoon' of ethnicity (1996: 191). This remains an approach within which he has difficulty taking ethnic attachments at their own *face* value.

The second dimension of Rex's approach to conflict that requires further exploration pretty much follows on from the above: his argument for 'egalitarian multiculturalism' (1996) seems to be in interesting tension with his long-standing views on society as a system of conflict – in the best case, balanced and managed conflict – rather than co-operation. In talking about an ideal of egalitarian multiculturalism, he draws upon a recent thread in European social theory that is concerned with the emergence in modern societies of a public sphere as a space of common participation that can hold complexity and heterogeneity together. In his ideal world of egalitarian multiculturalism, the public domain of national politics and culture would be open to all on the same terms, while various different communities or ethnies, with their own cultures, would each have their private spheres or domains in which to go about their everyday lives and invest in the continuity of their customs and values.

This is another point of view – which, it has to be remembered, Rex self-consciously offers as an *ideal* – that fits at best uncomfortably with the present times. The French affair of the headscarves is merely symptomatic of a wider problem that appears in two aspects. The first is the necessarily ethnic/cultural character of the public sphere in modern nation states: majorities are ethnics too, which means that there is no ethnically neutral civic-national culture. It is a contradiction in terms. The second is the difficulty in reconciling universalist – actually Western – discourses of human rights with the particularities of local and ethnic ways of life with which they may conflict.

In terms of Rex's long-standing theoretical scheme of things, this isn't the heart of the problem, however, and it is precisely here that revisiting his core theoretical work, as I have done in this brief discussion, pays dividends. Put simply, Rex's understanding of the place of conflict in society, as elaborated in *Key Problems* and *Social Conflict*, doesn't throw into doubt the possibility of multiculturalism; indeed it could be said to recognise the plural and heterogeneous nature of all enduring social arrangements. What it does instead, however, is to suggest the utter implausibility of peacefully co-existent (egalitarian) multi-culturalism. As an ideal it is remote and, arguably, a political distraction. Some sort of balance of forces is imaginable, but probably nothing else.

Empirical sociology

Unlike most of us, John Rex has written at least two genuinely magnificent books. After *Key Problems*, the other *is Race, Community and Conflict*, the study of Sparkbrook in Birmingham that he did with Robert Moore in the early 1960s. An account of complex relations between the local English and the immigrant Irish, Afro-Caribbeans and South Asians, its split focus on housing, voluntary associations and religion, combined with an exploration of generational change in the migrant communities, makes for a rich and many-layered text.

Its impact, too, was enormous, at first political and subsequently sociological. As Stuart Hall wrote when reviewing it for *The Listener*: 'They bring us close in to a familiar, recognisable part of our large industrial cities and the detailed character of life there. At the same time, they give us theoretical tools with which to understand the social processes by which ... such places come to exist at all.'[3] Hall gets to the heart of this book's qualities. If *Key Problems* was the first British social theory, *Race, Community and Conflict* was among the first properly theorised works of empirical sociology in Britain. However, it wore that theory – derived in part from the Chicago school and in part from *Key Problems* – lightly and remains an object lesson in how to write a properly sociological research report without having the theoretical tail wag the substantive dog. For this reason if no other – and there are others – it still has a huge amount to teach any apprentice sociological researcher. It is also a powerful confirmation that theory is the servant of systematic empirical inquiry, rather than an end in itself.

But something else also distinguishes *Race, Community and Conflict*. It is a very personal book. It is clear from Robert Moore's reflections (Moore 1977) that doing the research was a powerful – indeed, formative – experience for both authors, each in their different way. I think I am correct in saying that for each of them it was their first serious field study, and the excitement, enthusiasm and vigour of novices at work shows through. What's more, the combination of participant observation with local survey data enables the account to work at different levels, and to bring to life the situation in Sparkbrook at the time. By comparison, Rex's subsequent research in Birmingham, *Colonial Immigrants in a British City* (Rex and Tomlinson 1979), confined itself to interviewing and a large sample survey and reflects sociologically different times. A valuable enough study in its own right – which isn't damnation by faint praise – it is the product of a discipline that, in its research practices at least, had by then become a thoroughly routinised 'normal science'.

The increasingly respectable world of institutionalised sociology and higher education has, one suspects, never been particularly comfortable for John Rex. The intellectual and personal fire that illuminated the pages of *Key Problems* and *Race, Community and Conflict* has, to his great credit, never actually gone out. In a world of committees, academic and other politics, and ever more difficult issues of resource management, that fiery spirit has often made him an awkward customer. That he chose to work in the particularly demanding and conflictual arena of 'race' and ethnicity – although given his background in South Africa 'chose' is probably a poor choice of word here – did not make matters easier. Those of us with more than a passing interest in sociology and the study of ethnicity and 'race' have, however, a host of reasons to be grateful that he did.

2

John Rex: Some Reflections

AN INTERVIEW WITH KAMPTA KARRAN

KK Professor Rex, could you tell us what your boyhood was like, where you were born and what were the conditions during your childhood?

JR I am classified as a White South African and I am of the fifth generation born in South Africa. I was actually brought up in the town of Port Elizabeth which at that time was rather different, perhaps, from other cities in that the majority of working class people in that town were white and they were also English speaking. My whole up-bringing was in the context of a society which basically made racist assumptions about the people around us. It was a hierarchical order dominated by whites. Then there were Coloured people who were distinguished from Blacks and who spoke Afrikaans (i.e., the language of the Settlers of Dutch descent rather than one of the Bantu languages). And there were the vast majority of Black people and there were the Indians. In my normal White South African up-bringing we were trained to see those groups as constituting some sort of hierarchy. I supposed, if it hadn't been for the War and if I hadn't gone to university, I would not have easily been shaken out of those beliefs.

In point of fact, I was born 1925 and in 1943 joined the services which introduced me to a much larger world. I was two years in the British Navy abroad and became conscious of the peculiarity of the South African situation. So when I went back to South Africa I was already beginning to ask questions which were answered for me when I went to university. If it hadn't been for the war I wouldn't have been able to go to university. There was a special grant scheme for ex-service students which made it possible for me to go.

I went to Rhodes University and the President of the Students' representative Council was Ian Smith who later became Prime Minister of Rhodesia. The moment that I arrived at the University the Students Representative Council led by Smith had decided to withdraw the University from the National Union of Students because it admitted the non-white colleges. The result was that throughout my period of three years at Rhodes I was engaged continually in campaigns to get us back into this multi-racial organisation. That necessarily involved the process of politicization. One had to look for some sort of organisation which was a means of expression. There wasn't at that stage a Liberty Party but there was a Communist Party. Very often one thought, should I join the Communist Party? Actually, the Communist Party in the 1930s had a very mixed record in South African. It had originally grown up amongst white workers. I didn't join it.

On the other hand, the sort of analyst of the South African situation which I shared with my contemporaries amongst the radical students was essentially a Marxist one. When we looked at the great political divisions in South Africa we were inclined to emphasise not merely racial and cultural differences but the fact that the great bulk of the African workers had a very specific class position. There was the question of migrant labour and unfree labour. Much of the thought of the ideology of what became the African National Congress seemed to us to turn on that question.

KK What was the nature of the racism at that time? Biological? Theological?

JR I was at Rhodes which was a small White English-speaking University in Grahamstown. There were some non-racist people there. And indeed the fact that we were able to win our campaign to remain in the National Union of Students showed that we could eventually even command a majority. But most people who dominated the University when we went there held racist beliefs. Since they didn't intellectualise their position very much, it was hard to talk about the nature of the racism. But many people would say things like 'you can't train a black man to be a bricklayer because he does not understand the concept of the straight line'. Things like that were said all the time.

There was a belief that the racial hierarchy was the natural order of things. It was only ignorant people who came from other countries who didn't understand. I would have said, yes, it was old fashioned racism sometimes reinforced by the ideas that came from a particular interpretation of Christianity. The Afrikaner people regarded themselves as a chosen people were a particular destiny. So there was a combination, one had assumed, of biological racism reinforced by ideas of this kind.

KK Civilisation mission of that group?

JR Yes, you could say that.

KK You were going on to talk about the communist Party!

JR One always had this relationship with people who were Communists. Left liberals tended to be fairly close to communists in South Africa. I left South Africa when the Freedom Congress was held. It consisted of four elements: the African National Congress, the Indian National Congress, the Coloured people's Organisation and the Congress of Democrats for Whites. Most of the Whites who joined the Congress of Democrats were Communists. Relatively few Liberals joined it. There were some of course. The President of the Freedom Congress was Father Trevor Huddleston who was not a Communist and there was a slightly wider grouping. This was a crucial point in South African history.

KK You talked about the Indian Congress Party. What was the influence of Mohandas Karamchand Gandhi on the Indian Party and in the shaping of thinking at that time in South Africa?

JR Actually, Gandhi's influence in South Africa was not really a radical one. In his day, he campaigned for Indians' rights by passive resistance. He laid so much emphasis on passivity that very often he seemed to be quite complaint. But General Smutts did put him in goal. Although it was said that General Smutts used to visit him there and they used to talk about philosophy.

You see, the Indian community was divided obviously in several ways. We used to differentiate between the Indians who came over as indentured workers in the first place and then other Indians, who sociologists came to refer to as the passenger Indians, who paid their own passage. Some of the original workers came via Mauritius. Then you had the arrival of the Gujerati businessmen.

Within the Indian community you did get some Communist leadership which was partly based upon Indian trade unionism, partly based on middle-class intellectuals. There were two distinguished men, Dr Naicker and Dr Dadoo who were both Communists. The South African Indian Congress was quite close to the Communist Party. There were always other Indians who were much more middle class. I rather think, but I am not quite sure, that Gandhi's actual son was one of the more moderate anti-Communist people. And to this day, if one may just reflect on that for a moment, there is a division in the Indian community. Natal has a fairly considerable Indian working class population working in the factories. There are also rich and successful people in the Indian community. I think that, as change approaches in South African, quite a lot of those middle class Indians will throw in their lot with De Klerk and the Nationalist Party because they are frightened of blacks.

KK Who were your colleagues during that period?

JR At the University I was simply a young student. A big influence in my life, was my Professor who was a man called James Irving (a very wonderful person). He started his working life as a shipyard worker on Clydeside and got a scholarship through the W.E.A Cambridge, where he studied Anthropology. He taught in Nationalist China in the University of Nanking and then as an Extramural teacher in Yorkshire before coming to South Africa. A man of culture and learning, he taught us an awful lot and opened the world for us.

But the really important influence was the National Union of Students itself. Apart from the actual political executive of the National union of Students we had a research Council. One of the greatest experiences of my years at University was to go on an expedition to an area in Transkei where we divided ourselves up by different subject disciplines and studies all aspects of that area. I was in the group which looked at the educational system at the time. We had some very distinguished people in that team. The most distinguished was a man who'd become a very great geneticist called Sidney Breyner, who was closely associated with different people who did the work on breaking the genetic code, and so on, a man of enormous ability. The important thing about this was that people from a whole number of disciplines found themselves working in a politicised situation.

KK So you were in the Navy, then you were at the University and you were part of the struggle and then you left for England. What were the conditions that prompted that movement?

JR When I went to University I intended to become a minister in the Presbyterian Church in South Africa but I lost my calling there. Immediately after graduating I went to be a teacher in a Mission school in what was then Southern Rhodesia. To my surprise, after six weeks, the Immigration Department told me that I was, as they said, 'deemed undesirable' because of information received through their own Government. I had to go back to South Africa where I was unemployed I got a job with the, so called, Native Affairs department in Kimberley City Council, as Superintendent of one of the African villages. But I had only been there made to Leeds University was successful.

On the recommendation of my Professor in South Africa I was appointed an extra-mural teacher in Yorkshire. For about eight years I was simply doing extra-mural classes: sociology, social history and philosophy with working class people: steel workers, miners, agricultural workers. This experience brought me very close to the British labour Movement.

On the political level, I did at one stage become a Labour Parliamentary candidate, although I never actually stood in an election. The reason why I didn't go on with that was that I found that I had to give my time to rather a different kind of politics. And that was to help the young African political leaders from East and Central Africa to stop the spread of white supremacy to those areas. And so I spent a lot of my time arranging meeting for people like Tom Mboya, Kenneth Kaunda, Joshua N'komo. Most of those people came and spoke, and I was very much involved in that.

I also had to try to relate myself to British thought and academic life. So when I arrived in Leeds, I wanted to get in touch with British sociology and there was relatively little of it. It was mainly concentrated in the London School of Economics. In 1956, I became an internal lecturer in Leeds. I began to argue about sociological theory. This really was the basis of the argument. There were some very good people at the London School of Economics and they were concerned with problems of inequality and social mobility. They did quite a lot of statistical work of this kind. This administrative

approach to the question of inequality produced statistics for the
government on the assumption that it would then be corrected. It
seemed to me that even in England it wasn't as simple as this, that
one did have a society which was strongly based upon class conflict.
That meant that within society theory I became critical of the kind
of sociology that there was.

I wrote a thesis which eventually became my book *Key Problems
of Sociological Theory*. This wasn't about race or anything of the
kind. The emphasis was conflict theory. That really I suppose was
the start of my career as a sociologist.

One thing did happen during that time which is quite important
in relation to my limited connection with the Caribbean. In 1957
the theory Group of the British Sociological Association had one
section on the plural society of which I had not, at that stage, heard
anything of before. Suddenly I found myself in the Group which
was not talking in terms of mainstream British Sociological theory
but was talking about the plural society. Particularly, at that stage
we were discussing the ideas of J. S. Furnival. This was well before
M. G. Smith had written his book. So the first article I ever published appeared in the *British Journal of Sociology* called the 'Plural
Society in Sociological theory', in which I suggested that not simply
Furnival, but Malinowski in Britain and Myrdal in America, had
used a model of society which was very different from both the or-
thodox British sociology or the new kind of functionalist sociology
which was being imported from Harvard University, America. So
discussing the plural society became very important for me at that
stage on a theoretical level.

Then in 1962, I moved from Leeds to Birmingham and 1962 was,
in many ways, a terribly important year. There had been an upswing
in the rate of West Indian, Indian and Pakistani immigration in
British. There was a very imminent black presence in Birmingham.
Whole areas of the inner city were becoming increasingly black and
Birmingham was in a state of racist panic. I went to do research
in a state of racist panic. I west to do research in a particular area
of Birmingham called Sparkbrook which has for quite a long time
been the centre of Irish settlement. But now there were increasing
numbers of Pakistanis as well as some West Indians, particularly
from Barbados and St Kitts. The Jamaicans settled in a different part
of the city. I worked together with Robert Moore, my research assis-
tant, and we wrote a book called *Race, Community and Conflict*. We
drew on the theories of urban sociology particularly from Chicago

and also upon my own sensitivity to theories of class conflicts. Our study gave an account of what was happening to cities.

KK Did you, in the course of your research, take a strong look at inter-minority conflict? Or were you merely concentrating on minority/majority conflict?

JR We didn't really much. We found a situation in which the City Council discriminated against immigrants so that the immigrants were left to live in certain parts of the city. The housing entrepreneurs who actually provided housing for the people who left out tended, on the whole, to be Pakistanis. They bought old houses and housed their own kinsmen and fellow countrymen almost free and let off rooms to other groups: Irish, West Indians, some English people with problems. But that didn't produce inter-ethnic conflict between the Asians and the blacks. Many socialist people felt that this group of landlords would be in conflict with other people, but those who were looking for housing didn't in fact regard their landlords as their worst enemies because the landlords were putting a roof over their heads.

KK How did the Irish respond to the Pakistanis?

JR The Irish are a very different question. The Irish were conscious of being white and there was a process of what urban sociologists call 'succession' going in what was their area, Sparkbrook, which was gradually being taken over, principally by Pakistani's. Indeed, there was a great deal of Irish racism and racial discrimination. The labour Party club in Sparkbrook, when I first went there, was an all Irish working class place. When I said to someone once, 'don't you ever have black people here?', all the person could say was 'we did have a black man here and he was a pianist who played the piano'. Of course, that situation is now enormously changed. In Sparkbrook, 80 per cent of the management of the Labour Party is now Pakistani.

KK Would you say that the influx of black immigrants, Pakistanis and West Indians, created for the Irish an opportunity to be integrated into white majority culture? Or was that integration already taking place?

JR Irish immigration into Britain had been going on for a century or more, it was still going on in the 50's and the biggest influx of immigrants in the 50s was still Irish. The Labour Movement in Sparkbrook was very largely an Irish organisation. Many of the city councillors were Irish. As immigrants, the Irish were subjected to discrimination but they could also get help and there was a steady flow of Irish people towards the better suburbs.

KK   So the coming of the Blacks did not facilitate Irish integration into white majority society?

JR   No. there was a steady process of integration for Irish people, although in the early 60s there were still Irish people arriving in quite large numbers and they were poor and they were struggling.

KK   At that period did you observe any conflict between landlord (Pakistani) and tenant (West Indians), as classical Marxist theory would want to suggest?

JR   No.

KK   In the literature, one observes that the race relations disclosure tends to focus on white/black conflict. What about conflict within the black community: conflict between the Pakistanis and West Indians, or Asians and West Indians?

JR   Of course in the years after 1962 to the present day, has a very considerable growth of Indian and Pakistani business, so that there is now a middle class, including quite a lot of poor shopkeepers, amongst the Asians. But that has not had a political expression in terms if division between those communities. One of the things about the British situation, as opposed to that of Europe is, of course, that most of these immigrants have the vote and they started to get involved in the Labour Party. There have been Indian and Pakistani councillors. There have also been West Indian councillors. Looking at Birmingham as a whole, it is surprising how little expression there has been of inter-ethnic hostility. Even in the 1985 disturbance in Handsworth, when two Asians who ran a shop actually dies during the riots, there was no great Asian hostility toward the blacks.

KK   But do you see this non-expression of hostility in a manifest form, in an overt form, as meaning that the conflict is not there. Could the conflict be of a latent type? I am asking this, particularly in connection to Asians seeing fellow Asians being asked to leave countries like Uganda and Kenya. Blacks used to live in certain areas suddenly see them being taken over by Asians.

JR   I can see that there is a basis for latent hostility between Asians and Blacks, both because of the East African situation and because of

developing differences of class interests. But I would say that it is
as yet found relatively little political expression. There are growing
numbers of Asians but I haven't seen much sign of any sort of hostility against the blacks on the part of Asians. I think it is latently there.
If I speak privately to Indians who are successful in business, they
may express some racist ideas. One very important factor, of course,
is that although it has never been a majority organisation, the most
effective political organisation amongst the Indians was the Indian
Workers Association, which was Marxist. So long as there was that
sort of political leadership in place, the scope for the development
of Indian anti-Black racism was curtailed.

KK Now, Professor Rex, let us shift our focus to a conceptual issue.
There is this debate between what people like to call the racialisation discourse versus the race relations discourse. I don't know if
you care to comment on that?

JR Unfortunately, in this debate in sociological literature, I think I have
been gravely misrepresented by the sociologist, Robert Miles. In
fact, there are many points on which I agree with him. Although
I often said that I owe basically a kind of Marxism, in which I laid
great emphasis upon migrant labour and class conflict. And indeed
in the book which I wrote in 1970, *Race Relations in Sociological
Theory*, I make it quite clear that I regard the conflicts which exist
as not having any kind of racial or even ethnic overtones, but as being material conflicts which are then rationalised by the powerful
in terms of racist theories.

Now I was amazed when Miles wrote a book suggesting that
I have said these problems should be conceptualised in terms of
races. I think it is true that where people are in a state of conflict
then the visibility which a particular group has because of its colour
or culture makes it easier to mark it off. But the conflict is a conflict
over jobs, housing and things of this kind. There isn't really that
much difference between my own position and that of Miles. But
Miles has used the specific word 'racialisation' and, therefore, seems
to think that his position is quite different from my own view.

Now if you are asking me the question, 'are there races in the
world?' ... I was a participant in the UNESCO Experts Commission in 1967, International Experts Group, about the nature of race
and racism. We said, very specifically, that in a scientific sense the
term race as used by biologists is a classificatory concept of relative
usefulness to biologists, but that it has no relevance to the political differences amongst human beings. That was the basic conclu-

sion of our findings. If one is concerned with actual political sociology, 'race', as such, is not an important factor. We are talking about
conflicts of a different kind indeed. If someone asks me 'are there
races?', I would say, biologists recognise that there is a broad difference between groups which overlaps somewhat between Negroid,
Monogoloid, Caucasoid and which involves different physical ap-
pearances. The fact that I may say that doesn't mean that I say this
is a cause of conflict in itself.

KK How is it that landlords who were Asians and tenants who were
Blacks saw themselves not in conflict when they were classified by
difference? Was this seeming consensus a result of a stronger other
that they wanted to confront together?

JR Yes, I think the fact was that the people who got into entrepreneurial
positions were first of all in very low grade entrepreneurial positions. They themselves were subjected to racism on the part of the
white authorities. The experience of suffering racial discrimination
was strong enough to outweigh the sort of class differences which
occurred.

KK Do you not think the little difference one finds between some of
your works and those of others has to do with the 'race' vs. the
'ethnic' conceptualisation? It is felt in some quarters that 'ethnic'
as an explanatory variable dilutes the larger discourse concerning
the racialisation problematic.

JR I have said that too. One of the things we said in our UNESCO
statement was that when racial theories became discredited people found other bases for justifying inequality. Very often they said
these bases were ethnic, but the problems were essentially the same.
Because the terms 'race' is so misused in popular discourse I am
inclined to drop it from sociology altogether and to say there are
groups of people who are distinguished by a phenol-typical appearance or by culture. And when they can be clearly distinguished they
may be oppressed or exploited as a group.

Really, the more inclusive category is ethnic. But I give this warning in my book, Race and Ethnicity, that there is a tendency amongst
anthropologists when they talk about ethnic differences to under-
play the importance of conflict. I have always said that when people
use the term 'ethnic', it makes society seem less conflict-ridden. The
common theme running through all my sociology has been the emphasis upon conflict. Now there may be some situations of culture

difference. But there are a set of problems in the world of oppression and exploitation of one group by another. It is this area that the
sociology of race and ethnic relations has to deal with. It is always
about conflict.

One colleague of mine at the London School of Economics once
said 'there is no such thing as good race relations because, if there
were, nobody would be talking about them'. I think, myself, I prefer to use the term ethnic as the more inclusive term, but always
with emphasis on ethnic conflict. I want a general theory in the sociology of race and ethnic relations which can include things like
black/white relations, but can also include the conflict in Northern
Ireland.

KK Within the conflict school, there is a tendency to locate the debate
in two scholars; one traditionally termed bourgeois, and the other
radical. They are Max Weber and Karl Marx respectively. It is said
that your own work seems to straddle the works of these scholars.
Where does your Marxism stop and your Weberian thinking start?
Or are they on the same continuum?

JR I don't think that anyone who has seriously read Weber would say
that his sociology is not based on a realistic understanding of conflict. There is always a great deal in common between the realistic
political sociology of Weber and Marx. If for instance you take the
very important thing that Weber wrote on the city, he could very
well have written at the front of that book: 'the history of all societies is the history of class struggle'.

Now what ultimately is the difference between Weberian notions
of class conflicts and Marxian versions of class conflicts? I think
it is basically concerned with the labour theory of value. Marxism
involves the assumption that because of the way in which value is
developed capitalism will eventually run into crises and at that stage
there will be a transition and a coming of a new era.

JR Marxian economics is based on the labour theory of value and by
virtue of the economic argument leads to the notion that eventually
there's a crisis in which the working class overthrows the system and
creates a new system based upon proletariat hegemony.

Weber explicitly accepts the *marginalist* theory of value and hew
doesn't accept the labour theory of value. Weber also does not accept the whole economic argument about the inevitability of capitalist crisis. That doesn't mean that in Weber's sociology conflict
ceases to exist. It simply is something that is going to go on for ever.

It simply is something that is going to go on for ever. There are other interests in the world who will always be engaged in conflicts with one another.

In emphasizing this aspect of Weber's work in terms of conflict theory I do produce a version of Weber which is a very 'Marxised' one. On the other hand, when I look at Marxism, there are certain parts of it about which I am agnostic, such as the labour theory of value. Therefore, my account of class conflict does involve dropping some Marxist assumptions. To that extent I am giving a Weberianised form of Marx. I am really not concerned with theology. I think, actually, that what I like about Weber is that his concept of class and other things are much clearer than they are in Marx. Marx wrote in terms of that Hegelian legacy where the concepts which he used were actually much less clear then Weber's. But I am particular concerned with a sociology based on conflicts.

KK You have absorbed aspects of the works of Marx and Weber in your thinking. In the future, this synthesis may be referred to as the 'Rexonian' model. Would you car to comment on a 'Rexonian' model of society?

JR One thing about most of my work is that it is deeply pessimistic. It doesn't have any of the optimistic assumptions of the enlightenment, that we are going to move towards a future in which conflicts will be overcome. I wrote a book once called, *Sociology and the Demystification of the Modern World* which was the least successful book I ever wrote. In that, I tried to give my views on this question. I, in fact, developed an account of the major structural problems of the First World, the Second World, and the Third World in that book. But none of them involved the optimistic assumption of a move towards a more perfect future. I had my own particular idea of the nature of the capitalist society, the nature of communist society and the nature of 'third world' society, which I tried to set out in that book and one cannot sum them up in a short space.

It is interesting that that book was written in 1973. The structures which seemed to be something which were going to go on almost forever in the societies of the 'second world' and the communist societies have collapsed. We now live in a different kind of world where temporarily people in the West, some sociologists in the West, now have the comfortable assumption that there is only one kind of possible society and that is a capitalist society. Indeed, of course, there is this well known book which I haven't read, by the man called Fukuyama entitled, *The End of History*, which states that these major problems are never going to occur again.

As I see it, the capitalist world, in the wake of the end of the 'cold war', is one in which Western capitalism gives a higher standard of life overall than the communist world was able to do. But, if one looks at contemporary capitalism, one first finds that with the ending of the war economy, recessions in them to which people can't see an end. These are societies in which there are considerable sections of the population who are left out of the prosperity, who don't have jobs and who may be unemployed over several generations. And of course, such societies, to some extent try to keep such people alive and not rioting by various welfare measures. If one looks at the United States today one finds there's a big debate about the under-class. This is a rather unsatisfactory concept, but it draws attention to the fact that capitalist prosperity leaves out a large number of people. Also, if one looks at this, not just in terms of single nations but the capitalist world at the present time, a similar pattern unfolds.

I am very much concerned with research in Europe. One has a very strong conception of enormous prosperity and efficiency in the European Commission area. But also, in the notion of fortress Europe, the rest of the World is left out. From the point of view of successful capitalist Europe, there's the rest of the world where people can be left to die, where there can be great ecological disasters and political breakdown, where large numbers of the population are dying of Aids and so on. Also one gets perhaps the most disgustingly awful phenomenon of all in the Central American countries, namely, the actual shooting of surplus children, in counties like Brazils and Guatemala and so on. So you have a society which becomes more rationalised and efficient, but for whom a lot of people are surplus.

In America particularly, a very important phenomenon in this triumphant capitalist order, is the drug problems. Enormous numbers of people in this society are in fact being destroyed by drugs. If one says in the wake of the cold war, 'now we have successful capitalism', let's look at the structure of capitalist societies and see what they are actually about.

KK There are two important issues in your sociological discussion. These are your sociological discussion. These are your conceptions of the multicultural society and the plural society. How are these tied to your pessimistic version of humanity?

JR Let us briefly and succinctly refer to the literature on the theory of plural society. In Furnival's case, referring to Indonesia, he said there are separate ethnic groups each leading a separate moral existence. The groups meet only in the market place, and in the market place there is brutal inhuman exploitation. There is no common will.

Smith, on the other hand, talks about the societies juxtaposed. I always think Guyana is the best example of what Smith was talking about, of a society in which there are basically three groups. There is the group of people of Indian origin who are the blacks who are descended from the slaves and there were of course the white colonialists. This involves three nearly complete institutional systems, an Indian one, a black one and a white one. But they are incomplete in that, according to Smith, they do not have their own separate political institutions. The political order depends upon the domination of the society by one of the groups.

Both Furnival and Smith are talking about a society based upon different ethnic groups with different economic positions and political positions in the society, but essentially unequal.

Of Course, it seems to me that South Africa is a plural society. When I was there, the first time for forty-two years in the summer of 1991, I went to the cities like Capetown, Port Elizabeth and Durban and many people say these are nice cities. But then you ask the question 'where do the black people one sees working here or shopping here actually live'? They take you on the other side of the motorway around the mountain and you see a different world entirely of the shanties and, worse then shanties, where the squatters live. And you say 'what is the rate of unemployment in these areas' and people say anything up to 80 per cent. When I was looking at that, I was reminded of Furnuval theory. Now this was the plural society.

In Europe, at the present time, people talk about multicultural societies and sometimes they talk loosely and they say multicultural or plural societies. I do think that many people who talk about multiculturalism assume a situation of inequality. I think there is a concept of the ideal multicultural society which distinguishes it from the notion of plural society and that is one in which cultural diversity and equality of opportunity are coupled together. Of course, this was the basis of a famous statement by Roy Jenkins in England in 1968. People may criticise that statement but it is very important that he does hold the two ideas together.

If anybody talks about multiculturalism and fails to talk about equality, then what he is talking about is something more like plural society, not necessarily with the harsher aspects of brutality and exploitation, but still an unequal society, and it is more like a plural society. But it is possible, I think, in Europe and in Britain to fight for the ideal of a democratic multicultural society.

KK The difference between a multicultural model of society and an antiracist model of society is often highlighted in the literature. What are your comments of this affair?

JR First of all let us look at what I call the French model in France today. Very often, antiracist organisations lay emphasis upon equality of opportunity, and more generally on equality. Everybody in France should have the same tights and the society should be generally more egalitarian. It is possible to hold that view and to say we want people to abandon their separate cultures, and some would even say it is desirable that they should abandon their separate cultures so that all can be treated equally. I understand that position and to some extent I respect it, but it leads to the development of hostility to minority cultures which can it lead to racial conflict. I am really opposed to a simply egalitarian society which has contempt for the cultures of people. I am opposed to a so–called multicultural society which doesn't recognise the importance of equality of treatment for every individual. I'm groping towards the idea of a multicultural ideal, a democratic multicultural ideal, which achieves both aims, which has a place for the separate cultures but, nonetheless, in the public sphere, in the search for jobs and houses and political rights, treats all people as equals.

KK Now that is one of the positions that the antiracists also comment upon. They are arguing that if we start with the assumption that we will treat everyone as equal in the public domain, one would find that those who start with a position of disadvantage when they approach the institutions of the public, will still be at a disadvantage. So how do you reconcile that within the concept of multiculturalism? Or could this only be reconciled within the antiracists framework?

JR When that is said, most people would go on, and indeed I would go on, to say that, since these inequalities rest upon historical wrongs, it is necessary within your ideal to say that people who start with a disadvantage should be helped. It is necessary for actions to be taken to help them to have genuine equalities of opportunity. I think I am perhaps less committed to the notion of affirmative action in all the forms in which it is taken within the United States and I actually don't want to see a situation in which people who are classified as disadvantaged are continually moulded into a charitable regime. This itself involves a certain kind of racism so I do like an emphasis upon getting people to a position where they have genuine equality of opportunity, but not a position where some are going to be specially helped and cared for by the state and some aren't.

There is, of course, a separate question, that is, the question of equality of opportunity versus equality of outcome. I think of opportunity versus equality of outcome. I think that one out the things that has been established in the tradition of European democracy, because of the struggles of the working class, is that the working class has established that not merely everybody should have equality of opportunity but that there is a basic minimum, and perhaps quite a considerable minimum, of social rights, which everybody should have and that goes beyond the question of equality of opportunity.

KK   To enter into the realm of justice!

JR   Yes.

KK   Finally, Professor, what do you see as the way forward for black people?

JR   I think that many of the problems that are called race relations problems are not simply problems of people of different colour, race or ethnic group. The differentiation of people depends upon the political and economic structures of their societies. One of the interesting things about South Africa at the present time is that people are talking as though they envisage a society in the future in which relations between black and white, African and European will be irrelevant and all of these people will be the new South African.

I am saying that in the colonial and post-colonial world there are colonial and neo-colonial structures in which people who are distinguishable physically and culturally will be in situations of political conflicts. As far as the most advanced democratic capitalist societies are concerned, I think that there should not be de facto barriers to equality of opportunity. However, these barriers do exist. Therefore, it is very important that people who belong to the ethnic minorities and, particularly, the ethnic minorities who are of colonial origin, should retain their own organisations to fight for their rights. Maybe a point will come at which they may feel sufficiently secure to say 'we want our people to be assimilated into the mainstream. We don't want them to be distinguished as a separate community. But that time is not yet.' The very possibility of people making advances of this kind rests upon the fact that they have strong organisations which can fight for the rights of their respective communities and for individuals and population groups to make progress towards tolerance.

KK Thank you, Professor Rex, for this most interesting interview.

JR Thank you too Kampta. It was a pleasure talking with you. I wish you all the best in your studies and I hope that at some future date we can continue this discussion.

3

Race, Class and Ethnicity: A Mexican Perspective on the Sociology of John Rex

LAURA VELASCO AND OSCAR CONTRERAS

I N UNIVERSITY CIRCLES throughout Mexico during the 1970s and 1980s, social scientists were eagerly sharing a book entitled, *Problemas fundamentales de la teoría sociológica*, published by Amorrortu in Buenos Aires.[1] Its author was John Rex, a South African sociologist from the University of Leeds in the United Kingdom.

For many students of the social sciences in the 1980s, the small yellow book by John Rex became an essential reference in the articulation of a critique of structural-functionalist sociology, which, at that time, was almost a requirement for admission to the fraternity. Like the social sciences in general, sociology in Mexico was expanding and becoming institutionalized. In a matter of a few years, the number of students pursuing a sociology degree would rise from a few hundred to several thousand, concentrated primarily at universities in metropolitan Mexico City, but with an increasing presence in several regional universities.[2] In the classroom, teaching drew predominantly on dependency theory, the Latin American version of academic Marxism.

In this context, Rex's book was very well received, which quickly made it an indispensable reference on 'conflict theory', as opposed to the Parsonsian theory of social order. Rex, making a masterful use of functionalism's own categories, offered a very original version of the problems of order and social integration, by demonstrating the mechanisms that enable the persistence of a non-normative order based on class domination. Moreover, he insisted on the political utility of sociological knowledge in the struggle against inequality and injustice.

Paradoxically, at that time, almost no one seemed to appreciate the full importance of Rex's book, which contained much more than just a systematic and apt critique of structural-functionalism. Indeed, his critique was from the perspective of methodological individualism and was based on a conceptual strategy strongly influenced by the ideas of Max Weber. In that sense, the work of Rex far preceded later debates about Weber's legacy and the discussions on individualism that would occur in the Mexican social sciences only at the end of the 1980s and into the 1990s.

In England, the book had a notable impact. According to Herminio Martins,[3] it caused a sea change in the history of British sociology for two principal reasons: It was the first systematic and innovative work in sociological theory in many years by a South African-British sociologist and, moreover, it was a refreshing contribution from the Weberian legacy, producing a critique on the theoretical ideas about functionalism before that intellectual current became dominant in English sociology. Martin Albrow[4] agrees with Martins that the re-evaluation of Weberian thinking and the defence of methodological individualism in the 1960s make this work a key element in British sociological theory. For Richard Jenkins,[5] this book incontestably represents British sociology's first authentic contribution to general social theory.

Beyond the importance of this pioneering work, during the second half of the twentieth century, the work of John Rex became an essential reference in the debate on ethnic relations. His contributions to the discussion on pluralism in South Africa made it possible to think about that country in a way that was distinct from how classical authors, such as Furnival and Smith, had viewed other British colonies, such as those in the Caribbean. For the first time, the migrant workforce was deemed to be a central category that was the basis for asymmetrical relations and was intimately connected with the structure of social relations between racial and ethnic groups.[6] Rex pioneered the systematic and empirical study of race relations and urban conflict in South Africa, and once in England, he broadened this, based on his experiences with class issues and ethnic conflict. Currently, in the area of policy-making on cultural diversity, he is one of the most influential sociologists in England. In contrast to Mexico, where anthropologists were the principal spokespeople for ethnic difference, in England, sociologists played a much more active role in the analysis and

definition of the cultural profile of British society in the wake of India's de-
colonisation, the Caribbean migrations, and the recent arrival of Central
Europeans.

In Mexico, Rex's ideas on the study of ethnic relations were not as
widely disseminated as was his social-conflict theory. This may have been
due to anthropology's predominance in indigenist thinking, from the first
decades of the twentieth century until the beginning of the 1960s. Only be-
latedly, in the framework of dependency theory and the theory of internal
colonialism, did sociological theory venture into the debate on ethnic relations in Mexico. In that context, Rex's ethnic-relations theory resonated
favourably with sociologists like Rodolfo Stavenhagen, who observed these
relations in the framework of the colonial relations between the Mexican
state and indigenous peoples and of class relations in Mexican society. In
particular, the chapter 'The Role of Class Analysis in the Study of Race Relations – A Weberian Perspective',[7] in the book edited by John Rex and
David Mason, was read by generations of doctoral students in the Colegio
de México's Social Science program, which Stavenhagen directed.

John Rex was born in the 1920s in Port Elizabeth, South Africa, where
his father was a postal employee. John had a scholarship to study at the university, and, like many other descendants of British colonists, he received
his schooling in a racially-divided South Africa. A large part of his university life was framed by the domination of the National Party, which, at
the end of the 1940s, developed a policy of racial segregation that made
the separation of racial groups official. When Rex migrated to England, he
took with him the experiences of the struggle against racial discrimination
on the African continent, as did other academics born in British colonies,
such as the sociologists Percy Cohen and Robin Cohen, the writer Doris
Lessing, and the group of social anthropologists led by Max Gluckman at
Manchester. His academic life in England evolved in parallel with his ac-
tivism in the African nationalist movements and the labour and disarmament protests in England and Europe, and ultimately, his intellectual trajectory was shaped by his experience with England's immigrants.

After having taught at several English universities, Professor Rex
founded the Department of Sociology at the University of Warwick. Created in 1965, this university was based on a novel concept of higher
education that clearly aims at attaining excellence, and extending access to
higher education to a broader segment of British youth. From its beginning, the university's educational model had a strong research orientation,
and in its short existence, it has gained a solid reputation for its high academic level, its focus on research, and its successful connection with the
private sector, which is reflected in a noteworthy capacity to generate its

own income.[8]

The innovative nature of this university's environment can be appreciated even in the organisation of the campus, its modern and restrained architecture, its large gardens, and its pleasant community spaces, located principally around the Arts Centre, a lively cultural and performance venue, which is the second largest in England.

In the 2001–2002 academic year, as part of their stay in the Sociology Department at the University of Warwick, the authors of this essay had the opportunity to meet John Rex personally, and to talk extensively with him. At that time, he was professor emeritus of the Centre for Research in Ethnic Relations (CRER) in that department.

The Social Sciences building, which houses the CRER, has a spacious entry hall with sweeping staircases on each side. On the second floor, a few steps from the elevator, there is an office of modest dimensions, with a picture window at the back illuminating a big desk flanked by overflowing bookshelves. Behind the desk, in a comfortable chair, Professor John Rex leans over his computer to review his correspondence. He is a burly man, with large hands and a kind face. He moves with the parsimony of his almost 80 years of age, but he still has an enviable mental vitality and works as hard as a man half his age. His conversation reflects a great clarity and his demeanour is that of an enthusiastic host who is eager to get acquainted with his visitors. During a previous visit, we had arrived at this office to converse with the famous professor about his current work. His genial reception encouraged us to continue visiting him, and after several meetings, we decided to tape the conversations.

We felt it was important to share these conversations with the Mexican social science community,[9] not only because of the influence in Mexico and Latin America of Rex's ideas about social conflict and ethnic relations, but also because he is emblematic of a generation of sociologists who developed their ideas through direct participation in the great social struggles of their day. In that sense, Rex's intellectual and life experiences reflect a trajectory that is rare today: that of a rigorous academic who makes substantive contributions in his or her field of specialisation but who, at the same time, maintains a clear public commitment to, and an active militancy in, the struggle for a just world.

This reconstruction of the conversations with John Rex[10] is organised in three sections: his approach to sociology and his experience in the racial struggles in South Africa and Rhodesia (today, Zimbabwe); his experience with the labour and pacifist movements in England; and finally, the convergence of these life experiences with his academic formation and his intellectual exploration in the field of ethnic relations in post-migrant England.

England: experiences with class and race

LV/OC Let's talk about your move to England and your early years as a university professor.

JR Having been expelled from Rhodesia in 1949, I had to return to South Africa, where, strangely enough, I found a job working in what was called the Native Affairs Department in the city of Kimberley. This was an extremely interesting experience because it let me understand the way policy towards Blacks operated, how the police worked, and things like that. Meanwhile, I had applied for jobs overseas, particularly, one job at the University of Leeds and one job in the West Indies. Then one day, while I was sitting in my office, a policeman came to see me. He showed me a letter which said, 'Mr. Rex has applied for a passport to go to England or the West Indies. We understand that he is opposed to academic segregation and that he is a believer in the teachings of Marx, Engels, and Lenin'. And I said, 'Well, that is not an exact description of my position. I'll tell you what my position is'. But he interrupted me, 'No, that isn't necessary, we'll find out'. I made a statement to him anyway. In fact, at that time my ideas were very much caught up with those of Karl Mannheim and what he had to say about the role of intellectuals. I also told the policeman something that I had learned from my sociological studies: one of the bad things about the Communist world was that the Russians didn't let their citizens travel abroad.

With a certain amount of help, I obtained a passport and came to teach in England. With the support of Professor Irving, I went to teach at the University of Leeds, in a position which he himself had held many years earlier, working in the Extramural Department. I was a teacher for classes that were organised by the Workers Educational Association. For about four years, my students were mainly miners, steelworkers, and agricultural workers, and their wives, and I taught them sociology and philosophy. When I look back on those days, I think the standard of my teaching was terrible, but this experience brought me close to the working-class movement in England. Although I retained important links with Africa, I also began to identify very much with the English working class.

I was an extramural teacher for about seven or eight years. During that time, as part of my private, non-academic life, I also arranged political meetings for most of the African nationalist leaders, many of whom came from countries where they had no vote. I would arrange for them to address meetings in Leeds. A whole lot of people came and spoke at those meetings. Joshua N'komo, Tom Mboya (the leader of the African Trade Unions in Kenya), and Kenneth Kaunda are just some of the people who came. I introduced these African speakers to British trade unionists and also to the more liberal-minded people from the churches and similar bodies. We constituted quite an effective pressure group working through the Africa Bureau.

I am talking about 1960, when we – this group of British and South African activists – were participating in the labour struggles in England, the human-rights movements in South Africa, and various pacifist demonstrations at an international level. That year, Kwame Nkrumah organized this very big conference in Ghana to unite, under the idea of 'Positive Action', the pacifists opposed to the French atomic-bomb testing in the Sahara with the liberation fighters in Africa.[11] I was invited to go as an observer. It was a very important experience because, among other things, it was the first time that I had been involved in the politics of a 'one-party state', and I saw how it worked from the inside. At this meeting, organisations representing women, trade unionists, and youth participated, all controlled by the Convention People's Party that Nkrumah headed.

The conference put me in touch with many people from various countries. I met leaders from Somalia, Ethiopia, and Ghana. This experience heightened my interest in East Africa and Central Africa, as well as motivating me to continue collaborating to stop segregation and white supremacy in South Africa, Rhodesia, and Kenya.

LV/OC How did these experiences with the African nationalists and the rise of a Pan-African consciousness influence your political and academic work in England?

JR After seven years of teaching extramural classes, I was invited to teach sociology in the Department of Social Studies at the University of Leeds. It was a very exciting time. The year 1956 was the year of the Suez war and the Budapest revolution, and everything was changing. The students were excited and interested. For my part, I totally enjoyed my first year of lecturing in that department. I suppose, looking back on it, that the political concept which shaped my sociology was a rather simplistic, semi-Marxist one, based on the idea of developing trade-union consciousness, transforming it into political consciousness. But, these ideas were coupled with the other great thing that I became involved in, beside the nationalist struggle in Africa, which was the campaign for nuclear disarmament. I wrote a pamphlet at that time called 'Britain Without the Bomb', in which I advocated for what is called positive neutralism, which suggested that Britain should disengage from both the Soviet Union and the United States.

Now the nuclear disarmament movement in England really started in about 1958, with marches from the place where they made atomic weapons in Aldermaston. We would organise marches from there to London, which took up to four days. We had to camp overnight and start marching again the following day. These were wonderful occasions. I particularly remember a march in 1962, in which 100,000 people took part. It was organised by an extraordinary woman, Peggy Duff.

All of this meant that we, including those people in academic circles, had to argue about the nature of international conflict. The actual organisation of the marches came into the hands of the people who were running a magazine called the *New Left Review*. The *New Left Review* had been formed as a result of the amalgamation of the journal edited by E. P. Thompson and John Saville, called *The New Reasoner*, and the *Left Review*, which was run by a group of young men, mainly from Oxford, who were intellectually mostly Marxist. So, in 1960, the *New Left Review* was born. I was on this board along with a number of others who had not belonged to the two previous journals, including Raymond Williams, Ralph Miliband, Doris Lessing, Alasdair MacIntyre, and Norman Birnbaum. All these became a part of a new collective, which was organised largely by Stuart Hall, the editor, who was himself a Rhodes scholar from Jamaica.[12] He edited this magazine in an innovative and relaxed way. He sought a wide audience and experimented with new media trends. And he was very successful at this point. E. P. Thompson, however, really felt it was inadequate. He had come from a different style of organisation; he talked about party cadres, vanguards, and thing like that, and he would continually criticise Stuart Hall's way of running the *Review*. It wasn't a public or a really nasty debate, but it eventually led to a point at which Hall said, 'In a year's time, I am going to hand over to somebody else'. A problem we had to face was that we were paying very little money to Hall as editor of the magazine, only about £500 a year, and he was only able to survive by doing other work. Then, we had to find a new editor, and after several attempts, we decided that we needed to find someone whose views were very close to ours, who could write well, and who didn't need money. It seemed to me that the obvious candidate was Perry Anderson. So, we invited Perry Anderson to take over the *New Left Review*.

Behind the *Review*, there was a widespread social movement, in which many of us were involved. I was a chairman of the National League of Organizations, which was very active. The journal tried to be close to these movements, which was not easy. I recall that one time, one of our members, the leader of the National Union of Miners, a man called Lawrence Daly, said to Perry Anderson, 'Look, we want a magazine which can be sold in a pithead or at a factory gate'. Perry replied, 'Oh yes, that could be fine'. But, the first issue that came out began with an article called, 'Series and Nexus in the Family', by R. D. Laing. Anderson did not believe that working-class people could not participate in intellectual debates.

Under the leadership of Perry Anderson, there was a change of generation that we had wanted to see, but it also challenged us. Anderson had his own friends around him, so a new board was created. Its members were influenced by the French Marxism that was in vogue at that time, together with some recognition of the importance of Gramsci in Italy. People like myself who couldn't speak French were a little critical about this, seeing the new board as rich young men, who had all had French-speaking nannies.

Later, the *New Left Review*'s thinking was more critical and, much latter on, Perry Anderson wrote an interesting book called *Consideration of Western Marxism*, in which he was highly critical of nearly all of the French Marxist tradition. The only person he spoke well of was Ernest Mandel, the Belgian Marxist economic historian. The journal continued, and still continues today, and, for many people in Europe, it was regarded as a most important intellectual source. I taught students in Copenhagen, Malmö, and Lund, and when I asked them what sociology was about, they pointed to the *New Left Review*. They were particularly influenced by the ideas of Nicos Poulantzas,[13] who collaborated on the journal and who was at these universities at various times. Some of the students would only really listen to me if I could translate my own ideas into Poulantzian language.

LV/OC   Did Latin America figure at all in this intellectual landscape?

JR   Yes, around the issue of development. At that time there were figures like Andre Gunder Frank,[14] who had written a little pamphlet called, 'The Sociology of Underdevelopment and the Underdevelopment of Sociology'. The students were all very impressed by this. This made me take an interest in the whole question of the sociology of developing societies in a new way. Gunder Frank's view emphasised the importance of the colonial past in the formation of underdevelopment, and this book was important because it managed to spread the issue of development throughout Europe. As I understood it, there were different views on whether capitalism could contribute to economic development. One was Gunder Frank's view that all that Europe could do was promote underdevelopment in developing societies. A second view, amongst some British communists, was that some development was possible under capitalism. A third contribution to the debate came from the Brazilian Fernando Enrique Cardoso, who took a slightly different position. Cardoso is a very interesting man because he had studied in France, and he had worked through most of these ideas himself. I knew him as the president of the International Sociological Association. Later, when he became president of Brazil, he came to believe in the free market. Cardoso was probably the best sociologically educated president that there has been in any country.

LV/OC In the 1960s, you wrote a book that was very widely read in Mexico, Key Problems of Sociological Theory. Where do you position this book in your intellectual trajectory?

JR I wrote this book in 1961. In it, I criticise the tradition of what I call the bookkeeping style of social reform, which was done at the London School of Economics. What to me seemed to be philosophically much more positivist and functionalist was seen, strangely, as Marxist by the students of the influential David Glass. From my point of view, this formed part of a tendency that had originally been taught in anthropology but which now became important in sociology, through the work of Talcott Parsons and Robert Merton. In taking a stand against these two tendencies, I produced a version of conflict theory based on Marxism and the ideas of Max Weber. That led to me often being quoted along with Ralf Dahrendorf and C. Wright Mills.

That book was widely cited, but by the end of the 1960s, the ideas that I had developed there were coming under criticism from people who had read a lot more than I had, and I had much less influence. My 'simple' Marxism was superseded by French structural Marxism, and on the other hand, my interest in interpretive sociology, deriving from Weber, was superseded by ethnomethodology.

I tried to restate my position in 1973 in a book called *Sociology and the Demystification of the Modern World*.[15] This book received the worst reviews of any sociological book that has ever been written. I still stand by the ideas in this book.

LV/OC Your book addresses the issue of social conflict in abstract theoretical terms. However, it seems clear that behind your ideas was your contact with the working class and the African social movements.

JR In the 1970s, Anthony Giddens organised several conferences in which some British sociologists participated. I contributed to one of his books, where I explained my ideas about my conflict theory. But there is something that I must mention. During that time, I left Leeds for personal reasons, and I went to the University of Birmingham. I found it so horrible and commercial that I wanted to get away from the university. I spent a lot of my time in what was called the twilight zones of the city, not just slums, which would have been a misleading term. These were areas where immigrants had settled and were places I could relate to in terms of the theories of Park and Burgess. There, I found that people were developing a new type of community based on social work, in which they had to wrestle with the important question of the relationship between the immigrants and British working-class and middle-class white people. I remember one important thing which happened there. There was a street, and on one side of it, there were white people who had lived there for a long time, who saw that the area was deteriorating as it became populated with immigrants, and who were potentially racist. Across the street there were houses owned by Indians and Pakistanis, and they formed something called the Commonwealth Property Owners Association. A social worker, who was a brilliant woman (later on she went on to do great things in other ways), brought these people together. She set up an agreement between them in which the Association said to the white residents, 'For every pound that you spend in improving your property, we will spend a pound in improving our property, under the condition that the city council also spends a pound on improving the street paving and the lighting'. And that was the basis of the development of a different kind of community consciousness, which was politically important.

LV/OC In some ways, this is reminiscent of what you said about racialisation of space in Durban, South Africa.

JR Yes, indeed, for the two years that I was a teacher at the University of Birmingham, I was drawn into this exciting research on conflicts and the integration process for immigrants in English cities. I left Birmingham with the idea of going to the University of Hull, but by accident, I found myself appointed to the University of Durham where they knew almost nothing about sociology. In any case, they gave me a Chair in Social Theory and Institutions. I was very unhappy in Durham because of its upper-class traditions and closed atmosphere. I wrote to various friends to find out if there was somewhere else I could go, and I think that is why I was invited to come here to the University of Warwick.

Well, originally, I moved from Leeds to Birmingham for two years, from 1962 to 1964, and then I went to Durham, from 1964 to 1970. I came to Warwick in 1970, and I stayed. This department, which was going to have twenty-five teaching staff, was getting many students, so I could look around the country and recruit people. It was a marvellous opportunity. The central idea of the department that I had created in Durham and the one I have created here in Warwick is that all students should do a study of social institutions and also a study of sociological theory. Here at Warwick, in the first year, we gave them classical sociological theory based on Marx, Weber, and Durkheim, and in the second year, I had a colleague talk to them about modern developments in theory. And so we developed a very large sociology department.

I had a certain amount of difficulty because this was just after the student revolution in 1968. The structuralist Marxists on my staff were one short of having a majority in the department meetings. So they entered into an unholy alliance with our one ethnomethodologist. They had a point of view that was contrary to the orientation that I had encouraged for the department. My position had become very difficult. I went to Canada for a year, and I handed the department chairmanship to someone else. When I returned, I found life was still very difficult. At that same time, the Social Science Research Council of England was looking for someone to run the National Research Unit on Ethnic Relations, and I took that over.

Colonisation of England: migration, race, and ethnicity

LV/OC In the 1970s, Indian and Pakistani immigrants were already a very visible presence in English cities. How did this migration development enter into your sociological work?

JR The Social Science Research Council, as it was then called, thought that the universities had failed to develop sufficient research in particular areas. Therefore, they decided to fund their own units directly, and there were two in particular: Industrial Relations and Ethnic Relations. For five years from 1979 to 1984, I ran the Research Unit on Ethnic Relations for the Social Science Research Council, but at Aston University in Birmingham. I should say that in my own intellectual life, I now had to develop, theoretically, the relationship between social theory, on one hand, and a theory of ethnic relations on the other. I was writing about both of these things. In 1967, I had been a member of the UNESCO . The committee had begun to say, 'well, the biologists have this concept of race, and as we use it, it has no relevance to the political differences among men and women'. Therefore, we had to ask ourselves: if the concept of race has no scientific validity, what is racism about, and what does the sociologist have to say about racism?

I was very surprised in 1967 to find out how little had been written by sociologists theoretically about ethnic relations. I remember searching in a library at UNESCO and finding nothing. When I came back to England, I started to contribute to a series of books on sociological concepts. In particular, there was *Race Relations and Sociological Theory*, which was printed in 1970.[16] Much of my subsequent intellectual history has been concerned with arguing about the nature of ethnic relations.

LV/OC Do you believe that after the 1970s, the study of racial and ethnic relations has constituted a field of study that is independent from sociology?

JR As far as sociological theory is concerned, and particularly the history of sociological theory, there is a huge body of work written now about all aspects and issues concerning ethnic relations. Even though, in the mid-1980s, I managed to systematise the writing on the topic in the book *Theories of Race and Ethnic Relations*, written with David Mason,[17] I do try to keep up with people who are making these contributions, whose ideas are different from mine. Both the postmodernists and the Marxists are in this debate with me in the field of ethnic relations. There is, for instance, a journal called *Theory, Culture and Society*, which is all about postmodernism, and the editor, Mike Featherstone,[18] was a student of mine at Durham. He wrote a thesis on the 'Chicago sociology', but he now has become one of the big figures of postmodernist theory, which strongly criticises the concept of ethnicity. On the side of the Marxists, for example, is Robert Miles,[19] who mistakenly argues that I have defined the treatment of ethnic problems in England as a race problem, which was actually the opposite of the truth. On another front, I have had to respond to the challenges of developments in Marxism and urban sociology. In England, particularly, the Marxist sociologist Chris Pickvance,[20] a follower of the ideas of Manuel Castells, wrote about the new urban sociology from a Castellian Marxist point of view. According to these writers, in my work on urban sociology, I have dealt simply with the effects on racial discrimination of the actions of immediate gatekeepers, whereas a comprehensive urban sociology would have to deal with such matters as the ownership of land and interest rates. Rather than discouraging me, these criticisms have obliged me to place my work within a wider setting. Similarly, David Harvey's book, *Social Justice and the City*,[21] offered a Marxist explanation of why, in the city, the rich grow richer and the poor grow poorer. I do not claim to have contributed to these larger debates about political economy. My contributions to urban sociology are confined to studying the immediate gatekeepers, and how they create what I call 'housing classes'. Castells, however, presents me with further problems. Firstly, in his book, *The Urban Question*,[22] he broke out of the structuralist Marxist framework to offer a theory of social movements. This theory has been taken up by others, while Castells himself has moved toward a new theory, based on the notion of a network society.[23] I have to be modest about this. There are now ways of posing theoretical questions about ethnicity, class, and urbanism which are far more sweeping in their scale than anything which I have had to offer.

LV/OC   In the midst of this enormous number of theories, what do you believe is the principal challenge for the fields of study dealing with ethnic relations and cultural diversity?

JR   Every day, there are developments: new organisations which claim to provide an understanding of ethnicity and nationalism. We are trying harder and harder to respond to what is happening in society with theory. I heard of a new electronic journal, which will begin with a statement by Will Kymlicka,[24] about the importance of discussing the question of the applicability of Western European models of ethnicity to Eastern Europe. There are a host of new initiatives for studying the breakup of states after the collapse of Communism.

As far as sociological theory is concerned, I still believe in a particular kind of Weberian Marxism or Left Weberianism. What is debatable is a particular view of the epistemology of the social sciences. But it is difficult to go further in Weberian studies, which have produced enormous historical and theoretical scholarship. I try to follow this with the aid of one of Britain's leading Weberian experts, Sam Whimster,[25] and Gunther Roth, in the United States.

Meanwhile, I have also embarked on a whole new range of work dealing with the nature of multiculturalism and its governance both in Europe and further afield. This inevitably brings me in touch with debates about ethnicity and nationalism and the nature of transnational communities.

Part II

Key Problems in Sociological Theory: Exploring the Implications of John Rex's Neo-Weberianism

4

The Place of Values in the Study of Ethnicity and 'Race': Reflections on the Contribution of John Rex

MARTIN BULMER

IT IS SALUTARY to remember what a stir was made in the world by the publication in 1961 of John Rex's first book, *Key Problems in Sociological Theory*. Rex was a sociology lecturer at the University of Leeds, whence he had moved after a stint of extramural teaching on Teesside, which had followed his arrival in Britain from South Africa in 1949. *Key Problems* made a major contribution to orienting British sociology at a time at which its notable post-war expansion was just beginning [cf. Halsey 2004; Bulmer 2005]. The British Sociological Association had been established in 1950 [Platt 2003] and its Teacher's Section was acting as the leading edge of developing the subject. John, himself, was to chair the BSA later in the 1960s while heading the Sociology Department at Durham University.

This chapter has two aims, to focus upon one issue [among many] pursued in *Key Problems* and thereby to recapture John's approach to the place of values in sociological theory and locate it in relation to theorists such as Max Weber, Heinrich Rickert, Karl Mannheim and Gunnar Myrdal. Second, it examines a small number of value issues that have arisen in the study of ethnicity and 'race' relations, using examples from Myrdal's notable study of African-Americans, *An American Dilemma*, and the present Israel/Palestine conflict in the contemporary Middle East. John Rex's interests and sociological imagination have been concerned with 'race' as a sociological variable ever since his young days in Port Elizabeth, and these issues have been present in a muchof his subsequent work, receiving their first and most systematic statement in his first theoretical work.

Key Problems emphasised the role of theoretical models in orienting the sociologist to his or her research problems. John drew attention to the inadequacies of a sociological tradition dominated by empiricism and positivism. He castigated a tendency to rely on what were purportedly purely factual statements, in which 'left wing facts' were refuted by 'right wing facts' without acknowledgement of theoretical issues in their generation. He also criticised those who modelled sociology upon a 'positivism' which held that the social scientist operated in the same way as the natural scientist. The argument for being explicit about one's theoretical position was that one thereby avoided importing theoretical assumptions indirectly by using them implicitly in the form of undisclosed hunches about the way research data are selected and ordered.

Values played an important part in this congeries of problems. The empiricists, he argued, were engaging in debates in which they desperately sought to conceal the value-biases which pervaded their work. The positivists, on the other hand, falsely claimed that a value-free sociology was possible, ignoring the extent to which values pervaded all sociological work. *Key Problems* sought in particular to develop the action frame of reference as a basis for approaching research questions sociologically. Its source lay in the work of Max Weber, and it had been developed subsequently, according to Rex, by Karl Mannheim, Gunnar Myrdal and Talcott Parsons.

The key Weberian insight which provided the starting point was that we all select problems according to 'relevance for value'.

> The necessity of any element of a social relation, institution or system is only a relative necessity and depends upon the extent to which the ends and values achieved by the system are in fact desired by individuals and groups.... Given that we are concerned with the problem of how particular ends or valued states-of-affairs are to be attained, the sociologist may concern himself with causal or functional investigations to show what institutional relationships would favour their attainment. But the sociologist, qua sociologist, is in no better position than the layman to say whether or not a particular social end is to be desired. His task as a sociologist is to apply the

disciplines of scientific thinking to the discovery of causal relations
or the discovery of social means or ends (Rex 1961: viii).

The sociologist could not be expected to make value choices either for students or for the general reader, although sociology as a discipline might
expose more sharply the real, as distinct from the utopian, value choices
which face social actors.

> It is in this sense, and this sense alone, that sociology may be
> thought of as radical critical discipline. It will simply fall into bad
> repute if it fails to recognise this and seeks to compensate for the
> conservative ideological commitments of its recent past by embrac-
> ing a new political radicalism. On the other hand, if it does recog-
> nize its limitations, it will lay the foundations for a more honest and
> better-informed discussion of value-questions and earn a rightful
> and secure place in the university curriculum (Rex 1961: viii–ix).

The tone here is reminiscent of a work of John's a decade later, which ad-
umbrated the public responsibilities of the sociologist. *Sociology and the
Demystification of the Modern World* (Rex 1974) sets out the enlightening
role which sociology may play in challenging the comfortable assumptions
about the nature of society which people like to hold.

Key Problems, however, was a work of more austere theoretical purpose,
which devoted itself single mindedly to setting out the components of the
action frame of reference. The discussion of values was a key part of the
argument, and was discussed both in the context of the Parsonian action
schema, and Max Weber's conception of objectivity. The latter is the best
place to start.

Max Weber, it was pointed out in *Key Problems*, charged the sociologist with producing explanations which were both adequate at the level
of meaning, and causally adequate. Yet Weber was familiar with a tradition, particularly associated with Wilhelm Dilthey, which held that these
two types of explanation were incompatible and could not co-exist in the
same science. The task of the sociologist, which is completely different from
that of the natural scientist, is to understand symbolic modes of expression
or embodiments of meaning in social action, through *verstehen* (interpretive understanding).

Weber did not accept this position, and set against it two arguments.
The first is that there is a form of understanding in the social sciences which
can be set out in a manner not incompatible with the methods of science,
and second, that generalisation in the social sciences does not necessarily
depend on the existence of abstract systems of laws, which Dilthey thought

characterised the natural sciences, and from which the human sciences differed totally. The starting point for such an analysis is the understanding of rational action, and explanations can be constructed in terms of rationally constructed conduct. The sociologist can then go on to construct explanations of non-rational conduct – for example, religious belief – which are based upon hypotheses about human conduct which are susceptible to empirical investigation.

Second, Weber identified with other German predecessors, notably Heinrich Rickert, of the south-west German neo-Kantian school, who rejected positivism [cf Oakes 1988]. In his essay on objectivity [Weber 1949], argued that all science is faced with the problem of selecting from an infinitude of data that which is relevant to the problem being addressed. But, whereas in the natural sciences, the principle of selection is that it is the recurrent phenomena which are worthy of study, in the social sciences, the principle of selection must be that of 'relevance for value'.

> The significance of a configuration of cultural phenomena and the basis of this significance cannot however be derived and rendered intelligible by a system of analytic laws, however perfect it may be, since the significance of cultural events presupposes a value-oreintation toward those events. The concept of culture is a value concept. Empirical reality becomes 'culture' to us because and in so far as we relate it to value ideas. It includes those segments and only those segments of reality which have become significant to us because of their value-relevance. Only a small portion of existing concrete reality is coloured by our value-conditioned interest and it alone is significant to us. It is significant because it reveals relationships which are important to us due to their connection with our values. Only because and to the extent that this is the case is it worth worthwhile to know its individual features. We cannot discover, however, what is meaningful to us by a 'presuppositionless' investigation of empirical data. Rather perception of its meaningfulness to us is the presupposition of its becoming an object of investigation. Meaningfulness naturally does not coincide with laws as such, and the more general law the less the coincidence (Weber 1949: 76–77).

The discussion of this issue in *Key Problems* then moved on to a consideration of the writings of Karl Mannheim and Gunnar Myrdal on the problem of objectivity. Karl Mannheim was born in Budapest, became professor of sociology at Frankfurt University in 1930, and a refugee in Britain in 1933, following the rise of Hitler before he left Germany. He wrote *Ideology and Utopia*, a founding text of the sociology of knowledge, and this provided the basis for the discussion of his contribution in *Key Problems*. Mannheim was closer to Dilthey than Weber, arguing that 'it is clear that a human situation is characterisable only when one has also taken into account those conceptions which the participants have of it, how they experience their tensions in this situation, and how they react to the tensions so conceived' (Mannheim 1940: 40). There are certain terms which are so 'replete with valuations' that only a participant in the social system can understand them. Thus, it is necessary for the sociologist to enter into social situations as a participant if he is to be able to write significantly about them. This may necessitate the sacrifice of what is thought of as the detachment and objectivity of the sociologist, but it is necessary, because

> ...the purposefully oriented will is the source of the understanding of the situation. In order to work in the social sciences one must participate in the social process, but this participation in collective unconscious striving in no wise signifies that the persons participating in it falsify the facts or see them incorrectly. Indeed, on the contrary, participation in the living context of social life is a presupposition of the understanding of the inner nature of his living content. The disregard of quantitative elements and the complete restraint of the will does not constitute objectivity, but is instead the negation of the essential quality of the object (Mannheim 1940: 42).

Rex criticises Mannheim for psychological reductionism in confusing the question of why the sociologist is interested in a subject with the logical question of the validity of that knowledge. And he doubts that it is necessary to grasp a situation in its entirety. As Weber famously said: 'One does not have to have been Caesar, in order to understand Caesar'. One might construct a model of Caesar's motivation, without grasping every element in the situation.

Gunnar Myrdal was a Swedish economist who from an early age addressed issues of the value premises in economics, notably in his book *The Political Element in the Development of Economic Theory*, first published in Swedish in 1930 and in English in 1953, eight years before the appearance of *Key Problems*. Having published on economic theory and demographic issues in Sweden, Myrdal was recruited by the Carnegie Corporation of New York in 1936 to undertake a magisterial survey of the state of race relations in the United States, which appeared in 1944 as *An American Dilemma: the Negro Problem and Modern Democracy* (Myrdal, with Sterner and Rose, 1944).

Myrdal was commissioned by Carnegie to undertake the study because it was thought that no American scholar, whatever the colour of their skin, could be sufficiently dispassionate and achieve the necessary objectivity in

providing an account of American race relations. Myrdal addressed this
issue head on in his book, and, in an appendix on 'facts and valuations',
argued that the biases in the social sciences cannot be eradicated simply by
'keeping to the facts'. The social scientist himself is not immune to biases.

> In the light of the history of scientific writings on the American Ne-
> gro problem, the biased notions held in previous times and the op-
> portunistic tendencies steering them stand out in high relief against
> the better-controlled scientific views of today. Our steadily increas-
> ing stock of observations and inferences is not merely subjected
> to continuous cross-checking and critical discussion, but is delib-
> erately scrutinized to discover and correct hidden preconceptions
> and biases. Full objectivity, however, is an ideal toward which we
> are constantly striving, but which we can never reach. The social sci-
> entist, too, is part of the culture in which he lives, and he never suc-
> ceeds in freeing himself entirely from dependence on the dominant
> preconceptions and biases of his environment (Myrdal 1944: 1035).

Myrdal's answer to the value problem was to seek to make his value position
as clear as possible to the reader. Resort to 'the facts' or to statistical analysis
alone, or a refusal to draw practical or political conclusions from sociological work did not protect the sociologist. Myrdal argued that there was no
piece of research on the 'Negro problem' The only safeguard, in Myrdal's
view, was for the scholar to make his or her preconceptions explicit, and
he did this in two ways in *An American Dilemma*. Much of the analysis
was oriented to what Myrdal termed 'the American creed', an ideal typical
statement of the values embodied in the American constitution and Bill of
Rights. Values were thus explicitly introduced into the analysis, and the situation of people whom Myrdal termed 'the American Negro' and which
today would be replaced by 'African-American' was compared to the ideals set out in the creed. And Myrdal argued that the social scientist should
make their own values explicit in dealing with such a fraught and sensitive
issue as American race relations To that end, statements in the book which
he considered evaluative were printed in italics, to differentiate them from
statements which were empirical generalisations and summations of the
state of scientific knowledge.

In *Key Problems*, John Rex draws on Myrdal's methodological position in jutaposition to that of Mannheim. He argues that Myrdal implicitly recognises that power at the disposal of various groups in support of
their valuations actually determines the outcome in structural terms. And
that the balance of power can be reasonably easily objectively determined.
Myrdal, it may be argued, was more concerned with distinguishing facts

from valuations, and the distinction between the 'positive' and the 'normative' which has so preoccupied welfare economists. But his position is a distinctive one which has had some influence upon sociology.

Rex concludes his discussion of objectivity by arguing that Weber, Mannheim and Myrdal form a single sociological tradition. Facts are not just facts, but facts related to a purpose or end, and because there are many possible ends which may be pursued, two conclusions follow: (a) The criteria of relevance for the selection of problems to study may be determined by values. In this case, objectivity is achieved by making the scientist's values explicit. (b) Second, the social scientist must have regard to power.

> [T]he actual course of development of a social system will depend upon the balance of power behind the conflicting ends. In this case the course of development is capable of being relatively objectively determined. Nonetheless, the very notion of a balance of power is meaningless except in relation to groups pursuing conflicting ends and here again such ends must be made explicit (Rex 1961: 166).

In his subsequent work, which is not the primary focus of this chapter, John Rex has followed through this theoretical concern with values in an effective and distinguished way, indeed his contribution to the study and conceptualisation of 'race' and ethnicity has been characterised by a concern for the political and moral dimensions of the subject. Consider the following instances from his *œuvre*; they are selected merely as examples.

In his first major empirical study, with Robert Moore, *Race, Community and Conflict: A Study of Sparkbrook* (1967), which applied Robert Park's urban theory to Birmingham, and developed the theory of housing classes, Rex and Moore devoted a chapter to the policy implications of their research, and concluded:

> We should be inclined to say, if we were asked what the future of race relations in Britain's cities is likely to be, that a tendency toward segregation of coloured immigrants in cities will continue and that the inhabitants of these areas will more and more become the target of punitive policies and racial hostility. Nonetheless, we do not yet see this trend to be absolutely inevitable, and it is because we, as individuals rather than sociologists, wish to see it arrested that we have written this book (Rex and Moore 1967: 271).

Three years later, in *Race Relations in Sociological Theory*, John Rex set out his view of how contemporary race relations had been shaped by the institutions and practices of colonialism, not just in relation to slavery and various forms of unfree labour, but also in the emergence of the plural society in certain colonial territories. This fairly austere theoretical interest, first pursued in an article in the BJS (Rex 1959), was a continuing concern, in which he engaged in debate with an even more austere theorist of the plural society, M G Smith.

His period as Director of the SSRC Research Unit on Ethnic Relations, which he headed from 1979 to 1984, was marked by a major theoretical symposium edited by Rex and Mason (1986), which is the most impressive testimony to this theoretical influence in the field. A decade later, he was still engaged in the fray, with a foray into the intersections of nationalism, multiculturalism and migration (Guibernau and Rex 1997). This includes an incisive chapter on 'the concept of a multicultural society', written while he was heading the SSRC Unit, challenging the widespread use of the term without being clear what was meant.

> [A] anew goal has become widely accepted in British race relations, namely that of the multiracial society, but the meaning of this term remains remarkably obscure... Multiculturalism is a new goal for British race relations. It was not discussed much before 1968 and even today much research is directed by another and quite different value standpoint, namely that which emphasises equality of individual opportunity.... But more and more of the problems posed to us are not about equality and how it can be promoted, but about the multicultural society, which prima facie at least must mean a society in which people are not equally but differently treated. If in fact we pretend that multiculturalism and equality are the same goal under different names we are creating precisely that kind of fuzziness which Myrdalian principles would suggest that we should avoid (Rex 1997: 206).

John Rex's approach is important because it has identified the way in which values enter into sociological work, and the inescapability of addressing the issue of objectivity in any sociology of ethnic and 'race' relations. At this point, I am going to turn to the study of contemporary Israel/Palestine, and an experience of my own, to show how intractable are the problems of values and objectivity in the study of some contemporary ethnic conflicts. These are in principle no different from the difficulties with which Myrdal wrestled seventy years ago as he began work for *An American Dilemma*. There is a connection here with the work of John Rex, who in recent years has interested himself in the place of Muslims in western European societies. Others have drawn explicit parallels between Israel and John's native South Africa (cf Glazer 2003), though he himself has not concerned himself with the Middle East in his scholarly work.

My own direct engagement with the issues of academic objectivity and the problem of standpoint in the study of Israel came about in my capacity as editor of the international journal *Ethnic and Racial Studies*, when I started to put together a special issue in the late 1990s on '*Aspects of ethnic division in contemporary Israel*'. The proposed special issue provoked extended discussion at the ERS editorial board meeting in May 1997, where several members were concerned about the possible political implications of publishing an issue such as this.

Dr Haleh Afshar, a member of the Board, commented after reading a draft of my proposed introductory article:

> I dissent from the Board's decision to publish this issue primarily because it seems that by doing so the journal falls into the trap that majorities frequently fall into when dealing with minorities, that of taking the majority position as a norm and problematising that of minorities. In the case of Palestine this is all the more complicated since the minority has been created; the majority has been imported at the expense of the expulsion of the actual inhabitants of the land, many of whom are obliged to live in refugee camps outside their own country. The newly created concept of citizenship in Israel too is an exclusive concept which cannot accommodate the demands of the subordinated peoples that it has excluded on ethnic and religious grounds. If we are to conduct an ethnic and racial study of Israel, then we should do so in terms of the exclusionary policies of an occupying power that discards the peoples of this land. We should problematise the raison d'etre as well as the policies of the Israeli government and its army of occupation, rather than accepting their definitions and terminologies and seeing Palestinian nationhood and citizenship as problematical concepts that cannot be easily accommodated by Israeli discourse (H. Afshar, personal communication).

Dr Jan Penrose, another Board member, articulated the issue in terms of who has the power to define categories, like 'society', and to promote them in an international journal.

> The way in which society is defined has everything to do with how the situation in Israel is portrayed and consequently, with how solutions to the situation are identified and applied. Given that only one sociologist in Israeli universities is of Arab origin, it seems clear that Arab definitions of society in general, and of Israeli society in particular, will have much greater difficulty in achieving expression than those of Jewish academics. Under these circumstances, the decision to produce a special issue which is dominated by Jewish perspectives, however varied, makes the journal a potential vehicle for

the legitimizing of hegemonic views. However inadvertently, this situation also makes the journal complicit in the marginalization of alternative (in this instance Palestinian) views of the situation in Israel. The inclusion of one Palestinian author tempers this negative potential but it does not really move us beyond the token contributor status. Some might even argue that the token element makes the journal's complicity worse because it suggests a thin veneer of impartiality (J. Penrose, personal communication).

These challenges compelled me to say something in the Introduction to the special issue (Bulmer 1998) about my own standpoint in relation to the issues considered in the special issue. I am neither Jewish nor Arab. I had visited Israel twice: in 1963 when I had worked on a kibbutz for a month, and in 1997 at the invitation of the Israeli Sociological Association to speak at its annual conference. The articles which had been submitted and accepted by the journal, and the range of views which they represented, fully justified in my view the decision to publish a special issue, which has been strengthened by the addition of two further refereed articles, the second written by an Arab Israeli academic, immediately following my introduction, to provide a more general perspective upon theorizing Israeli society.

It was evident, I observed, that there were strong theoretical differences, reflecting the deep political divisions both between Jew and Arab, Israeli and Palestinian. Within the conflicting camps, the special issue made no claim to comprehensiveness, but neither did it contribute to 'the legitimising of hegemonic views'. My own observations were that currently sociologists in Israel were perhaps a somewhat marginal group, and certainly not pillars of the establishment nor bearers of the state ideology.

While I accepted the criticism that the field was dominated by Israeli Jewish scholars at the expense of Palestinian sociologists, there were and are very few of the latter. In such a situation, it cannot follow that one can say nothing about the two ethnic groups, and Arab definitions of Israeli society must be sought from various sources. Some Israeli Jewish sociologists have articulated views which give space and significant weight to Palestinian definitions of the situation. There was a convergence between some of these earlier theoretical statements and the work of Nadim Rouharla, a Palestinian Israeli working in the United States, who had recently articulated sharply (1997) some of the principal issues concerning Israeli Palestinians within the framework of a theory of collective identity. This penetrating analysis is not seeking solutions to political questions which to some, at least, appear to be impossible to find, but is searching for theoretical tools with which to understand a fractured society of exceptional complexity.

I also challenged one latent assumption of the two Board members quoted above, that views are best represented by scholars with particular backgrounds. As Max Weber remarked with reference to Caesar crossing the Rubicon, 'One does not have to have been Caesar to understand Caesar'. There is no necessity that scholarly objectivity requires that the scholar should be of a particular ethnic, religious, national, gendered or class origin in relation to the problem under investigation, in order to offer an adequate analysis of a particular problem. What matters in the study of contemporary Israel and its Jewish and Palestinian citizens is first a commitment to adequate theoretical understanding of the main issues involved, about which there is indeed disagreement, and second its close empirical investigation. Both qualities were demonstrated in the articles in the special issue. The particular origins of the scholars who produce these analyses is in my view a secondary matter, *pace* Karl Mannheim.

The wider issue of the responsibilities of the scholar in highly conflictual settings, whether they be in Northern Ireland, South Africa under apartheid, Sri Lanka or Kashmir, in which warfare and murder may be taking place, remains on the agenda. It is not, in my view, the task of a journal such as *Ethnic and Racial Studies* to extend the conflicts of the world into the pages of the journal, rather to seek to analyse the issues and structures involved in such conflicts in as dispassionate a way as can be achieved.

One could not do better, in my view, than to quote Max Weber:

> There is one tenet to which we adhere most firmly in our work, namely, that a social science journal.... to the extent that it is scientific, should be a place where those truths are sought which ... can claim ... the validity appropriate to an analysis of empirical reality (1949: 59).

This task is difficult enough, and is not to be confused with moral indifference or total detachment from the subject of inquiry. Nevertheless, a certain distancing of oneself from partisanship is probably a necessary corollary. The safeguard against partisanship does not lie primarily in the control over the individual, but in the exchange of views. As Weber wrote of the *Archiv für Sozialwissenschaft und Socialpolitik*:

> The peculiar characteristic of the journal has ... been ... that political antagonists can meet in it to carry on scientific work. It excludes no one from its circle of contributors who is willing to place himself within the framework of scientific discussion ... (I)n its pages no one will be protected, neither its contributors nor its editors, from being subjected to the sharpest factual, scientific criticism. Whoever cannot bear this, or takes the viewpoint that he does not wish to work, in the service of scientific knowledge, with persons whose

other ideals are different from his own, is free not to participate (1949: 60–61).

I tend to see the problem of Israel in longer-term historical perspective. No one side is right in the contemporary situation, and the best we can hope to achieve as social scientists is more adequate theoretical understanding of what appears at the present time to be a truly intractable situation which is so strongly invested with passion. Counterfactuals such as what if the Balfour Declaration had not been made, what if Israel had not come into existence, are of limited usefulness.

As Omer Bartov has observed:

> In Israel, debates on the recent past are mainly about the present. One never begins by speaking about the present, let alone the future, but always about the past. Who did what to whom, who did it first, worse, or better, who was whose victim? In Israel, people are not just interested in the past; they die or kill for it. Which is why, if ever there was any hope of following Leopold von Ranke's advice on writing history 'as it really was', Israel is definitely not the right place to try (1997: 13).

The Balfour Declaration and the period of British mandate were highly significant in the formation of contemporary Israel, yet many of the same problems of creating a system in which Arab and Jew could coexist within the same territory were apparent then. My father Charles Trevelyan (1870–1958), the Liberal and then Labour MP, who was 72 when I was born, was a close friend and in his early years a political associate of Herbert Samuel (1870–1963). Both were entering politics and parliament together and espousing liberal and radical causes. He was best man at Samuel's wedding at London's New West End Synagogue in 1897, claiming that he was the only gentile present (Morris 1977: 27). They remained personally close though diverging politically (Wasserstein 1992: 36–38). Samuel was a prominent member of Liberal governments, being Home Secretary during 1916 and holding other senior ministerial posts.

Herbert Samuel was appointed by Lloyd George as the first British High Commissioner in Palestine, a post which he held from 1920 to 1925. During his first three years as High Commissioner, Samuel's overriding aim was to devise a unitary and unifying political framework that would draw all the communities in Palestine, Arab and Jewish, Druze, Bedouin and Armenian, together. He sought, and failed, to create a single society in the territory over which Britain exercised its mandate. In 1923 he persuaded the British government not to withdraw from Palestine, as they were minded to do. He then resorted, very much against his own political inclinations, to attempt to deal with each community separately on the basis, not of national, but of communal institutions (Samuel 1945: 180–81). He supported the policy of Zionist development by the settlers, while conciliating the Arab opposition, thus permitting the creation of a Jewish semi-autonomous economy, an underground army, and the embryonic institutions of a national state.

Samuel's abandonment of the attempt to build a unified political community in Palestine and his recourse instead to a system in which the [British] Government of Palestine presided like an umpire over what were to develop into two rival quasi-governments prepared the way for the ultimate collapse of the Mandatory regime. In a sense, what Samuel created was a form of internal, or institutional partition of Palestine on a communal basis, a decade before the country's territorial partition began to be seriously discussed (Wasserstein 1992: 266–67).

One of his last official acts was the inauguration of the Hebrew University at a ceremony held in its large open-air amphitheatre on the slopes of Mount Scopus. This was a highly symbolic event, attended also by Lords Allenby and Balfour, the proceedings chaired by Chaim Weizmann. The tension between partisanship and disinterest is shown in the role of the proconsuls such as Samuel who created the conditions on the basis of which Israel eventually came into being. His was a colonial government, backed by military force, but hardly a conventional one. An analysis in terms of 'imperialism' alone is limited. Palestine was not a British possession, and Samuel and his successors became increasingly preoccupied with trying to hold the ring between the Arabs and the Jews. Reminders of this era persist. Amid the many paradoxes of contemporary divided Jerusalem, the Hebrew University displays a painting of the inauguration ceremony in 1925 and the High Commissioner's residence still stands near the Mount of Olives with its own gatehouse and is clearly identifiable, while in Tel Aviv the seafront walk between the beach and the town is named the Herbert Samuel Esplanade. These are ironic reminders, in the midst of profound contemporary conflicts, of the formative colonial period of this unique modern society in the eastern Mediterranean and of its complex internal divisions, some of which it was the aim of the special issue of the journal to examine.

Conclusion

This personal excursus into the dilemmas facing a journal editor brings us back to the discussion of values, and the relevance of Weber, Mannheim and Myrdal to the problem of objectivity. The importance of Weber is clear, in orienting us to the standpoint from which the sociologist begins his or her investigation. How far one may get with the analysis of the class origins of the scholar which Mannheim advocated is perhaps more open to doubt. Seeking to understand the views of members of the ruling class is a difficult enough task for the historian, but members of this class were not an undifferentiated mass. My father may have been a member of that class, though hardly a typical one (cf. Trevelyan 2006, chapter 4), but for various reasons connected with my family origins I did not grow up in that class or share his class position in my youth, how then can my interpretation of the Middle East situation of today be interpreted from the point of view of the sociology of knowledge as class determined or class influenced? Nor does the formulation of Gunnar Myrdal provide one with a self-evident solution to the issue of whose side one is on in the contemporary Middle East. Making one's biases explicit is useful advice, but it is not enough.

The conclusion one comes to is that John Rex's approach to the place of values in sociological inquiry has been a very stimulating and valuable one, which has pointed sociologists to be attentive to issues which otherwise they might have tended to ignore. His reading of the past of sociology, and his careful analysis in *Key Problems* has placed sociology in general and British sociology in particular in his debt, and these themes have been carried through consistently in his later work on ethnicity and race. Grounding such research and theorising in a well thought out methodological position in relation to values has been of exceptional importance.

5

The Long March with a Key Problem: Can Explanation and Understanding Be Linked?

MARGARET S. ARCHER

I N 1961, John Rex published *Key Problems of Sociological Theory*, which has rightly been called 'the first distinctively British sociological contribution to general social theory' (Jenkins 2005). In 1961, I entered the London School of Economics to read Sociology. These two events were related in both cause and effect. To account for the causal connection, we have to go back three more years and revisit the Aldermaston March of 1958 and a conversation that began, on the outskirts of Brentwood's interminable suburbs, between the author-to-be of *Key Problems* and a fifteen year old schoolgirl. To appreciate all of the effects would mean examining these two people's biographies and bibliographies over the next forty years.

Suburban Brentwood seems an unlikely setting for any life-changing event and perhaps only Max Weber, whose name I first heard under its dripping, pollarded trees, would have been open enough to recognise that a social encounter there, as anywhere, could result in matters becoming 'so rather than otherwise'. John has always found introducing sociology – his forte – to be irresistible and, doubtless, my pertinacious questioning hardly constituted resistance. As he flexed his sociological imagination, during that and other stretches of the route, touching on themes later to be developed in *Key Problems*, the girl who was already school-groomed for a degree in English Literature ceased being 'so' and wanted the 'otherwise' of becoming a sociologist, with an enthusiasm equalling his own.

Over the next few years I often reverted to that encounter (and its follow-ups, when John and I organised 'cost-to-coast' CND marches on successive New Years) because I was reluctant to chalk up its outcomes to an exercise of his 'charisma' or to a demonstration of chaos theory. Some light came when I first met the following sentence from C. Wright Mills, courtesy of the recently published *Key Problems*, '[t]he sociological imagination enables its possessor to understand the larger historical scene in terms of its meaning for the inner life and external career of a variety of individuals' (Mills 1959). The first issue was one of *verstehen*; how to understand the 'inner life' of a successful academic who had time for school kids' questionings? That was partially answered by reference to Max Weber's 'Science as a Vocation' in conjunction with what I had learned about John's 'larger historical scene' – his South African background and commitment to human flourishing, which exceeded opposing *apartheid*. It was only fully answered when I became familiar with the early work of Martin Hollis and his fertile idea that we *personify* our roles rather than merely discharge their obligations, including the small print. Putting the two together, John's way of interpreting his role of lecturer was a *personification of his vocation*; and that included taking school kids and their questioning on board.

Retrospectively, it seems not to have been pure happenstance that led me to juxtapose the names of Rex and Hollis because they shared another important concern. Both had a lifelong preoccupation with Weber's problem about how, or whether 'understanding' and 'explanation' could be combined or not – and both rejected Weber's own solution. 'Explanation' was, indeed, the second issue which the Aldermaston encounter posed for me, especially with reference to 'the larger historical scene'. It was one thing to have come to some understanding of the nature of this encounter in terms of the concerns and roles of its two interacting participants. But it was a completely different thing to acknowledge that the meeting would not have taken place at all without the 'historical scene' of CND in the late fifties, which had moulded our 'external careers' as marching protesters. And having concluded that, should one not then say that the encounter itself depended upon the particular historical position of Great Britain in relation to international (nuclear) relations?

Yet if this conclusion were drawn, then the 'structure' of international relations was being held to exert causal powers upon the interaction of two people, representing 'agency'. As I drew this conclusion (one I have held to ever since), this meant parting company with John, who has steadfastly hung on to methodological individualism as the way to combine the 'understanding' of agents with the 'explanation' of social systems, but also with

Structural Conditioning
T^1

Socio-Cultural Interaction

T_2 T_3
                        Structural Elaboration (morphogenesis)

                        Structural Reproduction (morphostasis)
                                                        T_4

Martin, who equally steadfastly maintained that 'there are always two stories to tell, one explanatory and the other interpretative, and *they cannot
finally be combined*' (Hollis and Smith: 87, emphasis added). Despite the efforts of Max Weber and his successors to act as marriage brokers, *Erklaren*
and *Verstehen* would never walk up the aisle together. Since I disagreed
with both, I was left with my 'Aldermaston problem', namely how could
'understanding' and 'explanation' march together? This paper represents
the latest of a long line of struggles with that problem.

One story about structure and agency?

Much of my work since *Social Origins of Educational Systems* (1979) has
been devoted to developing the 'morphogenetic approach'[1] to examine
how agents reproduce (morphostasis) or transform (morphogenesis) social structures and are themselves reproduced or transformed in the self-
same process. Stripped down to its chassis, this approach is based upon
two fundamental propositions: that structure necessarily pre-dates the ac-
tion(s) which transform it; and that structural elaboration necessarily post-
dates those actions, as represented in the following diagram.

This approach both respects the activity-dependence of every structural property at all times and the structural-dependency of 'social action'
in its conception and conduct.[2] However, it uses analytical (not philosophical) dualism to delineate different temporal phases – <Structural Conditioning → Social Interaction → Structural Elaboration> – to give an account of *structuring* over time and, with it, resultant changes in agential
constitution. Clearly the above is over-compressed, but I am neither trying
to introduce nor advocate the approach, but to make only a single point
about it, namely that morphogensis attempts to tell one story, though ad-
mittedly a complex one. It is the story of the mutually elaborative *interplay*
between 'structure' and 'agency', but also between 'objectivity' and 'subjectivity' over time.

Among the reviews received whilst this approach was being developed,
the most creative criticism came in a short article by Martin Hollis and

Steve Smith entitled, predictably enough, 'Two Stories about Structure and Agency' (1994). Effectively, this made me re-confront the 'Aldermaston problem'. The nub of the critique was that 'what matters is not that structure and agency both determined the outcome, not simply that we need to show how and in what ways and in what combinations they did, rather, the fundamental problem with morphogenesis is that it does not make sense of how we *integrate* structures and agents in a *single* story' (ibid.: 250). In fact, they were making two points. Firstly that the Morphogenetic approach, in particular, and Social Realism, in general, were wanting in their specification 'of *how* we integrate structures and agents into a single story'. Secondly, however, they were also maintaining that, in principle, this task could not be accomplished. There would always remain two stories, contra-Weber, whose difference in kind would ever defy the possibility of their combination. One story seeks to interpret subjective meanings and another story to explain objective interconnections in causal terms: '[t]o understand is to reproduce the order in the minds of actors: to explain is to find causes in the scientific manner' (Hollis and Smith 1990). The rest of the paper prolongs this discussion. In it, I want to concede that the criticism was justified and that more work needed to be done in order to answer the 'how' question satisfactorily. Yet in saying that, I am already disagreeing that the task of combining 'explanation' and 'understanding' is insuperable. I will proceed in reverse order because unless the task itself can plausibly be defended as tractable, all efforts to present a better mode of combination would be in vain.

Ontological Pluralism – objective and subjective ontologies

What leads some theorists to be so certain in their principled and anti-Weberian conviction that this combination of the subjective and the objective must ever lie beyond our grasp? In the case of these two authors it was their denial that 'agents and structures can be placed on the same ontological footing, as if they were distinct objects in the social world between which a relation holds' (Hollis and Smith 1994). However, Social Realists have never maintained that they are *distinct objects*, as opposed to ones possessing *distinctive properties and powers*. Given Realists' *stratified* view of reality, social or otherwise (Bhaskar 1990), there seems no difficulty about putting them on the same 'ontological footing', *if* what this means is that both sets of powers are real and that there is a relationship between them.

Yet, the very existence Hollis and Smith's claim for two stories does depend upon the *reality* of both the objective and subjective domains. Otherwise, one if not both 'stories' would be fictional, which is surely not what is being maintained. What seems to be at stake are the ontological *differences* between the two, rather than whether or not both are real. Certainly, the ontological differences between subjective agents and objective structures are great but in the thirty years since Popper differentiated between the Three Worlds, as ontological sub-worlds – the world of physical states, the world of mental states and the world of ideas – we have become accustomed to plural ontologies *and* to the interplay between them. What is important for the present argument is that Popper put his finger on the genuine oddity about World Two, the world of mental states, namely that it is ontologically real and yet it has a subjective ontology.

Conscious states like writing a book, planning one's career or deciding about marrying can only exist from the point of view of the subject who is experiencing those thoughts. They have what John Searle terms a first-person ontology (Searle 1999: 42), meaning they have a subjective mode of existence, which is also the case for desires, feelings, daydreams, beliefs and intentions. Only as experienced by a particular subject does a partic-ular thought exist. Just as there are no such things as disembodied pains, there are no such things as subjectively independent thoughts. Both are first-person dependent for their existence. However, you might object that whilst I cannot share my toothache with you, what am I currently doing but sharing my thoughts with you? In fact I do not agree that it is possi-ble to share my thoughts with you. That is, you cannot enter into my 'pre-monitionary notions' (James 1890: 281–2), which I internally sift, inspect, interrogate, distil and correct, prior to formulating sentences about them. Instead, what I am doing is sharing my *ideas* with you, as World Three ob-jects, ones that become permanently part of World Three when they are published.

However, the crucial point is not about sharing or epistemic access – the point is ontological. As Searle puts it, 'each of my conscious states ex-ists only as the state it is because it is experienced by me, the subject' (Searle 1999: 43). That is what makes the ontology of subjectivity distinctive. But there is no question about its reality; instead its existence underlines the fact that there are plural ontologies. Most other parts of reality have a third-person mode of existence, including social structures, given their emer-gent status and despite their activity-dependence. A thought does require a present-tense agent, doing the thinking in the first-person, but a structural property does not. Undoubtedly there are problems about linking the (first-person) properties of agents with the (third-person) properties of struc-tures and cultures, but these are fundamentally methodological and not ontological. And they are not insuperable, otherwise sociology would have been unable in principle to establish any connections between subjects 'attitudes', 'beliefs', 'outlooks' or 'reasons' and their socio-economic positions, gender, educational level, etcetera. Thus, we need to determine why the insuperable road block to 'one story' is held to derive from some intractable methodological and explanatory problems.

The crux of this issue seems to lie exactly where Max Weber first located it. On the one hand, agents interact in terms of rules and meanings (which are subjectively apprehended), whilst social institutions constitute a structured environment (objectively apprehended and causally explained). Whether or not this undoubted difference entails the principled impossibility of their 'combination' depends exclusively upon conceptions of 'structure' and 'agency'.

The conceptualization of an objective approach to social structure and a subjective approach to human agency is rather like an accordion. 'Science' and 'culture', as common representations of these two 'entities', can be held wide apart or folded closer together. If 'science' is basically conceptualized in Humean terms[3] (and 'culture' is basically conceptualized in Wittgensteinian terms, this makes for the widest gap between them, whereas the Realist version closes this gap. If causality is defined in a Humean manner for 'science', it is unsurprising that 'constant conjunctions' are held to be absent in the cultural domain and that the operation of causal explanation is doubted to work there. Conversely, realist theories of 'science' and of 'culture' minimise this gap, as is explicit in their defense of the possibility of naturalism. Causal powers are held to be generative mechanisms that are at work in both of these open systems, and human reasons are one category of causes. Equally, Realists do not acknowledge a self-standing hermeneutics because 'understanding' becomes a matter of grasping the causal efficacy of 'people'. Realism is thus 'concerned with actions which are practical, not just symbolic: with *making* (poesis), not just *doing* (praxis), or rather with doing which is not, or not only *saying*' (Bhaskar 1989: 146). Instead, to Hollis and Smith, for example, subjectivity is rooted in the *sayings* and *meanings* of a Wittgensteinian 'form of life', the influence of whose rules and norms 'is clearly not one of casual interplay' (Hollis and Smith 1994: 245). Yet, if reasons are causes, as the Realist maintains, then this difference between objectivity and subjectivity does not preclude examining the *interplay* between the causal powers of the 'people' and the 'parts' of society.

Bhaskar challenged the Humean conception of science and the fact that it leaves *hermeneutics as something entirely different and incommunicado* (Bhaskar 1989b: 132–152). Similarly, in *Culture and Agency* (Archer 1988), I challenged the conception of culture, as forming part of the 'myth of cultural integration', of which the 'form of life' is a latter-day example. Instead, causality is far from being foreign to culture. There are crucial causal relations between the level of the 'Cultural System', with its objective contradictions and complementarities, which profoundly condition the intersubjective level of 'Socio-Cultural' interaction, just as 'Socio-Cultural' doings causally modify the constitution of the 'Cultural System' over time. In short, Realist accounts of 'science' and 'culture' are based on the *same model of causal powers*, operative in the two domains, despite their *sui generis* differences. These powers are *necessarily* intertwined because actions, their conditions and consequences, span the two realms and thus cannot be divorced – which thus implies one story.

Two separate versions would both remain partial because each would contain large gaps, either about the conditioning circumstances under which agents live, act and develop or about their reproductive or transformatory consequences for structures, which otherwise must remain matters of structural parthenogenesis.

Strengthening the single story

If the argument presented above is valid, it can be agreed that these two domains have different ontologies, different modes of existence, but *without* this defying their combination into 'one story'. Nevertheless, Social Realists have not given an adequate account of *how* 'subjectivity and objectivity' are combined and this substantially weakens the solution they have offered to the problem of linking 'structure and agency'. Specifically we Social Realists have not given a satisfactory answer to the question 'How does structure influence agency?' In short, the Realist conception of the process linking the two is wanting. The next pages are spent amplifying upon the deficiencies of the linking process with which Realism had contented itself, but without agreeing that *in principle no such mechanism can be adduced to link the 'objective' and the 'subjective'.*

Central to the Critical Realist case is Roy Bhaskar's statement that 'the causal power of social forms is mediated through social agency' (Bhaskar 1989b: 26). This is surely correct, because unless the emergent properties of structure and culture are held to derive from people and their doings and to exert their causal effects through people and their actions, then Realism would be guilty of reification. Nevertheless, the linking process is not complete *because what is meant by that crucial word 'though' has not been unpacked.*

In Social Realism, the word 'through' has generically been replaced by the process of 'social conditioning'. However, to condition entails the existence of something that is conditioned, and because conditioning is not determinism, then this process necessarily involves the interplay between two different kinds of causal powers – those pertaining to structures and those belonging to agents. Therefore, an adequate conceptualisation of 'conditioning' must deal explicitly with the interplay between these two powers. Firstly, this involves a specification of *how* structural and cultural powers impinge upon agents, and secondly of *how* agents use their own personal powers to act 'so rather than otherwise' in such situations. Thus, there are two elements involved, the 'impingement upon' (which is objective) and the 'response to it' (which is subjective). Realists, myself included, have concentrated upon the former to the neglect of the latter.

Because of this one-sidedness, it is readily conceded here that Realism has been much more effective in specifying *how* the objective affects the subjective than vice versa. On the whole, I think Social Realism has satisfactorily conceptualised the objective side in terms of cultural and structural emergent properties impinging upon people by shaping the social situations they confront. Often this confrontation is involuntary, as with people's natal social context and its associated life-chances. Often it is voluntary, like getting married. In either case, these objective conditioning influences are transmitted to agents by shaping the situations that those agents live with, have to confront, or would confront if they chose to do x, y or z. Sometimes they impinge as constraints and enablements upon various courses of action and sometimes by distributing different types of vested interests or objective interests to different (groups of) people, which can enhance or reduce their motivation to undertake a given course of action.

However, since Realists are not determinists, what their account of 'conditioning' has omitted is why people do not respond in uniform fashion under the same structured circumstances. Subjects who are similarly situated can debate, both internally and externally, about the appropriate course of action and come to different conclusions. This is one of the major reasons why Humean constant conjunctions are not found between structural and cultural influences and action outcomes. At best, what are detected are empirical tendencies in action patterns, which are consonant with objective influences having moulded them. These must remain nothing more than trends, partly because contingencies intervene, given that the social system is open, but partly because a second causal power is *necessarily at play*, namely the personal power to reflect subjectively upon one's circumstances and to decide what to do in them or to do about them. Such inalienable powers of human reflexivity would generate variations in action responses even were it possible to achieve conditions of laboratory closure.

In short, the conceptualisation of this process of mediation between structure and agency has not been fully adequate because it has not fully incorporated the role played by human subjectivity in general. In particular, it omits the part of reflexivity in enabling agents to design and determine their responses to the structured circumstances in which they find themselves – in the light of what they care about most.

Let me now attempt to improve upon the Realist account of mediation. The process of 'conditioning' has been seen to entail the exercise of two sets of causal powers: those of the property that 'conditions' and those of the property that is 'conditioned'. This is clearest where constraints and enablements are concerned, the obvious point being that a constraint requires something to constrain and an enablement needs something to enable. These are not intransitive terms because if *per impossible* no agent ever conceived of any course of action, he or she could neither be constrained nor enabled.

For example, the mere existence of a top heavy demographic structure does not constrain a generous pensions' policy at all, unless and until somebody advances the policy of giving generous pensions. Only when that project has been mooted does the top heavy demographic structure in relation to a small active population become a constraint, *ceteris paribus*. Equally, in the cultural realm, if there is a contradiction between two beliefs or two theories it remains a purely logical matter, existing out there in the 'Universal Library' (Archer 1988: ch. 5), but is inert until and unless someone wants to uphold one of those ideas, assert one of those ideas or do something with one of those ideas. In other words, for an objective structural or cultural property to exercise its causal powers, such powers have to be *activated* by agents.

The proper incorporation of agential powers into the conceptualisation of conditioning entails the following three points. First, that social emergent properties, or more exactly the exercise of their powers, are dependent upon the existence of what have been termed agential 'projects', where a project stands for any course of action intentionally engaged upon by a human being. These projects, *as subjectively conceived by agents*, are necessary for the activation of social emergent properties, i.e., their transformation into powers. Second, only if there is a relationship of congruence or incongruence between the emergent social property and the project of the person(s) will the latter activate the former. Congruity or incongruity need not be the case. For example, if the agent's project was to engage in regular private prayer, no structural power on earth could prevent it though, of course, socio-cultural influences might be at work discouraging people's intentions to pray in general. When it is the case that congruence prevails, this represents a structural enablement and where incongruence exists, that constitutes a structural constraint. Third, and most importantly for this paper, agents have to respond to these influences by using their own personal powers to deliberate reflexively, always under their own descriptions, about how to act in such situations. What is unique about the reflexivity of human beings is that it can involve anticipation. A constraint or an enablement need not have impinged or impacted, it could just be foreseeable.

Hence, the efficacy of any social emergent property is at the mercy of the agents' reflexive activity. Outcomes vary enormously with agents' creativity in dreaming up brand new responses, even to situations that may have occurred many times before. Ultimately, the precise outcome varies with agents' personal concerns, degrees of commitment and with the costs different agents will pay to see their projects through in the face of structural obstacles and hindrances. Equally, they vary with agents' readiness to avail themselves of enablements. The one result that is rarely if ever found is a complete uniformity of response on behalf of every agent who encounters the same constraint or the same enablement. The deliberative process has nothing in common with cost-benefit analysis. It can be highly emotionally charged rather than being an exercise in instrumental rationality, although our emotions are always about something.[4] Elsewhere, I have argued that emotions (as distinct from moods) are commentaries on our concerns (Archer 2004: 327–356), which is also to plead that the *Wertrationalität* should not be issued a death certificate.

To deal adequately with this variation in agents' responses, when such agents are in the same social situation, does indeed mean addressing their subjectivity. It entails acknowledging their *personal powers*, in particular their power of reflexivity to think about themselves in relation to society and to come to different conclusions that lead to variable action outcomes. In short, without knowledge about their internal deliberations, we cannot account for exactly what they do. This can be quickly illustrated by considering the effects of different distributional placements of agents and the impossibility of deducing determinate courses of action from them alone. Suppose a collectivity of agents is well placed in terms of remuneration, repute and representation – or 'class', 'status' and 'power'. These positionings cannot in themselves be assumed to foster reproductive projects, despite all having much to lose objectively. To begin with the most obvious reason, not all agents are guided by their objective interests; they can choose to marry downwards, to take vows of poverty, to renounce titles or to chuck it all up for subsistence living. Thus, at best, this leaves a probability statement about the doings of 'most people most of the time', but to what actual courses of action do these probabilities attach?

Since there is no answer to that question, we are thrown back upon empirical generalisations of the kind, 'the greater the cost of a project, the less likely are people to entertain it'. Not only is that no explanation whatsoever (merely another quest for Humean constant conjunctions) but also, far from having eliminated human subjectivity, it relies upon a banal and highly dubious form of it. Instead, sociologists covertly recognise that sub-jectivity cannot be ignored but this 'recognition' consists in it being smug-gled in by social theorists *imputing subjective motives* to the agent, rather than examining the agent's own reflexively defined reasons, aims and con-cerns. Analytically, the result is the 'Two Stage Model' presented below. Ef-fectively, this Model transforms the first-person subjective ontology of the agent into a third-person 'objectivist' account proffered by the investigator.

1. **Structural and/or Cultural properties** *objectively* shape the situations that agents confront involuntarily and *exercise powers of constraint and enablement* in relation to –
2. **Subjective properties imputed to agents and assumed to govern their actions:** –

   – promotion of vested interests (Critical Realism)
   – instrumental rationality (Rational Choice Theory)
   – routine repertoires/habitus (Pragmatism/Bourdieu/Discourse The-ory)

Realists have to say *mea culpa* for we have often been guilty of putting im-puted responses to vested interests or objective interests into accounts of ac-tion as a kind of dummy for real and efficacious human subjectivity. There are many worse exemplars, and probably the worst is Rational Choice The-ory, which imputes instrumental rationality alone to all agents as they sup-posedly seek to maximise their preference schedules in order to become 'better off' in terms of some indeterminate future 'utiles' (Archer and Trit-ter 2001). Subjectively, every agent is reduced to a bargain hunter and the human pursuit of the *Wertrationalität* is disallowed (Hollis 1989). Bour-dieu, too, frequently endorsed an empty formalism about subjectivity, such that people's positions ('semi-consciously' and 'quasi-automatically') en-gendered dispositions to reproduce their positions (Bourdieu 1977; 1990). Such theoretical formulations seem to lose a lot of the rich and variable sub-jectivity that features prominently in his work on *La Misère du Monde*. In the cultural counterpart to the above, discourse 'theory' simply holds these ill-defined ideational clusters to have gained unproblematic hegemony over subjectivity.

The manifest inadequacies of any version of the 'Two Stage Model' are: (*a*) the failure to investigate anybody's subjectivity, (*b*) the imputation of subjective homogeneity to some given group, (*c*) the endorsement of re-flexively 'passive agents' and, (*d*) the foundational denial that the personal power of subjectivity needs to be understood. Sociology can neither dis-pense with the subjective nor can it make do with such impoverished ac-knowledgements of it. If this personal power is to be given its due, it seems obvious that to do so entails replacing the imputation of subjectivity by its investigation. Rather less obvious are answers about which aspects of human subjectivity sociologists should be investigating and incorporating. The strong suspicion, given the diversity of social theorising, is that any response would be contested because the answer itself would draw upon fundamentally contested concepts – and the greatest of these are 'action', 'structure' and 'agency' themselves.

Therefore, my response will remain within the context of Social Realism. For Realists to give subjectivity its due, whilst remaining faithful to their own explanatory framework, 'subjectivity' would be incorporated as a personal power of human agents, which is prior to, relatively autonomous from and possesses causal efficacy in relation to emergent structural or cultural properties. Clearly this would limit the tracts of people's subjective lives that are pertinent to social theory. For example, I presume no one would suggest that a dislike of spinach has causal powers beyond a capacity to disrupt family tea time. However, I want to advance a much more concrete response, namely that the aspect of 'subjectivity' to which Social Realists have failed to give its due is our reflexivity, through which we deliberate about ourselves in relation to our social circumstances. In other words, 'reflexivity' is put forward as the answer to how 'the causal power social forms is mediated *through* human agency'. It performs this mediatory role by virtue of the fact that we deliberate about ourselves in relation to the social situations that we confront, certainly fallibly, always incompletely and necessarily under our own descriptions, because that is the only way we can know anything.

Reflexivity is conceptualised as the Internal Conversation (Archer 2003) and advanced as the process which mediates the impact of social forms upon us and determines our responses to them. The Internal Conversation is put forward as the missing link in the Realist account of the interplay between structure and agency. Firstly, its mediation is essential to giving an account of precisely what we do rather than a statement about probable courses of action. And, in relation to constraints and enablements, agential responses can vary greatly: from evasion, through compliance, to strategic manipulation or subversion. Secondly, if it is held that agential subjectivity has itself been moulded by social influences, such as ideology, 'habitus' or, for argument's sake, 'discourse', it is impossible to ascertain for whom this is and is not the case without examining their inner dialogue. It cannot be the case for all, because 'the sociologist' has seen through these *attempts* at ideational misrepresentation in order to be able to describe them, but cannot claim a monopoly on this ability since the articulation of counter ideologies is hardly an academic preserve. However, if human reflexivity can be sustained as the missing mediatory mechanism, linking structure and agency, this would also have the effect of transforming the 'two stories' about 'understanding' and 'explanation' into one alone.

What kinds of subjective properties and powers are under consideration as constitutive of this mediatory process? The Internal Conversation designates the manner in which we reflexively make our way through the world. It is what makes (most of us) 'active agents', people who can exercise some governance in their own lives, as opposed to 'passive agents' to whom things simply happen (Hollis 1977). Being an 'active agent' hinges on the fact that individuals develop and define their ultimate concerns: those internal goods that they care about most (Frankurter 1998: ch. 7) and whose precise constellation makes for their concrete singularity as persons (Archer 1988). No one can have an ultimate concern and fail to do something about it. Instead, each person seeks to develop a concrete course of action to realise that concern by elaborating a project, in the (fallible) belief that to accomplish this project is to realise one's concern. If such courses of action are successful, which can never be taken for granted, everybody's constellation of concerns, when dovetailed together, becomes translated into a set of established practices. This constitutes their personal *modus vivendi*. Through this *modus vivendi*, subjects live out their personal concerns within society as best they can. In shorthand, these components can be summarized in the formula <Concerns → Projects → Practices>. There is nothing heroic or idealistic about this, because 'concerns' can be ignoble, 'projects' illegal and 'practices' illegitimate.

In short, it has been argued that our personal powers are exercised through reflexive internal dialogue and that the Internal Conversation is responsible for the delineation of our concerns, the definition of our projects and, ultimately, the determination of our practices in society. It is agential reflexivity which actively mediates between our structurally shaped circumstances and what we deliberately make of them. There is an obvious caution here; agents cannot make what they please of their circumstances. To maintain otherwise would be to endorse idealism and to commit the epistemic fallacy.[5] Indeed, if people get their objective circumstances badly wrong, these subjects pay the objective price whether or not they do so comprehendingly. Wrongly to believe that one can service a heavy mortgage results in foreclosure, with further objective consequences for obtaining alternative accommodation. What the Internal Conversation does do is to mediate by activating structural and cultural powers and in so doing there is no single and predictable outcome. This is because agents can exercise their reflexive powers in different ways, according to their very different concerns and considerations.

Thus, a 'Three Stage' process of mediation is being put forward, one that gives both objectivity and subjectivity their due and also explicitly incorporates their interplay.

(i)   Structural and cultural properties *objectively* shape the situations that agents confront involuntarily, and possess generative powers of constraint and enablement in relation to

(ii)   Agents' own configurations of concerns, as *subjectively* defined in relation to the three orders of natural reality – nature, practice and society.

(iii) Courses of action are produced through the reflexive deliberations of agents who *subjectively* determine their practical projects in relation to their *objective* circumstances.

The first stage deals with the kind of specification that Realists already provide about how 'social forms' impinge and impact on people by moulding their situations. This was summarised as follows in *Realist Social Theory*:

> Given their pre-existence, structural and cultural emergents shape the social environment to be inhabited. These results of past actions are deposited in the form of current situations. They account for what there is (structurally and culturally) to be distributed and also for the shape of such distributions; for the nature of the extant role array, the proportion of positions available at any time and the advantages/disadvantages associated with them; for the institutional configuration present and for those second order emergent properties of compatibility and incompatibility, that is whether the respective operations of institutions are matters of obstruction or assistance to one another. In these ways, situations are objectively defined for their subsequent occupants or incumbents (Archer 2003: 201).

However, these social features only become generative powers, rather than un-activated properties, in relationship to agential projects. Stage 2 examines the interface between the above and agential projects themselves, for again it is not the properties of agents that interact directly with structural or cultural properties but their powers as expressed in the pursuit of their projects. It is Stage 3 that has been missing in social theorising to date, but which appears essential in order to conceptualise the process of mediation properly and completely. In Stage 3, by virtue of their powers of reflexivity, agents deliberate about their objective circumstances in relation to their subjective concerns. They consult their projects to see if they can realise them, including adapting them, adjusting them, abandoning them or enlarging them in the deliberative process. They alter their practices, such that if a course of action is going well, subjects may become more ambitious, and, if it is going badly, they may become more circumspect. It is this crucial stage 3 that enables us all to try to do, to be or to become what we care about most in society – by virtue of our reflexivity.

This final stage of mediation is indispensable because without it we have no explanatory purchase on what exactly agents do. The absence of explanatory purchase means settling for empirical generalisations about what 'most of the people do most of the time'. Sociologists often settle for even less: 'Under circumstances x a statistically significant number of agents do y'. This spells a return to Humean constant conjunctions and, in consequence, a resignation to being unable to adduce a causal mechanism.

Conclusion

Neglect of the subjective contribution to mediation has the consequence that social forms are treated as intransitive, that is, simply as advantages or disadvantages. In effect, the presumption is that no one looks a gift horse in the mouth and that everybody gets down to cutting their coats to suit their cloth. Yet, 'advantages' are not intransitive because they have to be positively evaluated by the agent for some purpose. This is particularly relevant when the luck of having been dealt better life-chances than others is then presumed to mean that the advantages of 'keeping ahead' will dominate the activities of all who are so placed. This may be a common concern, but if it is, then it must have been subjectively adopted, for it is not one that can be blandly imputed to everybody – Tony Benn resigned his title in order to sit in the House of Commons. The conclusion is that if subjectivity is not properly investigated, it will be improperly imputed because it cannot be eliminated.

When a subjective ontology is introduced and agential reflexivity is investigated, three points are acknowledged on the agential side of the equation.

– That our unique personal identities, which derive from our singular constellations of concerns, mean that we are radically heterogeneous as agents. Even though we may share objective social features we may also seek very different ends, when in the same social situation.
– That our subjectivity is dynamic, it is not psychologically static, nor is it psychologically reducible, because we modify our own goals in terms of their contextural feasibility, as we see it. As always, we are fallible, can get it wrong and have to pay the objective price for doing so.
– That as agents we are active, for the most part, rather than passive because we can adjust our projects to those practices that we believe we can realise.

Without these points being taken on board, what are omitted are agential evaluations of their situations in the light of their concerns, and their evaluation of their projects in the light of their situations – whether they find themselves there voluntarily or involuntarily. In short, a full account of structure and agency and of the process mediating between them entails accepting and examining the interplay between two ontologies – the socially objective and the personally subjective. However, if this argument is sound, the conclusion is that it is indeed possible to produce one story rather than two, as Weber maintained, though not in the way he advocated doing it.

Part III

Commemorating John Rex's Contribution to Social Policy: Immigration and Racial Inequality

6

Child Deprivation: Minorities Ten Years On

ROBERT MOORE

IN THE MID 1990s I used the Sample of Anonymised Records (SARs) from the 1991 census to produce a simple analysis of social deprivation amongst children of different ethnic identities. This was published in 2000 as 'Material Deprivation Amongst Ethnic Minority and White Children' in *Experiencing Poverty*, a volume edited by Jonathan Bradshaw and Roy Sainsbury to commemorate the hundredth anniversary of Rowntree's pioneering study of poverty in York.[1] In this essay, I was attempting to test one of the limits of the SARs data through the study of children under school leaving age. Unlike adults in the census, children do not have occupations or marital statuses, they do not own cars or rent houses, they have no recorded educational attainments – so what could be said about their material conditions on the basis of census data? To what extent could we use the census to study key aspects of society as they impinged upon children?

I used the SARs to create an index of deprivation, which while not ideal, made what I believed to be the best use of the data available to measure material deprivation among children. It was constructed as follows:

The reasons for selecting these variables from the limited list available was set out in the original essay (ibid.: 146–149); the product was a five-point scale which was also used in a collapsed form as High, Medium and Low deprivation. Using the same components in 2001, the scale became a

Figure 1: Derivation of deprivation scores

Indicator	Value	Cumulative Score
Access to a car	Yes	0
	No	1
Housing density, person per room	> 1	1
	< 1	0
Adults in employment	2	0
	1	1
	0	2

six-point scale. The element 'adults in employment' was scored as two, minus the number in employment, but because, in 2001, a number of households had three persons in employment, this generated negative values if they lived at the lower density and had access to a car. These minus cases were merged with the zeros for the purposes of analysis. The index of deprivation derived from the CAMS is therefore comparable with that derived from the SARS.

The SARS comprise, in effect, a 1.8 million sample survey of the whole UK population based upon the census schedule – with derived variables added later by the administrators of the SARS. The data are published in a form that prevents disclosure of individuals, so the geography is restricted and the full range of values not made available for all variables (notably those relating to occupation). The 1991 sample was 2 per cent of the population, giving a sample of 184,708 children. The 2001 individual SARS comprised a 3 per cent sample with slightly tighter restrictions on the published data. This sample included 307,689 persons under the age of 16. We excluded from the analysis all those for whom ethnicity data or data needed to create the index of deprivation was imputed. This gave a total usable sample of 304,826 under 16s. Of this sample, 13.4 per cent were not White British, White Irish or 'Other White' compared with 9.8 per cent in the 1991 SARS. Thus about one in eight children in England is now from a 'visible' ethnic minority, compared with one in ten in 1991. As we shall see, the expansion of the ethnic categories used by the census in 2001 made strict comparability between 1991 and 2001 difficult.

In 1991, I divided the sample into those living in 'Poor England' and the remainder of England. Poor England was defined as the 21 local authority districts that appeared in the top 50 of Forrest and Gordon's 1992 tables for *both* material *and* social deprivation. Could the same local authorities be designated Poor England in 2001? The office of the Deputy Prime Minister, using seven 'domains' has created an Index of Multiple Deprivation for the UK. Twenty of the original 21 districts in Poor England feature in the top 50 districts on this index, with the other very close, half were in the top twenty (ODPM 2005). Thus, it seems safe to continue with the same definition of Poor England for 2001 data.

Let us first look at the population in general. The minority child population is not evenly spread geographically but as we would expect it conforms to the distribution of the whole minority population. Thus the minority child population is over-represented in the West Midlands, and markedly over represented in London, where it is 52 per cent of the child population of Inner London, and 33 per cent of the child population in Outer London. Roughly speaking every other child in Inner London is from a visible minority, and one in three in Outer London. Local concentrations of minority populations are well-documented and these are also reflected in the child populations: 57 per cent of the children in Tower Hamlets are Bangladeshi,[2] 29 per cent of Leicester children are Indian, 24 per cent of Bradford's children are Pakistani, and 15 per cent of Lambeth's children Black Caribbean. There are many local authorities with less than 5 per cent minority children; Blyth Valley and Easington being the most 'white' authorities, with the former having 99.1 per cent White and the latter 98.7 per cent 'White British' children (both without any White Irish and Easington with no 'Other White' either). Minority children are also over-represented in the local authorities that comprise Poor England where they form 37 per cent of the child population compared with 10 per cent in the remainder of England.

The Index of Multiple Deprivation is calculated by the ODPM for the smallest zones in the census – the output areas – and the index for each area is attached to each member of the CAMS to 'score' them according to their residence. The mean IMD scores for children therefore express the extent to which the children are living in deprived areas of England, which might itself be seen as a source of deprivation. But it is also the case that geographical concentration may confer certain social, economic and political advantages on minorities (see below).

Before turning to my own derived deprivation index we may examine the IMD scores for 'Poor England' and England as a whole. The *range* if IMD scores for local authorities is very substantial, with Liverpool at the top of the list scoring 49.8, and Wokingham, near the bottom, with a score of 5.1. The numbers in Tables 1 to 4 below refer, however, to the children – not the whole population. These tables are about young people's England.

Table 1: IMD scores, England

Location	Mean score	Number	S.D.
Poor England	40.2	38,090	16.4
Remainder of England	20.5	266,736	15.1
Total	22.9	304,826	16.6

Table 2: IMD scores, White ethnic groups

Ethnic Group	Mean score	Number	S.D.
White British	21.5	257,429	16.0
Irish (White)	23.0	1,167	15.7
Other white	22.2	5,345	15.8
All children all ethnic groups	22.9	—	16.6

Table 3: IMD scores, minority groups

Ethnic Group	Mean score	Number	S.D.
Caribbean (Black/Black British)	34.4	3,490	15.5
Indian	25.8	7,280	15.2
Pakistani (Asian/Asian British)	39.4	7,590	17.0
Bangladeshi (Asian/Asian British)	42.5	3,248	15.8
All children all ethnic groups	22.9	—	16.6

The standard deviations (S.D.) is a measure of the average difference of the scores from the mean score and therefore indicates the spread of children's scores.

The IMD scores suggest that children in the '1991 minorities' are the most deprived, with the notable exception of Indian children whose score is much closer to 'white' children. The 'mixed' category children score higher than the 'white' but substantially below the other minorities (again with the exception of the Indian children). When we turn to the CAMS-based index we see that for the ethnic groups with the 1991 labels deprivation has declined and that in 2001 the 'mixed' categories are still between the white and 1991 minority scores.

Tables 5 to 7 show the mean scores for all ethnic groups on the index of deprivation derived from the CAMS. The children's rank order only changes

Table 4: IMD scores, mixed groups

Ethnic Group	Mean score	Number	S.D.
White and Black Caribbean (Mixed)	31.1	4,051	17.2
White and Black African (Mixed)	30.4	1,054	17.7
White and Asian (Mixed)	23.2	2,612	17.1
Other Mixed	25.3	2,004	17.5
All children all ethnic groups	22.9	—	16.6

Table 5: Mean deprivation index scores (White categories), in England

	2001
White British	0.82
Irish (White)	0.97
Other White	1.19
All children	0.91
(All white children 1991	*0.96)*

Table 6: Mean deprivation scores, minorities, in England

	1991	2001
Black Caribbean	1.90	1.52
Indian	1.08	0.80
Pakistani	2.05	1.62
Bangladeshi	2.53	2.10
All children (all ethnic groups)	*1.03*	*0.91*

Table 7: Mean deprivation scores, mixed groups, in England

	2001
White and Black Caribbean	1.53
White and Black African	1.46
White and Asian	1.06
Other mixed	1.24
All children (all ethnic groups)	*0.91*

slightly between the IMD and CAMS calculations; of the 16 ethnic groups used in the 2001 Census four remained in the same rank position on the two scoring systems, ten moved up or down one or two places and Other White dropped four. The most striking case is that of the Indian children moving from seventh place on the IMD score to top (least deprived) with the CAMS index. This strongly suggests that the domestic circumstances of Indian children are less congruent with their locality than many other children – in other words less deprived Indian children are living in more deprived areas. Certainly when John Rex and I were observing the early settlement of Indian migrants in Birmingham in 1964–65, we noticed that businessmen, for example, were buying terraced houses in the area around Farm Park and to the west of the Stratford Road (as they were in Small Heath). These were not high status areas and still score poorly on the IMD. For example in 2004 Sparkbrook was the Birmingham ward with the third highest proportion of its population (89 per cent) living in Super Output Areas in the top 10 per cent for deprivation.

If we examine the data for children in the five ethnic groups who are in the *highest* level of deprivation (scoring 3 or 4 on the SARS/CAMS index), we find an unambiguous pattern; the rank order of the most deprived is the same in all regions.[3] Indian children are least represented in the most deprived, closely followed by the White British. Bangladeshi children are the most highly represented in the 'High Deprivation' category, followed by Black Caribbean and Pakistani children.

Unlike the 1991 Census, the 2001 Census asked a question about religion. What difference does it make to measure deprivation by religion rather than ethnicity?

The answer is 'not much'. Muslims have the highest mean deprivation score as do Pakistani and Bangladeshis. The Sikh and Hindu scores are in line with the Indian score. The Black Caribbean children are out of line with the Christian score but the label is too general for sensible conclusions to be drawn from this.

The number of earners in children's households is one of the three elements used to construct the deprivation index. Given that this is likely to be a crucial factor in the conditions of the children's lives (and to some extent the other two factors may depend on this one), then we should perhaps view the data separately.

Table 9 generates the same rank order as the CAMS index for half the ethnic groups and three quarters of those who move change less than one place between the two schemes. Whilst households with earners will have a wide range of incomes, those with no earners will, of course, have no earned incomes at all. Pakistani and Bangladeshis are lower on the CAMS

Table 8: Mean deprivation score, religious categories

Religion	Mean score	N	S.D.
Christian	0.8	198,976	1.0
Buddhist	1.3	502	1.1
Hindu	0.7	3,515	1.0
Jewish	0.7	1,348	0.9
Muslim	1.8	15,806	1.2
Sikh	0.7	2,515	1.1
Other religion	0.8	1,665	1.0
No religion	1.1	50,972	1.2
Religion not stated	1.2	29,527	1.2
Total	0.9	304,826	1.1

Table 9: Percentage of children in England living in households with no employed adult

Race	%
White British	16.2
White Irish	20.8
Other White	22.6
White and Black Caribbean	37.9
White and Black African	31.2
White and Asian	22.5
Other Mixed	26.0
Indian	12.3
Pakistani	30.6
Bangladeshi	36.5
Other Asian	26.8
Black Caribbean	30.2
Black African	39.2
Other Black	37.8
Chinese	17.0
Other Ethnic Group	31.5
All children	18.0

Table 10: Level of deprivation by age bracket 2001 CAMS

Deprivation level	Percentage of age bracket			N
	0–5	6–10	11–15	
Low	71.3	72.6	75.0	222,544
Medium	14.3	14.9	14.0	43,902
High	14.4	12.6	11.0	38,904
Total	100.0	100.0	100.0	305,350

ranking and Black Caribbean children higher, showing that the domestic circumstances exacerbate or mitigate their relatively low rankings on the earners scale. The variability of housing conditions and access to a car vary between households with no earners and need to be taken account of in any overall estimate of the relative deprivation of children.

The percentage of each minority group in the least deprived category has increased between 1991 and 2001 and, conversely, the percentage in the most deprived has decreased. In other words, during the past decade, children from all ethnic groups have moved away from the higher levels of deprivation. When we turn to the data for high deprivation – that is those scoring 3 and 4 in the CAMS index – we see significant differences between ethnic groups; 10, 14 and 16 per cent of White British, White Irish and Other White respectively are in the high deprivation category, but 22 per cent of Pakistani, 24 per cent Black Caribbean and 39 per cent Bangladeshi children. By contrast, only 7 per cent of Indian children are in this category.

Table 10 shows the percentage of children at each level of deprivation by age bracket. The 1991 study showed, in general, a decline in deprivation with age. Again, in 2001, we see in general terms that the percentage of children in high deprivation declines with age.

There are large differences between England and Poor England. In Poor England, 27 per cent of 0–5 year olds are in the high deprivation bracket and 22 per cent of 11–15s, while in the remainder of England only 12 per cent of the youngest age group are in the high deprivation bracket and 8 per cent of the oldest. High deprivation is therefore more common for all age brackets in Poor England and, even though it declines during the childhood years a little more than for the rest of England, it starts from a much higher base. The highest proportion of the most deprived are still, nonetheless, the youngest age group.

Perhaps the most striking figure to emerge from these data is the rapid rate of decline with age of high deprivation amongst 'Other Black' in both

Poor England and the remainder of England. This is a tantalising figure, because we do not really know what 'Other Black' means and I am undertaking research elsewhere to discover the effects of increasing the number of ethnic categories in the 2001 Census and how people may have reallocated themselves between 1991 and 2001 ethnic groups. Most importantly, we do not know how the data for these children would map back into the 1991 categories and perhaps change the profile of the five 1991 categories used for most of this analysis.

One factor may be important: the relatively low proportion of Pakistani and Bangladeshi women in our children's households who work. Sixty-five per cent of White British women work full or part time and 56 per cent of Indian women (albeit slightly more work full-time than White British women), whereas only 24 per cent of Pakistani and 19 per cent of Bangladeshi, women work. Conversely, 43 and 49 per cent of Pakistani and Bangladeshi women describe their occupations as caring for the family, compared with 16 per cent of Indian women and 15 per cent of all women. We may note also that younger (16–21 year old) Pakistani and Bangladeshi women in the children's households are working; over a quarter of Bangladeshis and nearly a third of Pakistanis (compared with half of young Indian women). That over 9 per cent of Indian children live in households with 3 or more earners compared with 4 per cent White British children suggests that many Indian children may live in households where there may be older siblings or relatives who are working. This is true to a lesser extent for White Irish, Pakistani and Bangladeshi children and may to some small extent mitigate the economic effects of low rates of economic activity amongst Pakistani and Bangladeshi women.

These differences in the trajectories of children of different ethnic groups need to be further explored by looking at each group separately. The original 2000 essay discussed Black Caribbean, Indian, Pakistani and Bangladeshi children. We will repeat this for 2001 but we also need to take account of the new categories used in the 2001 Census.

Black Caribbean children

Thirty seven per cent of Black Caribbean children live in Inner London, and 30 per cent in Outer London, with a further 14 per cent in the West Midlands. Within Poor England, over one half (56 per cent) of Black Caribbean children are to be found in Birmingham and the London Boroughs of Lambeth, Lewisham and Haringey. In the remainder of England they are less concentrated – 10 per cent are found in each of Brent and Croydon with smaller concentrations in Waltham Forest, Enfield, Redbridge and Luton. Ninety two per cent of the Black Caribbean children were born in the UK or Ireland.

In Poor England, 45 per cent of White British children live in detached or semi-detached houses, but only 24 per cent of Black Caribbean children. By contrast, 33 per cent of the latter live in purpose-built flats, compared with just over 10 per cent of White British children. Twenty per cent of the Black Caribbean children in the remainder of England live in flats, compared with 4 per cent of White British, making Black Caribbean children the children most likely to be living in flats anywhere in England. Taking England as a whole, 70 per cent of all children live in houses that are either owned outright or mortgaged, but only seven per cent in the highest deprivation bracket (52 per cent in Poor England with 6 per cent of the most deprived). Thirty one per cent of Black Caribbean children in Poor England are in owner occupied housing, but only six per cent of those in the highest deprivation. In the remainder of England, 46 per cent live in owner occupied dwellings but only 7 per cent of the most deprived. In Poor England, 37 per cent of White British children live in homes rented from the local authority or a housing association, and 70 per cent of those in the highest deprivation. For Black Caribbean children, the figures are 62 per cent and 84 per cent. For the most deprived children living in the rest of England, 69 per cent of White British children are in homes rented from social landlords, but 85 per cent of Black Caribbean children are so housed. This represents a small change from 1991, when in England as a whole, a higher proportion of Black Caribbean children lived in local authority or housing association dwellings. Since then, there has been a 7 per cent decline in this tenure and small increases in owner-occupation and private renting.

Ten per cent of all children live in single parent families and 14 per cent in Poor England. For Black Caribbean children, the figures are quite different; 40 per cent in Poor England, and 34 per cent in the remainder of England, live in single parent families (or perhaps, more strictly, single adult households). Seventy-seven per cent of England's children live with a married couple, but only a little over half of Black Caribbean children. There is a slight difference between the proportions of Black Caribbean and other children living with cohabiting couples with only a small difference between England and Poor England. The 'family reference person' (Wathan et al. 2001) for Black Caribbean children is more likely to be female than male in Poor England, and slightly more likely to be male in the remainder of England. This suggests that children in the poorer parts of England are more likely to live in a female-headed household. For Black Caribbean children, as for White British, there is a moderate association between living in female-headed household and deprivation (Cramer's $v = 0.28$ in Poor England and 0.27 in the rest of England). Black Caribbean children are the least likely of our five ethnic groups to have a person with long-term limiting illness in their household. Like their White British counterparts, very few Black Caribbean children live with people over the age of 65 (3 per cent).

Indian children

Within Poor England, 26 per cent of Indian children live in Leicester, 22 per cent in Birmingham, 16 per cent in Blackburn, 13 per cent in Wolverhampton and 11 per cent in Newham. Eighty-eight per cent of the population, therefore, lives in these six districts of the 21 districts of Poor England. In the remainder of England, the Indian children are more widely spread, but Brent, Ealing, Harrow and Hounslow in the west of London contain about a quarter of England's Indian children. There is quite a small population of Indian children in Inner London where it has much higher levels of deprivation than elsewhere.

Owner-occupation is very common for Indian households, 70 per cent of Indian children in Poor England and 82 per cent elsewhere (above the English percentage in both cases). Over half (51 per cent) of the most deprived Indian children live in owner-occupied dwellings. Forty-four per cent of Indian children in Poor England live in terraced housing (49 per cent of the most deprived children) and 31 per cent in the rest of England (but 44 per cent of the most deprived). Although Indian households strongly favour owner-occupation for the most deprived, the local authorities and housing associations nevertheless provide between a third and two fifths of housing. Perhaps the most striking statistic in all of the Indian housing data is that more than half of the most deprived group of children live in owner-occupied houses (White British, by contrast, 6 per cent). There has nonetheless been a slight move *away* from owner-occupation towards private renting since 1991. The contrast is seen most clearly between Poor England and the rest of England: 41 per cent of Indian households are in social housing in Poor England, but only 7 per cent in the remainder of England. For Indian children in high deprivation, 41 per cent occupy social housing in Poor England, but the numbers in this tenure are too small in the remainder of England to make any sensible calculation. Seventy per cent of White British children in the most deprived category live in social housing, wherever their location.

The less well-off Indian families may buy into cheaper terraced housing to a greater extent than poorer White British families; 25 per cent of the owner occupied houses of White British children are terraced dwellings, but 35 per cent of Indian. Only 60 per cent of all Indian children living in owner-occupied homes are in detached or semi-detached homes, but 73 per cent of White British children living in owner-occupation.

Just under 6 per cent of the Indian children in both Poor England and the remainder of England live in single parent households. Family reference persons are male for over 80 per cent of Indian children. There is no significant correlation between the gender of the family reference person and deprivation. Around one third of Indian children live with at least one person with long-term limiting illness. Ten per cent of Indian children have someone over 65 in their home, perhaps reflecting the more extended or multi-generational family structure that is typical of Indian culture.

Pakistani children

Ninety-one per cent was born in the UK or Ireland. Over one half (51 per cent) of Poor England's Pakistani children live in Birmingham, a further 12 per cent in Manchester and 10 per cent in each of Burnley and Newham. In the remainder of England, he Pakistani children are more widely spread, but about 15 per cent is in Bradford, with smaller concentrations in Rochdale and Waltham Forest.

Sixty-three per cent of Pakistani children in Poor England live in owner occupied homes. In England as a whole, there has been a decrease in the proportion of Pakistani children in owner-occupied houses by nearly 15 per cent since 1991. There has been an 8 per cent increase in private renting and 7 per cent in homes rented from local authorities or housing associations. Thirty-seven per cent live in detached homes or semis and 54 per cent in terraced houses. Interestingly, the more deprived are *less* likely to live in a terraced dwelling. Twenty per cent is in social housing, but 35 per cent of the most deprived. In the reminder of England, 50 per cent still lived in terraced houses (53 per cent of the most deprived).

Eight-per cent of Pakistani children in Poor England lives with a single parent, in England 7 per cent. Eighty-six per cent of Pakistani children lives in households with a male reference person in Poor England, and over 40 per cent throughout England lives with one or more person with long-term limiting illness (41 and 42 per cent). Nine per cent has an elder in the household.

Bangladeshi children

Amongst members of visible minorities, Bangladeshi and Black African children are the least likely to have been born in the British Isles. Eighty-seven per cent of Bangladeshi was born here. The largest concentration of Bangladeshi children in Poor England is to be found in Tower Hamlets where 60 per cent of the child population is Bangladeshi, comprising 45 per cent of Poor England's Bangladeshi children. Birmingham has a further 15 per cent and Newham 16 per cent. In the remainder of England, there are concentrations of Bangladeshi children in Camden, Oldham, Bradford and Luton. There are small numbers of Bangladeshi children elsewhere.

Unlike the other groups considered here, the modal form of housing for the Bangladeshi child in Poor England is a flat, and only 26 per cent live in owner occupation. In England as a whole, owner occupation has declined by 12 per cent for Bangladeshi children, who in 2001 where more likely to be living in rented accommodation than in 1991. There has been an increase of 7 per cent of children living in homes rented from local authorities and housing associations and a 5 per cent increase in private renting. The proportion of those living in terraced accommodation is higher for those in least deprivation in both Poor England and the rest of England. Bangladeshi children are less likely to live in owner-occupation than any other of the ethnic groups considered here. The exception to this is that the most deprived Bangladeshi children are *more* likely to be in owner-occupation than the most deprived White British and Black Caribbean children.

Nine per cent of the Bangladeshi children in Poor England live in single parent households. Without having appropriate data available, it is not possible to explain this *relatively* slightly lower level of married couple households, it might, for example, be an outcome of the disruption of family reunions by the processes of immigration control. All 'Asian' children, including Bangladeshi, are less likely to be in a single parent household than White British children. A slightly higher proportion live with a person with long-term limiting illness than Pakistani children (44 and 41 per cent). Ten per cent have an older person in the household.

Ethnic groups and housing choice

In *Race, Community and Conflict*, John Rex and I (1967 and see Hancock 1995) we suggested there was a hierarchy of desirability in housing in a large city, ranging from the multi-occupied dwellings of Sparkbrook to the owner-occupied detached houses of the suburbs. A few owner occupiers may have purchased unwisely and others may have been forced into it by lack of alternatives. Nevertheless, over 71 per cent of people in Britain live in an owner-occupied home. The desirability of owner-occupation is hard to deny. Some factors might, however, make a house in the suburbs less than attractive – the cost of upkeep, travel to work costs, separation from kin and friends. This might be especially true for minority families who may initially be seeking low-cost housing and wish to be near their work, their friends, shops and the other facilities that can be provided by a viable ethnic community (or 'colony' as we said in 1967). But it is also the case that the new arrivals in the 1960s had to take the accommodation that was available in the locations where they were seeking employment, whilst facing the additional constraints of direct and indirect discrimination in the provision of housing. Thus, the terraced houses of the northern towns and the East Midlands provided homes for immigrant textile workers, whilst other immigrants had to make do with the multi-occupied houses of the former middle class zone in Birmingham – where the remaining red-brick terraces also provided an *entrée* to owner occupation for some. The early choices by new arrivals were therefore very constrained (and public sector choices were even more constrained by direct discrimination by local authorities) and have themselves shaped the patterns of settlement that we now see.

One feature of the hierarchy of choice that is plain to see is that flats are the least preferred option and remain something of a residual form of housing for the most deprived families. Owner occupation is the choice of Indian and Pakistani families, even the most deprived. It is White British and Black Caribbean children who are most likely to be in social housing, especially the most deprived amongst them. The Bangladeshi children in Poor England are very likely to be found in social housing, especially the most deprived, although this reduced substantially for the remainder of England. In Tower Hamlets, where a high proportion of the population is Bangladeshi, the stock of terraced housing includes gentrified houses occupied by the very rich. It is not therefore surprising that many Bangladeshi children also live in flats and in social housing. However, unlike many other children the poorest Bangladeshi children are more likely to be living in owner occupation – perhaps because this was the only available accommodation in the desired location.

The ability to purchase a house depends on income and, in many parts of Britain, it is very difficult to purchase a house, or to service a mortgage, unless there are two incomes coming into the household. Table 11 shows the percentage of home owners and renters by the number of earners in the household. Less than 1 in 5 of the children's households with no earners were owner occupied, but over 80 per cent of households with two, three or more earners were in owner occupation.

There is a strong association between tenure and the number of earners in a household (Cramer's $v = 0.34$) and this association holds up for all ethnic groups, although it is slightly lower for Indian, Pakistani and Bangladeshi households. Indian and Pakistani one-earner households are over-represented in owner-occupation and Bangladeshis heavily underrepresented in owner-occupation. It appears that cultural factors interact with the economic status *and* the local housing market in ways that warrant further research.

In writing about Sparkbrook in 1966, we assumed that an aspiration to suburbia was built into the dynamics of city life (Rex and Moore 1967:

Table 11: Housing tenure and number of earners in the childrens household

	None	1	2	3 or more	N	%
Owner occupation	18.3	63.6	86.0	82.3	202,765	66.2
Social renting	59.4	25.2	8.8	12.7	71,987	23.5
Private renting	22.3	11.2	5.2	5.0	31,448	10.3
All tenures	100	100	100	100	306,200	100

9). There have been short-range moves to locations adjacent to the original locations of settlement and a trickle of affluent families moving to 'leafy suburbia'. By and large, the pattern that we observed in Birmingham in the mid 1960s with 'Asian' families seeking owner occupation, while Black Caribbean and poor white people rely more upon social housing, persists. In the mid-1960s 'social' housing meant council housing because housing associations were not today's large-scale housing providers. We foresaw the possibility of the suburban aspiration being modified (which was hinted at in the work of Oscar Lewis) by those immigrants who found the individual and individualised life of the suburb less desirable than the social life of the colony. We were also documenting the practical obstacles that were being put in the way of any newcomer who did hope to achieve suburban bliss.

We also wrote about the ways in which the immigrants might become part of British society (ibid.: 14–15). What was likely to distinguish the entry of migrants to the UK from the American experience was the existence of a welfare state. Whatever ill-will immigrants might experience in entering a steeply hierarchical society, they would nevertheless become citizens (see Moore 1993) acquiring the political, legal and social rights that this implied in Britain. Immigrants have been increasingly stigmatised and harsh measures introduced against them and their families, which imply that they will not enjoy the full rights of citizens – especially if, as latterly, they were asylum seekers or refugees. Muslim populations now finds themselves caught up in a moral panic over migration and terrorism and subjected to increased surveillance by the state, and abuse or violence by a minority of the white population. Many Muslims today must be glad that they do not live isolated lives in the suburbs. Alongside the development of policies which denied immigrants their citizenship, there has been an elaborate and now highly-institutionalised drive towards non-discrimination and multi-culturalism. The thrust of the two lines of policy are contradictory and reflect the sentiment expressed by Sparkbrook's MP when he asserted that 'without limitation integration is impossible, without integration limitation is inexcusable'.

Ethnic minorities in the occupational structure

Where are minorities in the occupational structure? If we divide the occupations of the 'reference adult' in the children's households into manual and non-manual, we find unsurprisingly that, for a high proportion of the children in high deprivation, the adults were in manual occupations; over 80 per cent for White British, Pakistani and Bangladeshi and 74 per cent for Indian children. In the case of Black Caribbean children, 67 per cent of the most deprived had adults in manual occupations. The 'non-manual' category is very broad and ranges from senior management and higher professionals to clerks and shop assistants. If we break this down further, we find that, for the majority of children in high deprivation living with adults in non-manual employment, the adults are in routine, low-skilled occupations. More importantly, however, most of these adults are not actually working. Unemployment and economic inactivity are the main characteristics of the reference adults in the households of the children in the highest deprivation. This observation needs to be treated with caution, however, because the number of employed persons in the household was part of the derivation of the deprivation index. Those Pakistani families who migrated to the northern towns in the 1960s did so in order to work in the textile industries – indeed they were recruited in Pakistan by northern employers. The collapse of textiles has resulted in high unemployment in these areas. So the children of these migrants now live within the 'colony' structure of thriving Pakistani communities standing on a very weak economic base that offers few occupational opportunities beyond 'working on the taxis or in a take-away', as one young man from Burnley expressed it.

Other minority children

Chinese children did not feature in the original article. Their IMD score is 22.5, close to that of the 'white' population, 24.5 per cent are in the high deprivation in Poor England and 6.9 per cent elsewhere in England. Of those Chinese children in high deprivation, 5 per cent live in owner-occupation in Poor England and 66 per cent in homes rented from local authorities or housing associations. In the remainder of England, the figures are 12 and 43 per cent. Two thirds of the most deprived Chinese children in Poor England live in single adult households and one third in the remainder of England. In Poor England and the remainder of England, 87 per cent and 79 per cent of the children in high deprivation live in households where the reference adult is in a manual occupation. Chinese children as a whole seem to enjoy material conditions similar to those of white children.

The 2001 Census saw an increase in the number of 'mixed' ethnic categories, categories which we might expect to increase in number at each census. What are the characteristics of these children enumerated as 'mixed'? For those living in two adult households, 70 to 80 per cent are reported as living in 'mixed partnerships'. This means the adults in the children's households will be 'White and Black Caribbean' or 'White and Asian' or 'Other' mixed' *etc*. This may not actually describe the child's parentage because, in some cases, a child may be living with partners, one of whom is not a parent. The 'ethnic' category may be taken to describe parentage rather than household composition, though there is no absolute guarantee that this is the case. For the children living in single adult households, the differences are reported as 'Different identities between generation only', the parentage, however, will remain 'mixed'.

Of the mixed categories, it is the 'Other Black' who have the highest levels of deprivation and who are more reliant on social housing. Their IMD score is third after Bangladeshis and Pakistanis, as is their mean deprivation score (1.7). In Poor England between 27 and 36 per cent of the 'mixed' children are in high deprivation, but a much lower proportion elsewhere, ranging from 14 per cent of 'other mixed' to 24 per cent of White and Black Caribbean. In both Poor England and the remainder of England, a high proportion of the most deprived are in single adult households, notably the White and Black Caribbean of whom 85 per cent live in a single adult household – a key component of the measurement of deprivation. However, with the exception of the White and Black Caribbean children, one half of all the 'mixed' children live in a two-adult household. Those that live in a single adult households are overwhelmingly with a female parent.

The introduction of the 'mixed' categories in the 2001 Census have thrown up some very interesting data that demands further research. For example, what is it about having parents from different backgrounds, or living in a 'mixed' household, that predisposes children to live in relative deprivation?

Some conclusions

The minority population of children is still largely located within what I have called Poor England, the 21 most deprived districts of England. They are, however, still the *minority* in all but a handful of districts. All children, minorities included, are less likely to be found in the most deprived category than in 1991 and over all their deprivation scores have improved. Deprivation as measured by the SARS/CAMS indexes at the two censuses shows a mainly stable pattern of deprivation, with the Indian children just edging White British children out of the top place with the lowest deprivation score in 2001. The Bangladeshi children meanwhile remain at the bottom of the scale with the highest deprivation score at both censuses.

The Black Caribbean children have moved up from seventh to fifth place but this might have been difficult to interpret because of the introduction of the 'White and Black Caribbean (mixed)' ethnic category in 2001, because we would not know whether the possible loss of 'mixed' children from the original Caribbean category might have influenced the outcome. The 'mixed' children have the same deprivation score as the Black Caribbean in 2001. 'Other Black' moved down from 6 to 8 on the deprivation scores. We have no way of knowing, but this category may include the long established black populations of the seaports who would therefore find themselves being overtaken by the children of more recent arrivals. My discussions with black people in Liverpool suggest that some may have used 'Other Black' in the census, though others stress either an African or Caribbean heritage. There are issues here for further research – not just about the census categories chosen by very long established black citizens but also about their economic and social position after a century of settlement.

Single parent and female headed households are more common for White British children and very much more common for Black Caribbean children, for whom this is a correlate of deprivation. 'Asian' children by contrast not only live in two adult households but are more likely to have older people present in their households. Unsurprisingly, those children that have working adults in their household are more likely to be in higher deprivation if the adults work in manual occupations or routine, unskilled non-manual occupations. Around a third of Black Caribbean, Pakistani and Bangladeshi children live in households without an earner, but only 12 per cent of Indian children.

Ethnic minority children are over-represented in what we have called 'Poor England', where they share high levels of deprivation with their White British counterparts. The exception to this are the Indian children, only 11 per cent of whom are in the high deprivation bracket in Poor England (the next lowest are the White British with 22 per cent). The parents of the Indian children in less deprived households have not re-located to less deprived parts of England; we have outlined some of the possible reasons for this, but it may also be the case that their relative 'affluence' derives mainly from the numbers of people working in Indian households, rather than any improved social or occupational status on the part of parents.

That more minority families now live in rented accommodation than in 1991 may suggest that, for some, owner-occupation originally secured them less than adequate accommodation and they are now choosing to be housed by local authorities, housing associations and private landlords. The housing associations will almost certainly be offering high quality accommodation, as may some private landlords. The Black Caribbean children who find themselves in council flats may not be so fortunate.

The story these data have to tell is largely one of stasis; whilst fewer children now experience the high levels of deprivation we saw in 1991, the rank order of the ethnic groups as defined by the census has altered only very slightly, save that Indian children seem to have improved their circumstances more than most, Black Caribbean a little. Black African, Pakistani and Bangladeshi children still experience the highest levels of deprivation, albeit absolutely less than in 1991. Furthermore, the characteristics of their deprivation, their domestic circumstances and location continue to differentiate 'Asian', black and white children from one another.

7

The Politicisation of Immigration

TOMAS HAMMAR

WE MET IN NICE at a meeting of one of the very first comparative research programmes on south to north migration within Europe, a programme initiated within the European Science Foundation (ESF), particularly for the study of cultural aspects of immigration. At that time, still after 25 years of large labour immigration into Europe, research on migration and ethnic relations had hardly begun in the social sciences and even less in the humanities. In hindsight, this is astonishing, for at the end of the 1970s the impact of immigration was already significant, not only on economic but also on cultural, social and political life.

John Rex had left South Africa in 1949. He had published his famous *Key Problems in Sociological Theory* already in 1961. Three years later he had founded the Department in Sociology at Durham University. In 1967, he was a member of the historical UNESCO international expert committee on the nature of race and race prejudice. More than 10 years later, when I first met John Rex in person, he was a renowned professor and director of the Centre for Research in Ethnic Relations at Warwick University (Martins 1993).

Unfortunately, the ambitious and progressive ESF-project was not well planned and funded. Each country was supposed to provide money for its own research team. The participants were not trained to work in a multidisciplinary comparative migration project. John Rex's helpful interventions were therefore much needed, and although he could not rescue the entire programme, his contribution resulted in a good book, edited by John, on the associations of immigrants in several countries (Rex et al. 1987; Oriel 1981).

When this happened in the end of the 1970s, European studies of migration and ethnicity had recently started in economics, demography and sociology, and slowly spread into other disciplines: anthropology, geography, linguistics, political science and others. But a truly multidisciplinary study of *International Migration and Ethnic Relations*[1] was still only a dream in a few scholars' minds. John Rex was one of the foresightful few who already at that time understood the importance of an open discussion, vivid exchange of theories and models and international cooperation across universities and faculties.

IMER studies are often said to comprise two major fields of knowledge: international migration and ethnic relations, and especially the interrelations between these two fields. Great attention is paid to the long term consequences of migration and the emergence of multicultural societies. Most IMER research has been mono-disciplinary, but as cross-disciplinary projects are indispensable in this field, a number of special research institutes have developed in Europe.[2]

Just as research has been spread across many different institutes, many governments have splintered rather than coordinated immigration policy[3] as, for example, when one agency has been charged with migration control, and another with the integration of immigrants. Also in political debates and in the media, control policy and integration policy are often discussed as if they were independent of each other.

The politics of migration and ethnicity

International population movements appeared first, immigration control came second and integration only third. Post 1945, large labour immigration to Europe was an established fact long before any of the immigration countries had activated control policies. Only thereafter, as a response to the immigration of many millions of families, were integration policies devised and implemented. This is, in short, an historic sequence. It must not be taken for a cause-and-effect relation, however. The explanation is far more complex, and I shall mainly focus here on some specific political factors, such as the politicisation of migration and ethnicity, the emerging anti-immigrant opinions, the role of the political parties, and the gaps between rhetoric and practice in immigration policy.

By the end of the twentieth century, the tradition of handling immigration as an apolitical issue was abandoned. I remember how happy we were in my Swedish research network, when migration was suddenly internationally recognised as a significant political issue. We hoped that our reports would be more widely read, and our studies better funded. We did not yet expect the other consequences of this politicisation as, for example, the impact of immigration on national elections and electoral strategies. We did not imagine that populist anti-immigrant parties would gain 10–20 per cent of the national vote, nor that the polls would register even higher rates of opinion hostile negative to foreigners and black immigrants, and opposed liberal migration control and a generous integration policy. Since then, the major political parties, both in government and in opposition, have found it necessary to adjust their policies to regain what they had already lost. I want to discuss why so much prejudice is voiced, and how so few can gain so much influence on a strategy of fear over the effects of public opinion.

The apolitical tradition

In the early 1970s one by one of the governments of Europe stopped all recruitment of foreign labour. When one state tightened its regulation, other neighbouring states practised the same cure. The same mutuality still operates, with EU-member states searching for ways of co-operating on control. A common European control and asylum policy is not yet established, but it is about to take shape. In contrast, the integration policy tends to remain country-specific, based on each state's national interests, and social welfare ideology.

International migration has a long apolitical tradition in Europe. It has only recently become a highly politicised issue, and we tend to forget that this is an abnormal rather than a 'normal' situation. The ideal of classical liberalism is a world of free trade, and of free movements of capital and populations. The states shall not interfere and regulate emigration and immigration, but leave migration to market forces. From 1914 to 1945, during the two world-wars and the serious depressions in between, states had to make temporary exceptions of these liberal principles. They were forced to use extraordinary control measures. Migration control thus started as a national emergency administration, handled by the 'aliens police', labour market bureaux and welfare agencies. If allowed, appeals were adjudicated by courts. Partners within the labour market were actively involved, but seldom the political parties.

All this changed after the Second World War. Immigration returned to being mainly an economic issue. Even in the early 1970s, when the import of labour became regulated, policy decisions of great significance were generally taken with little public debate or parliamentary discussion. The politicisation of migration occurred 15 years later, at the end of the 1980s and the beginning of the 1990s.

For several reasons, immigration policy has thus long remained apolitical. A comparative analysis, 'European immigration policy', published by a group of scholars commissioned by the Swedish Government in the beginning of the 1980s, found that political parties had for years refrained from intervening in immigration issues, leaving even fundamental policy decisions to civil servants, jurists and experts in the field, but also, interestingly, that the political parties in Britain and Switzerland were exceptions.[4]

We concluded that an early politicisation had been promoted in Britain by the electoral system and in Switzerland by the institution of referendum. In contrast to a system of proportional representation, where the vote goes to a party ticket in a large electoral district, the vote in a majority system is given to a person running in a single candidate constituency. The majority system gives an individual candidate an opportunity to defy the party platform in order to gain votes, for example, from people sympathising with racist and xenophobic ideas. We all remember Enoch Powell's notorious 'rivers of blood' speech in April 1968, which contributed to the Conservative victory in the general elections two years later, but also to Powell's loss of status and influence in the party.

The Swiss referendum on 'over-foreignisation' in 1970 was launched as a popular initiative. It was defeated but only with a small margin: 46 per cent of the voters supported the proposal by James Schwarzenbach to reduce the number of foreigners in Switzerland to less than 10 per cent of the *Swiss population*. From this moment and as a direct reaction to the strong anti-immigrant vote, the Swiss Federal Government formulated a new control policy intended to keep the size of the foreign population under a 'global ceiling'.

Both in Britain and in Switzerland the political parties have preferred not to politicise immigration. Zig Layton-Henry (1992) has described in detail how Commonwealth immigration from 1962 was restrained and stopped by a long series of legislative acts, and how these restrictions were often supplemented with anti-discrimination legislation. Control and integration policies were both shaped with an eye on public opinion.

In 'European Immigration Policy' we had little to say about three questions which would soon dominate the interests of both policy makers and academia: 1. refugee immigration, the so called abuse of the right of asylum, and illegal immigration; 2. the inefficiency gap between policy goals and policy outcomes in control as well as in integration policy, and 3. the politicisation of immigration. In the last 20 years, from 1985 to 2005, European immigration control has become more and more restrictive. But immigration to Europe has continued as before in spite of the many attempts to constrain it (Cornelius et al. 2004).

In the first edition of the book by Cornelius et al. (1994), both control and integration policies were discussed in the chapters about different countries, but in keeping with the new political climate, control was given most attention. The theoretical framework was based on two broad and vague theories. According to the first hypothesis, control and integration policies tend to converge in most immigration countries. The second hypothesis claims that there is a growing gap in all countries between policy goals and policy outcomes. Many examples are given but the gaps are hard to measure, because policy goals are ambiguous and vaguely defined, because the consequences are often unintended, and also because reliable statistics are seldom available. Most well known is the policy gap between the goal (or myth) that guest-workers on temporary contracts will return to their country of origin, and not – as the outcome has actually been – settle down for good and bring their families to the country of immigration. Even sophisticated modern control measures are easily circumvented and therefore inadequate. Border controls and visa regulations may be rigorous and still not do the job. The agencies responsible for administration or adjudication are not efficient enough and, even worse, they fail to implement the aims of the official control policy, and often no one intervenes to correct this neglect (employer sanctions in the USA is one example.)

The editors of the second edition (Cornelius et al. 2004) conclude that control policies are getting more ambitious and more restrictive, but still fail. Government interventions are not able to reduce 'unwanted' migration flows: 'more often they simply re-channel the flows and create more opportunities for people smugglers to cash in on the traffic' (ibid.: 41). Even when there is full evidence that new and improved methods are not working, governments continue to invest in them, because they want to show the public that they have not lost control over immigration. Opinion functions here as a restrictive constraint against a too liberal policy, but public opinion may also function in the opposite direction as a liberal constraint against too tough restrictions.

The second point, the liberal constraint, is made by Wayne Cornelius and colleagues who maintain that immigration countries, which violate human rights and humanitarian values, run the risk of a broad public backlash. In their opinion, neither a complete free immigration, nor a too restrictive system is the solution. States have to protect their national interests and cannot in the global economy allow themselves to lose control. The states can both alone and jointly exert some influence upon immigration but they cannot completely control it. If the present policy were less restrictive, it would, in their view, better serve the countries' demographic and economic interests, for example to meet the markets' demand for selected labour immigration. A more liberal policy would also remove the worst consequences of the current asylum policy, perhaps even restore those civil and social rights, which for years have been extended to domiciled foreigners, but which are now in many countries being revised or curtailed.

If the authors of this study are right, and I think they are, the present policy is excessively restrictive both because of politicisation and public opinion. A third factor is the competition between the immigration countries. No one wants to be known as more generous than the other. States compete in control restrictions and sometimes also in tough treatment of asylum seekers, refusing them access to work and temporary integration. Probably such deterrent actions have no impact on the international migration flows in general, but perhaps some impact on the distribution of immigrants across the countries.

The consequences of politicisation

In Europe in the second half of the 1980s the political status of international migration suddenly shifted radically. This previously low-level domestic policy issue was transformed into a matter of major signatories for both national and international politics. Immigration was put on the agenda at many summits of European political leaders, and serious attempts were made to coordinate the member states' national control policies (Messina and Thouez 2002).

I have described the apolitical system of immigration politics as administration rather than policy making, and as characterised by consensus rather than conflict (Hammar 2001). Policy decisions were taken behind closed doors, and members of the decision-making elites were not politicians but bureaucrats, experts, and representatives of organised interests. This corresponds to Gary Freeman's well known definition of 'client politics', namely immigration politics managed by strong organised interests. In a non-transparent power system, the level of open political conflict remains low, and the outcome tends to be a liberal and expansive immigration policy, rather than a restrictive one.

When the apolitical tradition was abandoned in the 1980s, the term 'client politics' became too narrow for a full description of immigration policy-making in Europe. The economic interests (the market), which had shaped the policy of immigration up to this point, were replaced by the political parties. To understand this politicisation, we have to use both political and socio-economic explanations. 'Party politics' replaced the 'client politics' because in some cases politicians wanted to dos. In others, because they were forced to do so. The shift was scarcely radical, however, not a shift from no politicisation to a full and permanent one, nor was the previous 'client politics' completely abandoned (Freeman 1995).

In a commentary from the 1994 version of *Controlling Immigration*, Gary Freeman suggested a third hypothesis in addition to the two already mentioned (the first one, on policy convergence and the second one, on the inefficiency gap between official policy goals and actual policy outcomes) (Freeman 2002). The great puzzle was, Freeman wrote, 'the large and systematic gap between public opinion and public policy'. In his view, the immigration policy of most liberal states is more liberal than public opinion as expressed in surveys and elections. Citizen-voters are 'sceptical if not hostile toward immigration' and even when the policy has become more restrictive, it is still more liberal than public preference.

To tackle this puzzle, Freeman looks for a broad theory of immigration politics linking public policy and the public opinion. He deals with post-industrial change theories, spatial theories (about contests for dominance in the use of space) and international trade theories. All are valuable and interesting, but they have a strong economic bias, and forget about theories on policy making in various democratic and electoral systems (parliamentary system, proportional representation and majority vote systems, referenda etc.) and they also neglect different types of political party systems (membership parties, interest and ideology, electoral machines). Missing especially are the formation of public opinions and political parties' strategies in relation to politicisation and depoliticisation.

Politicians and parties may act in one way under apolitical conditions, with an uninformed and uninterested public, and in quite another manner in a politicised situation, where sensitive and complex information must be handled, and where the rhetoric is often poisoned by hypocritical oversimplification (Westin 1993).

A sensitive issue – public opinion and the political parties

It is surprising that the apolitical period in most European countries continued till late in the 1980s, many years after the arrival of millions of immigrants and the de facto settlement of many ethnic and religious minorities, competing with the native population for space, housing, work and education. In Britain and in Scandinavia, immigrants had early on been granted full domicile and socio-economic rights and often political rights, but they were still heavily exposed to prejudice and discrimination.

The direct politicisation had begun earlier in Britain than in most other European immigration countries. In several countries (for example in France, Denmark and Norway) populist parties had gained some representation in national parliaments but from the start not just on immigration, but on a variety of other issues: taxes, unemployment, criminality, housing, welfare service, health and education, etc. Migration only later became the core issue of new extreme parties. It is in itself a highly emotive issue, attractive to heterogeneous groups of voters, dissatisfied for various reasons. For these voters, migration represents something more than the realities of immigration control and integration policies. Immigration is regarded as a symbol for a great and generalised anxiety, shared by many people, and as a national rallying point.

Charismatic and strong leaders have been quite successful in politicising latent and tacit anti-immigration attitudes. In countries with proportional representation, populist parties have received more than 10 per cent of the votes and seats in some national elections. If no majority can be formed without their support, they might even have an impact on the parliamentary situation. In such cases they have, as Jörg Haider's Austrian Freedom Party in the year 2000 or Pia Kjærsgaard's Danish Peoples' Party in 2005, held the balance of power in their hands. They have secured cabinet posts, and gained access to decision-making about immigration, 'their own policy issue', perhaps even the power to determine the country's immigration policy (Bauböck 1999; Fenger-Grön, C. et al. 2003).

These situations have been exceptional, but already the risk that something like this might happen, has had an impact on policy programmes and decisions of many parties. In the 1990s, an attempt was made to start an anti-immigrant party in Sweden, and during one legislative term a populist party 'New Democracy' held eight per cent of the seats in the parliament. The five old political parties, which were well organised member parties with faithful voters, had long been able to exclude new parties. Financial and legal impediments were used to keep new parties out of parliament, among others, a threshold: to gain representation a party must obtain four per cent of the national vote. In contrast to neighbouring Denmark and Norway, Sweden has so far been spared from a successful anti-immigrant party. But to play safe and shield off the risk, the two major, leading parties (the Social-Democrats, s and the Moderates, m) have both incorporated into their own immigration policies the restrictive demands made by anti-immigrant parties (Hammar 1999).

We may conclude that a system of proportional representation tends to be less efficient than a majority vote system in excluding new populist parties, but that the major parties in both systems have adapted to demands to restrict immigration, to avoid the risk of losing votes and power.

Unlike in Denmark and Norway, the traditional party system has survived longer in Sweden, and the populist parties have therefore been less successful there. But the future is uncertain and change may come quickly. In all the Scandinavian countries, the rate of party membership is falling, and so is the interest in politics. Party preferences shift a lot from one election to the other. Politicians often complain that they are met with disbelief and contempt, and voters complain that they all the time have to listen to empty political rhetoric.

Immigration management

The politicisation of immigration has developed into a kind of a vicious circle. Restrictive immigration control has brought about more hostility towards immigrants and therefore again more control. The consequences are almost entirely negative, and many political parties would like to see at least a partial depoliticisation, moving immigration away from the political battle fields. Pleading for a better immigration policy, they now often use a term borrowed from business administration: they hope for better 'immigration management'.

'Looking ahead to a managed migration agenda', Sarah Spencer (2003: 21) tries to find all sorts of remedies for the present politics of migration. In the introduction to a reader with essays on the politics of immigration, she proposes a number of policies for a better management of immigration. In the present European asylum crisis, she argues, priority should be given to investments in just and generous systems for asylum determination, systems able 'to provide well-founded, faster and fairer decisions'.

The weight of this proposal is well documented in a recent Swedish dissertation on asylum determination (Norström 2004). The task of immigration officers, responsible for the asylum determination, is in Sweden, as everywhere primarily to discriminate between genuine and bogus refugees. The decisions are officially not political, but legal-administrative. As shown in this dissertation, immigration officers tend to develop a kind of professionalism, characterised by mistrust towards all those asylum seekers who do not bring any identification documents, who tell the same story as all the others, and who have paid for being smuggled into the country. After years in a climate of mistrust, they may not be aware of the obvious risk that they make biased, unfair and negative decisions.

It is difficult to find a just and efficient determination system, and such a system would cost the governments a lot, more than policy makers are likely to spend. Migration policy has suffered too long from the inefficiency gap between policy aims and policy outcomes. At the same time, it has suffered from a corresponding gap between on the one hand a hypocritical rhetoric of fear scenarios, vague promises, and outright gildings and on the other hand a practice, coloured by professional mistrust, prejudice opinion and contempt for humanitarian values.

As the inefficiency gap remains great and cannot be measured, and as migration forecasts cannot be verified, policy makers have advantages in public debates about asylum seekers, detentions and deportations etc. Politicians may have access to secret information not available to others. But instead of seriously explaining all relevant facts, they often bluntly assure that in cases of this sort the right of asylum has been and always will be held sacred. In the worst case, they may conceal or deny facts, even when a country's decisions have been criticised by the UN Commission on Torture or by Amnesty International. The symbolic nature of the immigration issue may sometimes induce politicians to use outright hypocritical rhetoric, just to win a few extra political points.

Sarah Spencer writes, 'governments must be truthful with the public' (2003). They should, for example, explain to the public why refugees should be protected and why families should be allowed living together. Governments 'should be open about the benefits and the costs, and realistic about the limitations of what can be delivered' (ibid.). Unfortunately, representatives of most governments would probably just answer that they are already open and truthful.

Two constraints on the public opinion

In the last two decades of relatively large and non-wanted refugee immigration to Europe, we have discerned two parallel trends. The control of immigration has successively become more restrictive and the immigration issue has been politicised. The public debate has been intensive, and populist parties have shown that the immigration issue, thanks to the symbolic power to capture public opinion, may carry a significant electoral weight. The voters' discontent therefore sets bounds to the immigration policy: politicians must not adopt a liberal policy. They have to keep immigration under control.

If this is called the restrictive constraint of immigration policy, there is also a liberal and democratic constraint: politicians may observe fundamental civilised rules, expressed in international law, in human rights, in the right of asylum, and in the international conventions about family reunion and about children etc. Here is the dividing-line: asylum seekers, over-stayers and 'illegals' must not be abused and treated in inhuman ways. Immigration authorities should listen to their arguments, consider their predicament, and make decisions within a reasonable time. They should, for example, not be allowed to deport families which have already spent several years in the country.

The political problem of politicisation is, however, that the restrictive constraint is constantly overemphasised by politicians, while the liberal and democratic constraint is largely neglected. It is too easy for policy makers and immigration officers to blind themselves to what is really going on in their own policy implementation, and to hide behind an empty rhetoric.

8

'Race Relations': The Problem with the Wrong Name

STEPHEN STEINBERG

> Which deception is most dangerous? Whose recovery is
> more doubtful, that of him who does not see or of him
> who sees and still does not see? Which is more difficult,
> to awaken one who sleeps or to awaken one who, awake,
> dreams that he is awake?
>
> —Søren Kierkegaard

IN THE FEMININE MYSTIQUE, published in 1963, Betty Friedan came up with an ingenious formulation for the malaise she detected among middle-class suburban housewives. She called it 'the problem that has no name.' Implicit here is a critique of sociological practice. Except for a few pieces by those rare women in American sociology – for example, Helen Hacker's 1951 article on 'Women as a Minority Group' – the categorical subordination of women was not even on the radar screen of the sociological establishment. 'Sexism' had not yet entered the sociological lexicon. The idea that women were consigned to uphold the patriarchal family and the suburban dream was beyond the sociological imagination. The relegation of women to traditional roles was accepted by the male professoriate as an unquestioned fact of life.

Thanks to Daniel Horowitz's biography (*Betty Friedan and the Making of The Feminine Mystique*), we now know that Friedan was no ordinary housewife who arrived at her epiphany through experience and introspection. She was a seasoned political activist who had been schooled in radical thought at Smith College in the 1940s, worked as a labour journalist for two decades, and was steeped in the feminist thought and politics of the 1950s. By the 1960s Friedan was also a suburban housewife, but she brought a conceptual and ideological lens to this experience that allowed her to see clearly what was opaque to most others. Friedan knew better, but as a skilful rhetorician, she refracted social reality through the lens of the average suburban housewife when she wrote that this was a 'problem that has no name.'

Race in America presents quite another situation: a problem that has been misdiagnosed and mislabelled – a problem with the wrong name. The term that has dominated sociological discourse on race for seven decades is 'race relations.' Ponder for a moment the implications of applying this designation to the subject at hand. In the 1930s, when Robert Park introduced 'race relations' into the sociological lexicon, blacks were a totally downtrodden people. All but 13 per cent fell below the poverty line. Three-quarters lived in the South where they were denied elementary rights of citizenship, were subjected to an all-encompassing system of racial segregation, and were threatened with violence and death for even minor deviations from a debasing system of racial etiquette. During the 1930s, there were 119 lynchings. Yes, Robert Park had a point: 'race relations' were a problem. Small wonder that mainstream sociology still celebrates his perspicacity!

How is it that we apply such benign language to such a malignant problem? It is rather like diagnosing a melanoma as a skin rash, and prescribing a topical salve. Putting the wrong name on a problem is worse than having no name at all. In the latter instance, one is at least open to filling the conceptual void. In the first instance, however, words lead us down a blind alley. They divert us from the facets of the problem that should command our attention, and as the analogy to melanoma suggests, they lead to remedies that are ineffectual or worse.

Sociology can hardly be accused of turning a blind eye to the problem of race. As Franklin Frazier pointed out in 1947, the first two treatises on sociology in America concerned race (actually, they were pro-slavery tracts), and sociology has since produced an enormous body of research and writing on race and racism. But is this a case of seeing and still not seeing? What is the conceptual lens that the sociologist brings to the study of race? Does it illuminate or does it obscure? And what are we to say of a field whose very name – 'race relations' – is already an artful obfuscation?

What terminology would more accurately capture the essence of race in America? The right name, I submit, is 'racial oppression'. This in fact was the term used by Marxist writers in the 1930s, and it entered sociological parlance in the 1970s with the publication of Bob Blauner's *Racial Oppression in America*. Unlike 'race relations', 'racial oppression' conveys a clear sense of the nature, magnitude, and sources of the problem. Whereas the race relations model assumes that racial prejudice arises out of a natural antipathy between groups on the basis of difference, 'racial oppression' locates the source of the problem within the structure of society. Whereas 'race relations' elides the issue of power, reducing racism down to the level of attitudes, 'racial oppression' makes clear from the outset that we are dealing here with a system of domination, one that entails major political and economic institutions, including the state itself. Whereas 'race relations' implies mutuality, 'racial oppression' clearly distinguishes between the oppressor and the oppressed. Whereas 'race relations' rivets attention on superficial aspects of the racial dyad, 'racial oppression' explores the underlying factors that engender racial division and discord. Whereas the sociologist of 'race relations' is reduced to the social equivalent of a marriage counsellor, exploring ways to repair these fractured relationships, the sociologist of 'racial oppression' is potentially an agent of social transformation.

As Thomas Pettigrew suggested in 1964, the ultimate fallacy of the race relations model was that it placed more importance on reducing prejudice among whites than on improving conditions among blacks. Think about it: here was a praxis that ministered to the oppressor rather than the oppressed! In effect, black aspirations for deliverance from poverty and racism were put on hold while whites underwent a therapeutic transformation. What clearer evidence that sociologists, despite their best intentions, have practised white social science?

I hope it is clear that I am raising issue not just with the term 'race relations' but with the entire paradigm that the term represents. Other terms of discourse are equally problematic. In 1984 Barton Meyers, a psychologist at Brooklyn College, wrote an incisive paper entitled, *Minority Group: An Ideological Formulation*. Meyers argued, much as I do here, that the term 'minority group', coined by Louis Wirth in 1945, presents 'a distorted understanding of reality', whose effect is 'to make obscure, especially to subordinate groups, the prevailing system of power and the intentions of the powerful'. Needless to say, his proposal to expunge 'minority group' from the sociological lexicon, and to substitute 'oppressed groups', has fallen on deaf ears. Is it that we hear, but we still do not hear?

The terms 'prejudice' and 'discrimination' are also ideologically laden. Marxists have long argued that prejudice and discrimination are the mere epiphenomena of systems of racial domination. Oliver Cox wrote sardonically: 'If beliefs per se could subjugate a people, the beliefs which Negroes hold about whites should be as effective as those which whites hold about Negroes.' The tendency in social science has been to reify prejudice, to treat it as a problem unto itself, and to pretend that racism could be ameliorated by disabusing whites of the distorted beliefs that they harbour about blacks. This set of assumptions has given rise to a stream of redundant studies, conducted over five decades that chart the prevalence and distribution of prejudiced beliefs. We measure – with meticulous care – but we measure the 'wrong' things, or more exactly, the epiphenomena of racism. Or we measure the right things – glaring inequalities between blacks and whites in wealth, status, and power – but we attribute them to the wrong causes: to deficits in human capital or to aberrant or dysfunctional cultures that are said to perpetuate poverty from one generation to the next.

'Discrimination' suffers from the same problem. Instead of focusing on the historical and structural processes that reproduce racial inequalities from one generation to the next, discrimination is reduced to the level of discrete acts by discrete individuals. However, far more is involved here than individual acts of discrimination, even as they constitute larger aggregates. We are dealing here with the systematic exclusion of an entire people from whole job sectors through all of American history. To describe this as 'discrimination' is to trivialize the issue, to elide its institutional character, and again, to obscure its magnitude and sources. I prefer the term 'occupational apartheid,' which captures the systemic character of the problem, and provides a logic for affirmative action – which is aimed, not at atomized individuals, but at large-scale organizations, such as corporations, unions, and universities.

As I argued in *Turning Back*, the racial crisis of the 1960s provided stark proof of the failure of the race relations paradigm to explain, much less do anything about, the forces that were tearing American society apart. This opened up the canon to radical and minority voices that had long been cast to the periphery. In *Racial Oppression in America*, Blauner explicitly rejected the race relations model and, picking up on the rhetoric and politics of Third World movements, he used the term 'internal colonialism' to describe the encapsulation and plight of blacks and other Third World groups in America. Another key conceptual innovation was proposed in a book that was a collaboration between a political activist and a political scientist. In *Black Power*, Stokely Carmichael and Charles Hamilton drew a distinction between 'individual racism' and 'institutional racism.' The latter, they said, did not depend on intentional acts of racial animus, but was embedded in established and respected institutions of society. Here was a truly revelatory way of looking at racism, one that avoided the reductionist tendencies within sociology, and that treated racism as a systemic problem that required systemic change. Despite these theoretical advances, the insurgent sociology of the 1960s never developed a fully-fledged alternative paradigm. Reflecting the racial backlash in the society at large, mainstream sociology has reverted to the language and logic of 'race relations.'

Like the Confederate flag, the race relations paradigm has endured the challenges of history. A recent study published in Race and Society examined the 34 course syllabi included in the 1997 edition of the ASA's publication on Teaching Race and Ethnic Relations. All but one course had prosaic titles such as 'Minority Groups,' 'Minority Relations,' 'Race and Minority Relations,' 'Race and Ethnic Relations,' and for a new but equally obfuscating twist, 'Race and Ethnic Diversity.' The exception was a course entitled 'White Racism,' which aroused fierce controversy when introduced at the University of Connecticut.

One might argue that the Chicago sociologists who pioneered the study of race were 'products of their times.' But why is it that sociologists are still wedded to these same obfuscating categories seven decades later, as though the Civil Rights Revolution never happened? Why is a course entitled 'White Racism' seen as a provocation? Why has sociology failed to develop a discourse that illuminates, instead of obscures, the systemic character of racism?

Like Cox and Du Bois in an earlier time, the proponents of a critical sociology on race are reduced to carping from the sidelines. It is fundamentally a question of hegemony: of which perspectives prevail; which command resources; which are central to intellectual discourse, both inside and outside the academy; which are influential when it comes to the formation of public policy. To pursue the question of hegemony, one would have to examine the web of relationships among elite universities, professional associations, government, the media, book publishers and book review editors, 'dream teams,' and those all-important foundations – which together constitute a power elite that has a decisive influence on discourse, intellectual production, and social policy.

Nowhere is the hegemonic status of the race relations paradigm more evident than in the recent report issued by the advisory board for President Clinton's Initiative on Race. The initiative itself illustrates the schizophrenic split between social reality and the construction of that reality that is endemic to the race relations model. Here is a President who helped to instigate and enact the repeal of welfare, removing billions of dollars of subsidies to poor minority families; who signed a crime bill that has increased the prison population to over two million people, two-thirds of them black and Latino; who promised to 'mend, not end' affirmative action, and yet did little or nothing to oppose Proposition 209 in California, and presided over the quiet dismantling of affirmative action policy.

Instead of public policies to attack structural racism, Clinton provided us with the spectacle of a national conversation on race predicated on the assumption that dialogue 'helps to dispel stereotypes,' and is 'a tool for finding common ground.' However, these bland assumptions are not politically innocent, as Adolph Reed argued in his column in *The Progressive* (December 1997):

The problem isn't racial division or a need for healing. It is racial inequality and injustice. And the remedy isn't an elaborately choreographed pageantry of essentializing yackety-yak about group experience, cultural difference, pain, and the inevitable platitudes about understanding. Rather, we need a clear commitment by the federal government to preserve, buttress, and extend civil rights and to use the office of the Presidency to indicate that commitment forcefully and unambiguously. As the lesson of the past three decades in the South makes clear, this is the only effective way to change racist attitudes and beliefs.

The report finally issued by the Commission represents at once the nullification of the 1968 Kerner Commission Report, and the reinstatement of the race relations model as the intellectual framework for race policy in America. Whereas the Kerner Report confronted the nation with the harsh reality that it was 'moving toward two societies, one black, one white – separate and unequal,' the Franklin Report provides a reassuring illusion of 'One America in the 21st Century.' Whereas the Kerner Report presented the grisly facts about racial inequality and racial conflict, designed to galvanize the nation to action, the Franklin Report is replete with platitudes about 'accomplishments, challenges, and opportunities.'

The most glaring point of difference pertains to social policy. The Kerner Report concluded with 73 pages of policy recommendations that envisioned a comprehensive program of economic development and social reconstruction targeted at poverty areas and racial ghettos. Not only does the Franklin Report lack any major policy initiatives, but there is no sense of crisis that the three pillars of anti-racist public policy – affirmative action, school desegregation, and racial districting – have all been gutted, effectively bringing the Second Reconstruction to an unceremonious end.

It is true that the Franklin Report includes an endorsement of affirmative action, albeit a tepid one, along with a litany of proposals for reforming housing, health care, education, and criminal justice. Its main emphasis, however, is on bridging the racial divide through dialogue. Nero has been subjected to the judgment of history for fiddling while Rome burned. In this case we are asked to dialogue – and the Commission's report provides us with a dazzling array of alternatives: One America Conversations, Campus Weeks of Dialogue, Statewide Days of Dialogue, meetings, forums, conferences, public service announcements, and visits to the One America Web Site. Finally, the Franklin Report concludes with a section entitled 'Ten Things Every American Should Do to Promote Racial Reconciliation.'

It is as though Durkheim concluded his masterpiece with 'Ten Things That Everybody Should Do to Avoid Suicide.' Or Weber offered ten tips for succeeding in business. Or Marx advocated a WPA-style jobs program for the lumpenproletariat. If the President's Advisory Board on Race has displayed an abysmal failure of sociological imagination, who are we to blame but the sociologist of 'race relations' who has betrayed the promise of sociology's intellectual tradition by reducing social facts down to the level of individual predispositions? What can we hope of a Presidential commission or the public at large if sociologists, despite their assiduous labors, still do not see that good race relations are unattainable – indeed, inconceivable – unless there is a basic parity of condition between the black and white citizens of this nation?

Note

This paper was originally published in 2001 in *New Politics*, 8(2) <http://www.wpunj.edu/~newpol/issue30/steinb30.htm>. Accessed 7 January 2007.

Part IV

Race Relations in the City: Revisiting John Rex's Local Studies of Race Relations in Birmingham

9

Sparkbrook, Housing Classes & the Market Situation: Forty Years On

TAHIR ABBAS

I FIRST ENCOUNTERED John Rex's work on race and ethnicity when I was a postgraduate student at the University of Birmingham, reading a masters degree in economic development and policy. In writing my dissertation on the economic development and decline of Small Heath, a somewhat disadvantaged ward of south Birmingham where I was born and grew up in, I was introduced to his work. His writings encouraged me to research ethnicity, ultimately moving me to the Centre for Research in Ethnic Relations at the University of Warwick in 1995 to begin my doctoral research. Having a background in economics and economic development and policy, I was interested in questions of economy and society and, in particular, the 'hot potato' that seemed to afflict ethnic minorities, the subject of education, which, essentially, is a route out of poverty and way in which to achieve upward social mobility for many racialised minorities. Not wanting to move beyond my depth, my study focused on South Asians in Birmingham, hoping to keep my research nearer home, and being semi-autobiographical in some respects, too. I was encouraged to find that John

Rex had researched Birmingham not just once but on two occasions, help-ing to put the study of cities and the subject of ethnicity on the global soci-ological map. Any self-assured sociologist with anything to say about eth-nicity knows about housing classes and the urban sociology of race and ethnicity, as derived from the studies in Birmingham.

I worked on my study, getting on with reading and thinking about the extensive research that already existed on ethnic minorities in education in Britain. The many numbers of interviews I had to carry out meant being locked away in analysis for much of my first two years. When I did emerge from my office and when I finally mustered the confidence of being in the same room as John Rex for more than one minute, we ended up talking about New Labour, which had just come into power in 1997. He suggested that things did not look any different in terms of political ideologies and I rejoined that New Labour actually is more akin to 'New Conservatism', at which he growled approvingly. I had won him over. I began to write up my research, presented it at conferences, and publishing short pieces where the opportunities emerged. John Rex read a piece in *Dialogue*, entitled, 'British South Asian Youth: A New Diaspora' (1997). He wrote to me and asked me meet with him – we sat and talked extensively. The article was a summary of a longer paper on further college students and their retrospective expe-riences of school and perspectives on further and higher education (Abbas 2002). I alluded to questions of class analysis, ethnicity and the impact of religion and culture on identities in the sphere of the education system to explore the essential drivers of educational achievement. I got many an-swers but also more questions, too. Needless to say, John Rex and I have remained in touch and have been talking about Birmingham, education, class and ethnicity since then. In more recent periods Muslims in Britain have also become an interesting point of discussion.

The subject of this chapter is a more specific analysis of the work of John Rex and his study of housing classes in Sparkbrook, Birmingham (Rex and Moore 1967). I discuss the developments to the locality over time and the issues that emerge today. Recent debates in relation to market situations and Muslim minorities and their urban inter-ethnicity are elaborated upon in an effort to explore the extent to which Rex's Weberian class analysis of the market situation of housing still resonates today. To this end, it is im-portant to first elaborate on Marxian accounts of ethnic class relations that were popular at the time of John Rex's work in Sparkbrook. Second, the details of the Sparkbrook study and the concept of 'housing classes' is anal-ysed, taking into consideration the lengthy critiques it encountered. Finally, the current position in Sparkbrook is explored, making specific reference to what has changed or otherwise, given forty years of economic, social, political and cultural development.

Economic structure and social conflict

The concept of exploitation is central to Marxist understanding of history and contemporary society. But not all social conflicts can be immediately reduced to the struggle between exploiters and exploited, and to explain these conflicts other concepts are required. An important one is that of oppression: the systematic discrimination by one social group against another on the grounds of characteristics either inherited (skin colour, gender) or socially acquired (religious belief, sexual orientation). The experience of oppression cuts across class lines, although the experience is more or less severe depending on where its victims are placed within the class structure. Some forms, like the oppression of women, have persisted throughout the existence of class society, while others, like modern racism, are specific to capitalism alone (Miles 1982). Sometimes the reasons, or pretexts, for the oppression of a group may change over time. During feudalism, for example, Jewish people were persecuted for their religious beliefs, but as capitalism developed, persecution increasingly took place on the grounds of their supposed race. Whatever the reason or pretext, however, ruling classes throughout history have instigated or endorsed the oppression of different groups in order to maintain or create divisions amongst those over whom they rule. Recently, groups have been subjected to oppression on the grounds of their ethnicity and religion. The most extreme form of such oppression has become known as 'ethnic cleansing' (Ahmed 1995).

Marxists seek to explain ethnic relations by incorporating ethnicity as an element in the analysis of the capitalist mode of production. One view is to show the ways in which ethnic divisions serve to further the interests of capital. Here, the view of class as the primary form of social division is emphasised. Apparent ethnic inequalities are in fact manifestations of class relations between bourgeoisie and proletariat. Capitalists exploit ethnic divisions to manipulate and divide the working class. Furthermore, ethnicity and racism are merely ideological constructions that mystify and conceal real material formations – and to legitimate and perpetuate prevailing relationships of exploitation and domination.

A more satisfactory type of Marxist approach, however, treats racialised groups as distinct types of labour. In Britain, South Asian and African-Caribbean workers can be viewed as a 'racialised fraction' of the working class (Phizacklea and Miles 1980). Stigmatising minority ethnic groups by attributing racial differences permits them to be discriminated against, and used to fill the types of jobs that are rejected by the white ethnic majority. Ethnic minority workers, thus, occupy distinct labour market positions, and are more disadvantaged than their white fellows. Another concept is the notion of 'migrant labour' (cf. Castles and Kosack 1973). It is argued that capitalist employers use migrant labour as a source of cheap, highly exploitative labour. Migrant labourers supplement the indigenous proletariat, especially in the 'dirty' jobs, which are hard to fill. Because of their migrant status, such workers (especially guest workers with temporary work visas) can be expelled to their home countries when their labour is no longer needed, and without any cost to the state (i.e., no welfare benefit payments). However, such approaches restrict the concept of 'ethnicity' to situations involving labour. Cultural Marxists consider the way in which racism and imperialist dogmas have been used in advanced societies to strengthen the cultural hegemony of the ruling class. Racism does not merely serve to legitimate class domination but also informs the meanings working people impute to their experiences, and the way they live out their own class position.

The Marxist analysis, nevertheless, has certain limitations. First, non-class forms of division are ultimately seen as less important than class relations, and as determined by them (if not reducible to them). Second, there is a tendency to see racialised groups as though they were all part of the proletariat. However, greater petite bourgeoisie numbers are beginning to emerge from the ethnic minorities and more are found at all levels of the class structure (but not always at the very highest levels). Third, ethnic relations have a different existential location from class relations. Racist attitudes and practices occur among the white population as a whole. They cannot be reduced to economic factors alone.

Stratification by ethnic group is a particular problem for classic Marxist accounts. Traditional Marxism discounts the problem altogether, and sees 'race' as a mere epiphenomenon, distinguishing the fundamental split between the real, traditional classes. This is the sort of Marxism that Parkin (1979) rebukes as being unable to deal with the genuine complexities of stratification, especially of the 'new' forms. The general Marxist retort to Parkin or any of the other Weberians is that they have isolated and listed a number of social processes like closure or structuration but do not give any systematic account of them. The approach does not explain what puts ethnicity or skin colour on the agenda so prominently or what makes it a potent basis for systematic discrimination in capitalism. There are two possible approaches here. First, racism is impossible to understand without understanding imperialism (non-Marxists have also said this, but for Marxists, imperialism is itself inspired and driven by economic pressures). In the process of imperial conquest, white Britons encountered persons with different cultures and skin colours – and conquered and exploited them.

These events led to a class ideological distortion: cultural differences and skin colour were taken as signs of inferiority. The subdued, conquered and demoralised state of the colonised was seen as an attribute of their culture, rather than as a result of superior technology. That ideological legacy and imperialist context helps centralise skin colour as a factor in the processes of closure in Britain. Second, stratification by ethnicity serves capitalism. The 'underclass' is a modern substitute for the classic 'reserve army of the unemployed' which keeps wages low, divides the work force in both real and ideological terms, and buffers the economy against booms and slumps, etc.

Miles and Brown (2003) argue for the need to move beyond presenting racism as 'functional' to capitalist development, and a cultural analysis that neglects the economic basis of capitalism and social relations of inequality. Defining racism as functional to capitalism is to presuppose the nature and outcome of its interactions with economic and political relations, and with other ideologies. This assumes a homogenous ruling class inevitably and necessarily derives economic and/or political advantage from its expression. The use of racism to limit labour does not advantage employers experiencing labour shortages. Civil disturbances will not help capitalists whose business will be disrupted. Nor will the state wish to increase expenditure to maintain social order. Racism is a contradictory phenomenon – what is 'functional' for one set of interests will be 'dysfunctional' for another. In general, all the multiple factors mentioned in the Weberian approaches can be fitted to Marxist models (Giddens 1982). The 'social formation' is a complex one in modern Marxism, with three or four 'levels' ('economic', 'political' and 'ideological', 'cultural') according to Althusser (1977). 'Race' is functional at each of these levels. This leads to an exploration of Weberian approaches and the extent of the overlap.

Race and class: the development of 'housing classes'

There is a considerable overlap between Weberian and Marxist thinking in relation to ethnicity. Both perspectives see ethnic inequality in primarily economic terms and analyse ethnicity in terms of its link to class. Weber distinguishes different kinds of groups within a particular society, using the concept of status. Weberians suggest that ethnic groups could be seen as negatively privileged status groups. Processes of 'social closure', involving exclusion and demarcation, are used to mark out the social boundaries between groups and maintain the hierarchical ordering of the society. Some Weberians try to combine Marxian and Weberian concepts. They explain the position of ethnic minority workers in terms of a mixture of class position, capitalist needs and minority status, arising from the colonial past.

Similar to Marxism, Weberians agree that 'race' is an unreal category. For this reason, it cannot be a base for actions in the way that class is. Therefore, the formation of 'racialised groups' must be linked to broader economic processes. For Castles and Kosack (1973), it is clear that racial discrimination has a number of social dimensions. Labour markets inevitably link with other social and political goods in their 'distributive' processes. Immigrant workers face multiple discriminations, for example in terms of low wages and insecurity at work; in the political sphere, where they are frequently denied full citizenship rights and equal access to welfare provision; in local housing markets; and, in the education system.

Economic factors are not always somehow more fundamental than others. It is possible to pursue a Weberian strategy of complexity in stratification. This approach is exemplified in discussions of race in the major study by Rex and Moore. Utilising the theoretical categorisation of concentric zones of the city by Park and Burgess (1925), Rex suggested that the weakness of the theory was its failure to 'investigate sufficiently the relationship between the culture and society of one sub-community and those of another' (Rex and Moore 1967: 8). Rex argues that his theory of housing theoretical intervention was an attempt to make sense of the processes underlying Park and Burgess's theory of 'urban zones', which was developed in the 1920s. The point of departure for this study was the settlement patterns of groups of migrants from Britain's former colonies, principally the Caribbean and South Asia. The post-war economic boom in Britain created particular labour shortages that were filled by migration from the former colonial dependencies. The areas that experienced the greatest influx of migrant workers were in the South, the West Midlands and the North. At the town and city level, the areas that received these migrants, and which later provided the space for community reconstruction, are referred to as 'twilight zones'. They emerged near to the city centre and were within easy reach of places of work. Rex and Moore's starting premise is rejection of the assumption that the process of migration and settlement itself had a deleterious impact upon housing conditions within Birmingham, leading to the emergence of the 'twilight zone'. Rather, they argue that it was through the operations of discrimination within the housing allocation system of the city council that necessitated the concentration of migrant and post-migrant groups in certain types of housing in specific areas of the city.

Rex and Moore argue that, in being squeezed out of local authority housing, an alternative was found by migrant groups in the form of lodging houses in areas within the city's 'middle ring', one such area being Sparkbrook. These areas were also in the process of being vacated by members of the majority population, whose economic mobility manifested itself in the form of relocation to the suburbs and home-ownership. These two categories, i.e., home ownership and residency in lodging houses, formed the two ends of the 'housing class' schema, with home-ownership constituting the most and lodging-houses the least desirable of housing types. The theory of 'housing classes' was a development of a Weberian (as distinct from a Marxian) concept of class, whereby competition within a range of markets other than the labour market was considered to have class defining features (Sarre et al. 1989). Rex and Moore (1967: 274) defined six classes overall; 'the owner of a whole house; that of the owner of a mortgaged whole house; that of the council tenant – a) in a house with a long life and b) in a house awaiting demolition; that of the tenant of a whole house owned by a private landlord; that of the owner of house bought with short term loans who is compelled to let rooms in order to meet his repayment obligations; and that of the tenant of rooms in a lodging-house'.

Rex and Moore argue that much racial conflict can be understood through exploring basic urban processes and problems, and they key urban process is that of competition for scarce but desirable housing. Where Marxists identify two main classes in terms of relationship to the means of production, Rex and Moore utilise a more flexible Weberian position which defines a variety of classes according to given 'market situations', with one such market being housing. This led to the notion of 'housing classes' to determine groups which occupy various positions of strength in the housing market and its system of allocation. These classes do not coincide with the Marxian classes, although there is some relationship with them, since one Marxist class would consist of several housing classes characterised by different interests and market situations. Rex and Moore are interested in the ways in which people define their own class membership. In this, they suspect that everyone would aspire to the 'suburban ideal' of 'relatively detached family life'.

But in relation to the disadvantaged positions of former new Commonwealth economic migrants and their experience of purchasing 'private' sector housing, invariably problems are faced. Indeed, in the immediate post war period there were two main ways in which British working class people sought to improve their housing conditions. If they had a sufficient and secure income they could obtain mortgages from building societies and purchase good family housing, usually in the suburbs. If, on the other hand, their wages were too low or uncertain, they could turn to the council for houses to rent. The existence of such options in the field of housing, however, had little meaning to African-Caribbean and South Asian workers in the 1950s and 1960s. But estate agents, building societies and vendors were able to and did discriminate freely against ethnic minority applicants and house purchasers were forced to buy in restricted areas. Furthermore, with irregular forms of finance, so far as the rented council sector was concerned, the points system was used to discriminate systematically if indirectly against ethnic minorities. While it is true that both of these forms of discrimination were weakened after the passing of the 1969 Race Relations Act and with the abatement of the housing shortage in the public sector, the fact remains by that time many immigrant groups had been forced into making long-term housing commitments, quasi-ghetto conditions had emerged. Moreover, once this kind of segregation had started, it perpetuated itself. New buyers chose to stay in the segregated areas because of the existence of communal facilities and because they felt that there they had protection. Thus there grew not merely a system of urban segregation but a situation in which the social bonds of a segregated residential community were at least as powerful as those engendered by working class membership. In Marxian terms, while immigrant workers might have been members of the working class, as a class-in-itself they did not share in the types of bonding and social consciousness which existed in the working class as a whole and formed if anything their own separate 'class-for-itself'.

Rex used Weber's account of classes (Weber 1968), taking on the notion that class situations were market place situations arising from the differential distribution of poverty including domestic as well as industrial property. Rex drew attention to the position of inferior housing classes, yet just as in the case of colonial societies, Rex recognised that these essentially economic positions were overlaid by a social and political order. Rex argued that there was a complex social ordering of the population based upon both class and status, i.e., social stratification. Thus, if the term 'underclass' was to be used in analysing these metropolitan societies it should refer to both the economic positions (involving inferior status of employment) and social position (viewed as bottom of the current stratification system) in metropolitan capitalist societies. Such an 'underclass' Rex saw as involving others as well as immigrants from post colonial societies but also that colonial status indicated in Britain above all by colour meant that there was a higher statistical probability of postcolonial immigrants being assigned to this 'underclass'.

This concept of housing class was widely debated in urban sociology, however it was criticised by Marxists influenced by the new urban sociology. Rex's critics were uneasy about his use of the term class in relation to housing. To them, class conflict in the capitalist mode of production was a notion confined to the conflict of those who created and those who gained surplus value. Castles and Kosack argue that the housing market can *only* be secondary to the labour market in defining class position, in the sense that the ability to compete in the labour market is highly dependent upon income. From this perspective, to assert the independence or equal importance of ownership of private property to labour market participation in line with Weber cannot be easily sustained. Whilst some recognised that the housing issue did have a degree of independence, critics disagreed with Rex and Moore's assertion that differential rights were controlled by immediate 'gatekeepers' in the urban system. His critics argued it was the constraints imposed on the gatekeepers by factors such as the cost of land, by rent levels and the rate of interest. Rex also encountered criticism from Miles (1982) on the definition of 'a race relations situation' and his account of the structure of colonial and metropolitan societies. Miles argued Rex's analysis was conceptually inadequate from a Marxist position. Solomos (1982) refers to Rex as reductionist and economistic Marxism, although Rex (1994) asserts that Solomos fails to recognise that all of his specifies what he means by 'relative autonomy' in theoretical terms, rather than leaving the problem at the purely abstract level. Rex is also accused by Gilroy (1980) of 'counter insurgency', whilst others indict Rex for stereotyping African-Caribbean people and therefore helping in their repression. A particularly sensitive point concerns the question of the African-Caribbean family, where Rex is apparently implying a cultural deficit model (Lawrence 1982). In response to these criticisms, Rex argues that it is not simply appropriate to regard African-Caribbean people as victims or only having universal human characteristics, though they share these with the indigenous people, it is also important to find out how they have been influenced by their own culture and what their group aspirations are.

Rex's methodology may give some credence to his distinction and description of African-Caribbean people. It concerns differentiation, which has to be made between the use of ideal types and political stereotyping. Given Rex's Weberian methodology, the use of ideal types is essential in sociology; they are developed to interpret empirical reality and the need to be refined in the light of evidence. Political stereotypes are used in political conflict to denigrate and damage one's opponents. This is something Rex believes occurred in relation to the writers from the Centre for Contemporary Cultural Studies. Consequently, it could be said the criticisms are legitimate in so far as they show that Rex's ideal types are crudely developed or inconsistent with empirical facts. Much less legitimate is the criticism involving an imputation of motive, specifically that Rex is simply offering political stereotypes because of an anti-Black political position based on Rex's reference and relationship to African-Caribbean people's earlier colonial experience in British society and its link with contemporary African-Caribbean youth culture. However, for Rex, part of the process of understanding these new creative developments involve seeking to appreciate the social structures previously developed under conditions of colonialism. Even Gilroy (1987), who criticised Rex for insisting on a class analysis of the so called 'race relations problematic', underwent a change to his own ideas. Gilroy now believed that people seek fulfilment and liberation in new ways, and the confrontation between employer and employee is no longer the main confrontation between the individual and society. Rex (1996: 26) feels that Gilroy 'like many postmodernists exaggerate the changes which have occurred'. He states, 'in my own view struggles concerned with employment are still amongst the most important structuring factors in politics. On the other hand I take some satisfaction in the fact that my emphasis on housing classes in my earlier work would now seem to be acceptable, since they would undoubtedly count as social movements'.

The points of disagreement lie in the different social science and methodological philosophies, and largely between those conveying an economic framework, such as Robert Miles, and those suggesting a sociological framework, such as Paul Gilroy, Eric Lawrence and Stuart Hall. But Ratcliffe (1999) suggests that there are other issues that stem for 'a constraints school' perspective, such that indeed ethnic minorities have no choice in their housing conditions because of either racial or structural discrimination. Their choices are limited by both external and internal factors in relation to market situations for housing. As Ratcliffe (1999: 13, original emphasis) adds, 'many have felt that the 'choice-constraints' framework produces a rather static and sterile form of analysis dominated by structure *versus* agency'. Dayha (1974: 77) also stresses that Rex and Moore place too great an emphasis on structural constraints faced by minorities, having 'imposed their own political perspectives on the immigrant housing situation...without providing sufficient evidence to support their various statements'.

Marxism of the type that was prevalent in social science teaching in the 1970s attempts to deduce an account of historical events and an interpretation of the behaviour of institutions and their agents. Rex's methodology by contrast began with the development of ideal types of action on the part of groups such as classes and ethnic minority communities on the one hand and social and political institutions on the other. Rex who starts with the construction of ideal types is bound to deal with the relationships between collective action of classes and ethnic minorities and the institutions and apparatuses of the state.

Sparkbrook today: market situations and Muslim minorities
In the post-war period, the first significant settlement of South Asians was mainly by male workers who had come to Britain for economic opportu-

nity but with the view that they would return. These were the 'pioneers' and theirs was a 'myth of return'. The passing of anti-immigration laws in 1962 and 1968 saw a sharp rise in numbers of migrants electing to stay in Britain. As a result, a substantial increase in the sponsorship of village kin and the settlement of migrant families occurred (Anwar 1979). A third wave of migration took place in the 1970s as East African Asians sought refuge from political unrest in Uganda, Kenya and other African countries (Mattausch 1998).

At the time, large numbers of South Asians settling in Greater London and in the industrial cities of the West Midlands, West Yorkshire and Lancashire, an out-movement of the British middle class from the industrial inner and middle ring neighbourhoods to the outer suburbs was already in process (Ward 1983; Whitehand and Carr 2001). This movement left a significant percentage of the industrial heritage largely redundant and open to conversion and transformation by the new urban immigrant settlers. Settlement first took place in spatially defined areas within the major industrial areas in Sparkbrook corresponding to the late-Victorian and Edwardian (1875–1918) inner and middle ring neighbourhoods. Racialised housing policies limited choices to these localised parts of British cities. Rex and Moore argued that a combination of racial politics, discriminatory practices, policies and labour exploitation were ways of maintaining the spatial segregation of the 'other'.

The highly regular and well differentiated layout of the industrial urban landscape, characterised by regular streets, two storey terraces governed urban change, although these neighbourhoods offered a number of advantages for the early settlers. First, much of the terraced housing stock was vacant and therefore it was both cheap and non-competitive, with the added advantage of being capable of absorbing large numbers of male workers. Second, the High Street, a major through road of commercial activity connect the neighbourhoods to the city centre, made these areas readily accessible to the central business, commercial and industrial districts for employment opportunities. It was around these established urban centres that South Asian landlords began to establish a strong transnational network through the *biradari* (patrilineal and extended kinship and village networks). They sponsored fellow *biraderi*-members and lodged them in their homes shaping a process of chain migration which continued to influence patterns of settlement within specific geographies in British industrial cities. This form of spatialised *biradari*-based social organisation had its benefits at the outset. It created an environment of social welfare and cohesion in an antagonistic environment; and it fostered the perpetuation of traditional norms, values and beliefs amongst the newcomers (Peach 2000). With the arrival of families from the mid-1960s, the village-kin group, as a residential unit, began to develop into nuclear households of owner-occupied properties with people living in close proximity to each other (Dayha 1974). Peach (2000) has shown that through social processes of intermarriage and proximity the persistence and stability of the South Asian cultural group were able to accommodate differences.

Until the 1960s, the West Midlands region, with Birmingham at its centre, was one of the fastest growing. Strength was in a strong manufacturing base in vehicles, material manufacturing, and engineering. During the 1970s and 1980s, however, the region suffered severe industrial decline with the city of Birmingham particularly affected. Unemployment rose far faster than new jobs were being created with some wards in the inner cities decimated as are result, including Sparkbrook. As the indigenous population moved out of inner Birmingham, through a process known as 'white flight', South Asians and African-Caribbeans were trapped in the inner city areas. Subsequently, these areas become further impoverished with new employment being created elsewhere and in other economic sectors. It is only recently that the expanding service sector has begun to make an impact on the fortunes of the city. The effects of de-industrialisation, technological investment and the internationalisation of capital and labour have left a distinct impression on some parts of the city.

By the late 1980s, however, a combination of natural increase and a new wave of migration marked a sharp rise in the number of South Asians. This period is characterised by the settlement of the outer suburbs but nevertheless still maintaining close social ties with local and transnational South Asian *biradari* (Shaw 2000). Indeed, close proximity to South Asian business, the mosque, good schools and transport has shown to be a primary factor for the stability of social groups in particular areas of the city. Thus within these social geographies and urban landscapes new relationships were spatialised from the most personal and intimate of relationships – the family group – to those based on religion, commerce, education and politics.

Discussion

In Birmingham today there are noticeable ethnic and religious communities, past and present, living in reasonable harmony with each others. This is irrespective of how successfully or otherwise the local state has managed its multicultural and pubic policy relations (Abbas and Anwar 2005). More recently, Birmingham is becoming home to Eastern Europeans and Northern and Eastern Africans gravitating to the city and moving (or being moved) to already densely populated South Asian Muslim areas. These new Muslim

groups arrive to live and work in the city and want to be near existing established Muslim and other ethnic minority communities. As 'refugees and
asylum seekers', new Muslim migrant groups can often find it harder to integrate into society. Much of this is a function of limited economic, cultural
and social capital as well as the facts of racism and discrimination. New and
existing Muslim groups experience issues in accessing employment, housing and education, while at the same time are vulnerable to hostility from
dominant society, where public option whipped up by media sensational-
ism and right-wing nationalism is especially unsympathetic.

The 1991 Census found that Birmingham contained seven per cent of
all ethnic minorities in Britain. Twenty-two per cent of the city's population was of ethnic minority origin, with nearly twice as many South Asians
in comparison to African-Caribbeans. Birmingham Pakistanis constituted
the largest single ethnic minority group comprising seven per cent of the
total population of the city. The 2001 Census confirms these trends. The
largest ethnic minority group is Pakistani comprising just over 10 per cent
of the total population of the city. Today, there are 1m people in Birmingham, with about of third that are non-white. In 2001, there were an estimated 23,318 ethnic minorities in Sparkbrook, representing an estimated
82 per cent of all people in the ward. This compares with an average of 34
per cent in Birmingham as a whole, 14 per cent within the West Midlands
region and 13 per cent in England and Wales. From 1991 to 2001 there is
an increase of 13 per cent in the ethnic minority population.

During the 1990s and more recently, there has been an intake of European and Middle Eastern Muslim 'refugees and asylum seekers' from such
places as Bosnia, Kosovo, Afghanistan, Somalia and Iraq, but the demographic profile today is dominated by Muslims from South Asia, and, principally, from Pakistan and Bangladesh (approximately half of all Muslims
in Britain are 'Pakistani', of which it is estimated more than three-quarters
are of 'Kashmiri' origin). In a city of 1m people, Birmingham Muslims account for 14.3 per cent of the population, with Pakistanis numbering just
over 104,000. This number is twice as large as the highest concentration of
Muslims outside of London. In 2001, nearly one in ten of all British Muslims were to be found in Birmingham, arguably home to the world's largest
expatriate Kashmiri community (ONS 2005). In more recent years, a number of bourgeoisie South Asians have moved to affluent neighbouring wards
and into relatively exclusive housing but remain in relative spatial proximity to the ethnic ties from which they stemmed. Sparkbrook today largely
contains a whole host of migrant communities and existing established ethnic minority groups. Invariably, the profile of Sparkbrook is one of Muslim

communities, new and existing, living in an area that contains the support networks and entrepreneurial profile relevant to a set of religious and cultural needs and aspirations.

As John Rex enters his eighty-second year, it is clear that his work on the study of ethnicity, and in particular competitive urban landscapes that impact on the experiences of racialised ethnic minorities, albeit in a post-welfare globalising and increasingly fractured world, maintain its importance in the annals of sociology, past and present. The world has changed and so has sociology to reflect the increasingly complex social relations that underpin it and no less so in relation to ethnicity. His continuing legacy in the academe sees 'race', ethnicity and multiculturalism in all aspects of various teaching and research faculties, with the concerns around institutional practices and economic infrastructure remaining important in continuing analyses of ethnic minorities. In an era where global economic activity motivated by neo-conservative political hegemonic projects results in changing geographical boundaries and their relationship to the means of production, with Muslim minorities at home and abroad subjugated by dominant paradigms, the 'othering of others' operating within a neo-orientalist framework, and with increasing polarities between rich and poor, minority and majority, Muslim and non-Muslim, Rex's analytical framework in relation to housing classes in understanding complex, post-industrial inter-ethnic relations remains eminently useful. For all the criticism and debate that the Rex and Moore study of Sparkbrook generated, to conceptualise a more flexible Weberian position which defines a variety of classes according to given 'market situations' remains an important intellectual frame of reference, particularly given the recent and developing concerns in relation to the British Muslim community in the light of the events of 9/11 and the 'war on terrorism' at the global level – and the 2001 northern disturbances and the events of 7/7 at the local level. The local and global and inextricably linked for Muslims, as well as non-Muslim majorities. The ways in which the economic, political, social and intellectual impact on Muslim-non-Muslim relations are invariably manifestations of differing market situations.

Acknowledgements
I would like to thank Dr Richard T Gale, Department of Sociology, University of Birmingham, for his valuable comments on an earlier version of this chapter.

10

Exposing The Urban Systems Driving Ethnic Integration and Conflict: Our Debt to John Rex

FRANK REEVES

A MAJOR NEW STUDY of race and ethnic relations in Birmingham in the British West Midlands is urgently needed. Far from there being too much research and too little action, as community groups are prone to assert, far too much action is taken without understanding of cause or effect, or of the likely consequences of intervention. A study of the kind envisaged would draw insights from the sociology and social economics of the city, and of race relations, and show how various systems relating to the economy and employment, housing and consumption, and education (as a means of status allocation or social mobility), coupled with sub-systems affecting family life, health, culture and leisure, all come together to exacerbate or alleviate racial inequality.

Only by the exposure of these structures and processes will it be possible to draw up a comprehensive strategy and to take effective action to promote equality and alleviate continuing ethnic conflict. Currently, there are many uncoordinated strategies, often based on interpretation of national statistics, intuition, or business-as-usual assumptions, with little or no understanding of the region or city as a Leviathan-like socio-economic system, uncontrollably dispensing rewards and penalties as it moves onward.

Two of John Rex's studies of urban race relations, arguably the most in-
fluential, were undertaken in Birmingham. The first, *Race and Community
Conflict*, co-authored with Robert Moore, and published in 1967, focused
on the area of Sparkbrook on the south-east side of the City. The second,
Colonial Immigrants in a British City, and subtitled, *a class analysis*, was
co-authored with Sally Tomlinson and published twelve years later in 1979.
It involved structured and unstructured interviews of people in the Soho,
Sandwell, Handsworth, and Newtown wards of the area, referred to collec-
tively as Handsworth, to the north west of the City.

Since these sociology texts whose fieldwork was undertaken in the mid
1960s and late 1970s were written, however, considerable changes have
taken place in ethnic demographics, race relations, law, social policy, the
welfare state, politics (especially of immigration), the economy, and approaches to regeneration and regionalisation, as well as on the European
and international front.

Particularly in ethnic demographic terms, Birmingham has changed.
The 1961 census showed 29,000 New Commonwealth-born residents of
Birmingham, or under 3 per cent of the total population. The majority of
New Commonwealth immigrants at the time was from the West Indies
(16,298), with 10,156 from India and Pakistan. By 1971, the number of
New Commonwealth immigrants (excluding their British-born children)
had grown to 67,940, or 6 per cent of the total population. The majority
now was from the Indian subcontinent (35,400), with 25,365 from the West
Indies. By comparison, the 2001 census showed an ethnic minority population of 289,706 or 29.7 per cent, approaching one third of the total population of Birmingham. Of these, 104,060 (10.7 per cent of the Birmingham
population) were of Pakistani, 55,792 (5.7 per cent) of Indian, and 47,877
(4.9 per cent) of Caribbean ethnic origin.

In the Sparkbrook that Rex and Moore studied in 1964, the Irish were
the largest of the ethnic minorities making up 12.9 per cent of the ward, followed by the West Indians (8.7 per cent), the Pakistanis (3.6 per cent), and
Indians (2.0 per cent). By 2001, the Sparkbrook ward (although boundaries
are not conterminous with the Sparkbrook of 1964) had a black and minority ethnic population of 77.9 per cent, a figure including people of Pakistani
ethnic origin (40.5 per cent), Bangladeshi (10.4 per cent), and Indian (5.7
per cent). Black and black British made up a further 9.5 per cent. The Irish
population had fallen to 3.1 per cent.

In the four wards (Handsworth, Newtown, Sandwell and Soho) making
up the greater Handsworth studied by Rex and Tomlinson in the 1970s, 18.6
per cent of the population was born in the New Commonwealth, 9.2 per
cent in the West Indies, 7.8 per cent in India, and 1.6 per cent in Pakistan.

Together with their children born here, black and minority ethnic communities constituted roughly 30 per cent of the total population of the area. While ward boundaries once more had changed, in 2001, the Handsworth ward, for example, had a black and minority population of 81.5 per cent, 18.8 per cent of Black or Black British, 18.7 per cent of Indian, 25.2 per cent of Pakistani, and 10.9 per cent of Bangladeshi ethnic origin.

In both areas, what were then termed New Commonwealth immigrants, their offspring, and subsequent black and minority ethnic migrants, now formed four fifths of the population and an increasing proportion of that population was born and brought up in Birmingham.

Both of the Birmingham studies were written against a background of intense debate about race relations legislation and the public institutions needed to make it effective. The first Race Relations Act was passed in 1965, setting up the Race Relations Board and the National Committee for Commonwealth Immigrants (NCCI). By 1966, Roy Jenkins, the Home Secretary, was already proposing an extension of the legislation to cover employment and housing, and in 1968, the second Race Relations Act was passed, replacing the NCCI with the Community Relations Commission. In 1976, the current Act was passed, introducing the concept of 'indirect discrimination' to deal with behaviour that was discriminatory in effect, irrespective of proof of intent. The legislation also proposed a merger of the Race Relations Board and Community Relations Commission to form the Commission for Racial Equality.

Since the two studies of Birmingham, the Race Relations (Amendment) Act 2000 has strengthened the scope of the 1976 Act, extending protection against racial discrimination by public authorities and placing on them a duty to promote equality of opportunity and good race relations. The Human Rights Act 1968 provided for the enforcement in the UK courts and tribunals of the rights and freedoms, including freedom from discrimination, secured by the European Convention of Human Rights. European legislation following the Treaty of Amsterdam has reinforced discrimination law with the European Race Directive. Currently, the government is proposing to set up a Commission for Equality and Human Rights which will replace the Equal Opportunities Commission, the Disability Rights Commission, and the Commission for Racial Equality, and combine their powers and functions, as well as take responsibility for new areas of discrimination legislation covering sexual orientation, religion or belief, and age.

In regard to recent social policy development, possibly the most significant event in the field of race relations has been the publication of the Macpherson report (Home Office 1999). It examined the murder of the black youth, Stephen Lawrence, using the concept of 'institutional racism'.

The report not only prepared the ground for the subsequent Race Relations (Amendment) Act 2000, but led to an increased willingness on the part of local authorities, the police, and other public bodies, to review the race relations impact of their policies and practices. For most authorities, the task of eliminating institutional racism, however, is now almost indistinguishable from the pursuit of the government's general drive for public sector service improvement.

Despite these and other changes in the last twenty-five years, many of the race relations issues raised by the two earlier Birmingham studies remain topical and, indeed, some, such as immigration, ethnic conflict, institutional discrimination, and integration, are receiving renewed attention. Immigration control, no longer simply of New Commonwealth immigration, is still a subject of debate, but its scope has now been extended within the context of the enlarged labour market of the European Union to include categories of asylum seekers, refugees, migrant workers from Eastern Europe and elsewhere, and persons entering through family ties from the Indian subcontinent.

Racial discrimination, especially its institutional manifestations, is still seen to be a major problem, limiting the opportunities of black and minority ethnic people and resulting in continued racial inequality. Racist ideologies, then expressed by immigration control associations and far-right political parties, such as the National Front, are now more cautiously articulated by candidates for the British National Party, wearing suits, (see REWM, February and June 2005). Since the 9/11 attack on the World Trade Centre and the reaction it provoked to Muslim extremism, there has been an increasing awareness of the Muslim community (especially in Birmingham), Islamophobia, and religious discrimination, although so-called religious discrimination may be a form of racism or xenophobia by proxy.

Rex and Moore, of course, would have been very aware of the Nottingham and Notting Hill race riots of 1958, the Dudley disturbances of the same year, repeated in 1962, and conflict in Wolverhampton in 1965. In Handsworth in May 1976, 28 people were arrested in the violence between National Front supporters demonstrating in support of Robert Relf held in Winston Green prison, and an anti-racist counter-demonstration of local black people living in the vicinity. In the Ladywood by-election campaign of August 1977, another National Front meeting ended in large-scale disorder on the Soho Road in Handsworth, with police cars and vans being overturned and set on fire. Further serious disturbances took place in July 1981, and September 1985.

Since 2001, following riots in Oldham, Burnley and Bradford, in which gangs from different ethnic backgrounds attacked each other and the police, and destroyed property, the government has once again been alerted to the existence of social divisions along lines of ethnicity, religion and culture. Prior to the rioting, Sir Herman Ouseley, former Chair of the Commission of Racial Equality, had produced a report on Bradford warning of a 'worrying drift towards self-segregation' and of the need to arrest and reverse that process (Bradford Vision 2001).

Following a series of official reports (Ouseley, Clarke, Ritchie, Cantle, Denham) highlighting social fragmentation and the polarisation of groups along ethnic lines, the government began to formulate a 'community cohesion' policy aimed at bringing together separate communities, building bridges between them, and developing an overarching culture of participatory citizenship. These emerging policies acquired a greater urgency in the aftermath of the 9/11 attacks and the 2005 tube bombings. In October 2005, conflict occurred again in Handsworth, this time between the black and the Asian communities (see REWM, November 2005). Interestingly, Rex's views on ethnic conflict and Rex and Tomlinson's insights into structural integration acquire a new significance in the context of the emphasis on 'community cohesion', but the government was clearly oblivious of earlier sociological theory when developing its policies on cohesion and integration.

In *Race Relations in Sociological Theory* (1970), Rex argued that race relations issues in metropolitan societies were characterised by restrictions on the social mobility of the members of particular racial groups or, as it was described in Parsonian terms, roles were systematically 'ascribed' rather than 'achieved' (p. 117). Race relations situations were to be found in cases where there was conflict between social strata or social segments.

This conflict was of several kinds, of which two, in particular, might apply to the situation in Birmingham. The first was the kind of conflict that occurred when a minority group sought to enter the stratification system from below, as in the case of the post-Second-World-War New Commonwealth immigration of black and Asian workers. The second came about when two or more groups competed for limited resources. The conflict between black people and Asians in Handsworth Lozells in October 2005 might easily be interpreted as an example of perceived ethnic competition, as might the decision in May 2006 of a substantial proportion of the Kingstanding ward electorate to vote for a British National Party candidate, campaigning for 'equality of treatment' for the 'indigenous white population' of Birmingham.

What then are the main features of John Rex's contribution to the theory and practice of local and regional work aimed at reducing racial discrimination, increasing equality of opportunity, and encouraging good race relations? Rex's work is so extensive and replete with ideas that any selection must always be personal, but the following elements retain their importance for most race equality practitioners.

Rex describes the city from the point of view of (1) the discipline of sociology, relying heavily on the sociological concepts of (2) social class and ethnicity. He is particularly concerned with the way urban structures and systems ((3) property and process) generate (4) housing classes. (5) Racial discrimination is situated and explained as emerging from the operation of urban systems of this kind. In his later work on Handsworth, Rex identifies four main urban systems – housing, employment, education and politics (6) which govern the distribution of life chances. These systems are deeply implicated in the government of relationships between the city's ethnic groups and affect levels of (7) social integration and (8) social conflict. Rex's sociology owes much to the work of Max Weber. It involves (9) listening to and understanding social actors and accepting (10) the possibility of rational action. Rex insists that it is possible for socially-conscious actors (11) to intervene to change the course of events.

1. The discipline of sociology

The most obvious and, therefore, usually neglected feature of John Rex's work is that it is sociological and, more especially, inspired by the sociology of Max Weber. Rex has distinctive views on questions such as the nature of the sociological subject matter, of social change, conflict and value, of the ontological status of micro and macro social structures and other social entities, of the kinds of proof and certainty that can be expected in social science, and of the relationship between sociologists' knowledge and common sense, ideology or myth (Rex and Tomlinson 1979: 297).

In the 1960s, the concepts of racial prejudice and discrimination were more frequently embedded in an academic discourse deriving from psychology, which gave the impression that they were a product of a general human tendency only manifested by a deviant minority with disturbed personalities. Rex repositions these important concepts in a distinctly social matrix and interprets them as behavioural strategies for realising group interests in conflict over scarce resources within the context of an industrial city's complex social structures. While he does not wish to claim that racism is a mere epiphenomenon caused by exploitation, oppression and discrimination, he rejects the view that the practice of racialism is something that arises from racially-prejudiced belief (Rex 1970: 117–8).

The psychological tendency, or (as I prefer to characterise it) the unanchored psycho-cultural approach to race relations, is regularly in the habit of detaching itself from social and economic determinants and of reasserting a worrying degree of autonomy, in contemporary race relations literature in, for example, discussions about the nature of prejudice, Britishness, multiple identities, or 'identities in Britain' (see, for example, some sections of The Runnymede Trust 2000). This kind of approach, practically manifested in race-awareness training, 'bridge-building', 'citizenship ceremonies', or public celebrations of multi-racialism and ethnic togetherness, and decoupled from the pursuit of racial justice and equality, is unlikely by itself to deliver much improvement to Birmingham's race relations.

It may be that fuller social contextualisation is simply neglected and is always assumed within the ongoing academic debate, but the questions of who thinks or utters an opinion, how widely it is held, why that particular opinion is popular, and whose interests it serves, too often go unanswered. The Weberian approach, on the other hand, invariably requires the expression of thought to be tied to social action in order to provide a unique sociological insight.

Rex is anxious to ensure that the sociologist's role is properly understood and does not suffer from over- simplification. Race relations research is not just about the quantitative monitoring of race relations to discover the relative life chances of different ethnic groups. While this kind of research will often have immediate political relevance, sociologists must ask more profound questions about the differentials they discover, and delve into the underlying social and economic structures and processes producing these results. Prior to simple studies of life chances, there has to be some understanding of what it means to belong to an ethnic group and the values that determine choice and action as a result of that belonging.

For Rex, it is important for people to understand that sociology is not an inductive science with the task of discovering empirical laws. Nevertheless, empirically-oriented social researchers continue to define their job in terms of testing hypotheses about the relationship between independent and dependent variables which always involves a ceteris paribus assumption, where matters are never ever likely to be equal again. Measurable attributes of sample populations cannot be divorced from the specific structures within which they occur, because the attributes are structurally located and have no meaning in isolation. Sociology requires a comparative study of structures – not a generalisation of attributes (Rex and Tomlinson 1979: 277).

Drawing on Weber, Rex goes on to develop 'ideal-typical' structural categories for the study of race relations, which are relevant to his research material and, when this is done, to compare these constructs with instances of their manifestation in the reality of the changing world – in this case, Birmingham (ibid.: 300). The constructs are thus not merely descriptors but 'yardsticks' (ibid.: 311).

In the Birmingham of 2006, much of what passes for research into race relations are the needs analyses and impact assessments required of public authorities under the Race Relations Act 2000. There is an assumption that the data gathered can be automatically translated into management information and used in a decision-making process that can readily effect change to increase equality, without any intervening layer of theorisation, or understanding of, or distinction between, cause and effect. This atheoretical approach to data gathering, and the superficiality of the action taken on the basis of it, is precisely why Rex insists on mapping out the parameters and purpose of the sociological research endeavour.

2. Social class and ethnicity

Rex is insistent on developing an analysis of the role of markets in relation to class, status and power. From a Weberian standpoint, the differential control of property leads to the emergence of different market situations in which groups have power to dispose of resources and to deny them to others. These kinds of 'class relationships', if extended to examining relationships between majority and minority, are extremely complex. Rex tackles this issue by exploring the differences between American and British society in the understanding and operation of social class and ethnicity and their accompanying social processes. In the United States, industrial conflict is to a large extent contained within the bounds of industrial society, whereas in Britain, people believe in the existence of social classes, there is still to some degree a class-conscious working class, and politics is conceived along class lines. The American dream is not of equality, but of open and fair competition in a land of individual opportunity.

In Britain, the labour and trade union movement is committed to collective bargaining, rather than to the hope of individual mobility as the means of securing justice in employment. Politically, it seeks to modify the operation of the free market in the workers' interests and, by the creation of welfare services, to provide workers with a social wage over and above the wage obtained by the individual employee. In contrast to this collectivism, the United States has an alternative value system of capitalism, individualism, and mutual aid.

Published in 1979, this account of collectivism in Britain may not appear as convincing now after eleven years of government by Margaret Thatcher (1979–90), seven years of John Major (1990–97) and eight years of Tony Blair (1997–). This has undoubtedly been what Stuart Hall (2003) describes as a prolonged period of neo-liberalism, entrepreneurial governance, and a reversal of Labour's historical commitment to equality, universality and collective social provision (Hall 2003).

The resultant weakening of the organised labour movement has a number of predictable consequences for race relations. It reduces the likelihood of mass collective action by workers from a particular ethnic group (for example, the Indian Workers Association), or of expressions of international and inter-ethnic worker solidarity, and it provides political space for alternative ethnic chauvinistic responses to structural inequality (as in the case of the British National Party).

With a reduction in the possibilities of collective social solutions, and an extension and institutionalisation of individual choice in traditional areas of public service provision, such as housing, education, and health, it becomes increasingly difficult to see how key issues of racial inequality can effectively be addressed. Trevor Phillips (2005) is right to speculate as to whether Britain's race-relations future will resemble the segregated cities and neighbourhoods of the United States, although this is not, of course, to postulate the emergence of American-style black ghettos.

3. Property and process within the city

Through his sociology, Rex sets out to show how elements of the urban social structure and conflict system contribute to sharpening or mitigating intergroup conflict between newcomers to the city and longer-term residents. Rex believes two aspects of the urban social system are of particular relevance to this exercise. The first is the system of differential distribution of housing opportunity leading to the emergence of housing class conflict. The second is the process whereby immigrants coming into the city are gradually socialised into the urban social system (Rex 1973: 3).

Race, Community and Conflict draws specifically on the theories of urban sociology to analyse the forces determining the lives of new and established communities of Birmingham. These theories are of two kinds: firstly, the urban zone theories associated with the names of Park, Burgess and McKenzie (Chicago school) and secondly, the rural/urban relational dichotomy deriving from the ideas of Tonnies, Redfield and Wirth.

For Rex, the distinction between various zones of the city, whether viewed as concentric rings, or as arranged in sectors, assists in identifying several sub-communities, each defined by specific housing (job and other) market relationships. The weakness of the Chicago school lies in its failure to investigate adequately how one zonal sub-community relates to, and is affected adversely or otherwise by, another. Rex proceeds to modify the theory by suggesting that in the course of the development of city life, various groups, defined by their relationship to property, become separated from one another, and create their own community life styles.

Firstly, an upper-middle class possesses property and the capacity to live without community and neighbourhood support. Secondly, a lower-middle class has access to inferior housing and other social facilities and aspires to an upper-middle-class life style. Thirdly, a working class acquires security 'in communal collective and neighbourly institutions fashioned in the course of struggle against economic diversity' (Rex and Moore 1967: 8).

Fourthly, a further development occurs when the lower-middle classes, including white-collar people and better-off artisans, leave the centre of the city for suburbia, in imitation of the life of the upper-middle class. Fifthly, their deserted homes become occupied by the city's social rejects and new-comers, who 'lack the defensive communal institutions of the working class, but who defend themselves and seek security within some sort of colony structure' (ibid.: 8–9). This last group does not enjoy an autonomous community life of its own but recognises its place at the back of the queue for a suburban life style. In other words, the city shares to some extent 'a unitary status value system'. This fifth category sees itself as temporary resident and in a transitional state.

Community institutions evolve here a means of providing short-term security and a defence against racism, until some kind of movement outwards can be made (ibid.: 9). Rex predicts that any attempt to combine and segregate the inhabitants of this area is bound to create conflict and lead eventually to riot.

The second kind of urban theory relates to migration from rural areas to the city, and is based on a typology of rural and urban community values. Rural society has affective, diffuse, particularistic and ascriptive relations that are maintained by informal social controls and rewards, while the social relations of the city are neutral, specific, universalistic and achievement-oriented and maintained by formal bureaucratic controls and rewards.

While Rex acknowledges that there is some dispute about this typology and its application, he highlights two features for attention: firstly, the presence in the city of public agencies exercising social control and providing welfare and secondly a social support network of kin and neighbours. From this it can be inferred that the longer newcomers reside in the city, the less they are likely to depend on their 'colony' and the more they come to rely on the city's institutions and their immediate family network.

This has a number of consequences for immigrants in the 'twilight area'. Not only are they constrained to live in a tight-knit community, perhaps even more tightly-knit than their rural community of origin, but they also

become part of an urban society where they have new rights and obligations as citizens. As part of this, they sign up to the city's status system and
to the competition to enter more prestigious sub-communities, although
not all will, or are meant to, succeed. In this competitive context, discrimination on the basis of race or origin acquires greater significance and must
be resisted both individually and collectively.

It is also important for the city as a whole, and for life in the neighbourhoods where immigrants live, that conflicts of interest are contained
and managed. Group ties of sufficient adequacy to provide a minimum of
emotional support must also be retained. Community life in the 'immigrant quarter' or 'twilight zone' results from achieving a balance between
these various imperatives.

On the basis of these two sets of theory, Rex set out the research endeavour: to find out 'who lives there, what primary community ties they
have, what their housing situation, economic position and status aspirations are, what associations they form, how these associations interact, and
how far the various groups are incorporated into urban society as citizens'
(Rex and Moore 1967: 11).

4. Housing classes

Rex is able convincingly to fuse perspectives from urban sociology and the
sociology of race relations to provide a new and original analysis of the
forces giving rise to racial separation. The emphasis is firmly on the social,
economic and political structures and systems affecting the lives of individuals. The two determinants of the structure of race relations in Birmingham
are unhesitatingly identified as the systems of housing allocation and job allocation, although the Sparkbrook study mostly focuses on the ownership
and control of housing.

On the basis of their access to housing, residents of the city divided into
three classes or categories: owner occupiers, tenants of private landlords,
and tenants of the council (Rex and Moore 1967: 36). People's associations,
interests, lifestyles and positions in the urban social structure were determined by their membership of one of these classes.

Owner occupiers had to have a certain amount of capital and level and
type of income. By virtue of their newcomer status and kind of occupation, immigrants found it difficult to obtain mortgages and were largely excluded from the class of owner-occupiers. Council house tenancies could
only be obtained on the grounds of need and length of residence. Selection was also based on domestic standards as assessed by Housing Visitors.
Tenants were not allowed to take lodgers. Most immigrants were excluded
on the grounds that they did not meet the length-of-residence criteria, but

were also rejected on the judgement of the Housing Visitors. The research team did not believe that 'the Housing Visitor was so free of prejudice that a coloured skin is not taken to imply low domestic standards' (Rex and Moore 1967: 27). If immigrants' standards were judged low, they were only ever likely to be admitted to inferior properties.

Whole-house private tenancies were in short supply because of demolition. Landlords were in a position to select tenants according to their preferences and, as nearly all landlords letting whole houses were white, black and minority ethnic immigrants were unlikely to gain access to tenancies of this kind.

The last of four accommodation options was that of owning or living in a lodging house. A tenant in a lodging house had to pay a high rent and accept overcrowded conditions, lack of privacy, and an absence of the choice of neighbour.

The three housing classes corresponded to the operation of three separate socio–economic systems: accommodation allocated through (i) a free market in housing modified by a credit system of mortgages, giving building societies bureaucratic control over selection, (ii) a welfare system using various bureaucratic criteria to select tenants on the basis of need, and (iii) a free market in the residential space provided by lodging houses for those who were unable to qualify for the other categories.

By restricting the conversion into lodging houses of larger properties to certain districts, the City Council was effectively restricting the dispersal of new arrivals and laying the foundation for immigrant-dominated areas, or 'ghettoes'. Certainly, New Commonwealth immigrants' choice of accommodation was severely constrained by the operation of the three systems of housing allocation.

A thorough review of the effect of the private sector housing market and the system for allocating social housing, together with research into the housing opportunities and aspirations of all Birmingham's ethnic communities is clearly essential to understanding the emerging distribution pattern of different ethnic communities across the city (see ECOTEC/EKOS 2005 report).

Lord Rogers, chair of the National Urban Taskforce, recently warned of the effects of the middle classes abandoning inner cities and causing a 'deepening racial and social divide', of increased 'ghettoisation' between rented and private housing, and of the inadequacies of social housing accommodating the poor. To this has to be added the difficulties associated with the overlapping and differently-funded regeneration bodies, the lack of power of local councils (compared to their European counterparts) to take action in the fields of transport and finance, and the growing evidence of the ineffectuality of government measures to tackle persistent inequality

(*The Guardian*, 23 November 2005).

5. Racial discrimination

The Sparkbrook study provides a detailed description of housing allocation, ownership and control, making it abundantly clear that individuals
and groups come to act against New Commonwealth immigrants at various stages in their search for accommodation. The strength of the analysis
is to show how these individual and separate acts, resulting in discriminatory outcomes, are generally expressions of competing sectional interests
(Rex and Moore 1967: 35) which combine as a total system or 'catch 22'
to exclude Irish and New Commonwealth immigrants from mainstream
housing provision, thus forcing them to live in the 'twilight zones' where
they are then blamed for the poverty of their own condition.

This example constitutes one of the earliest and most convincing cases
in British sociological literature of what has since come to be referred to as
'institutional discrimination'. This kind of systemic discrimination does not
exist in isolation. The study also highlights the action of the Housing Visitors who, on the basis of their stereotypical judgements, use their discre-
tion to make offers of various types of housing: low density pre-war council
houses, post-war council flats or houses, good houses taken into council
ownership, patched houses awaiting demolition, or houses awaiting demolition which have not been patched. The researchers found no case of West
Indian or other 'coloured applicants' being offered a council-built house
during their stay in Birmingham.

In the rare case where they qualified and were made an offer, it was
always of 'patched' houses. This is an incident of West Indian suspicion of
discrimination by Housing Visitors being confirmed by the researchers on
the basis of the evidence of outcome: a concept enshrined since 1976 in
race relations law as 'indirect discrimination'.

The study also draws attention to the way the consequent concentration
of New Commonwealth immigration in poor-quality housing was likely to
result in white people assuming that immigrants preferred and chose that
kind of housing, and indeed were the primary cause of the poor conditions
in which they found themselves. This kind of cycle or spiral of prejudice
and discrimination needs to be recognised in policy-making and has to be
broken.

Sociological interpretations and understandings of prejudice and discrimination, its causes, embeddedness, and role, are often forgotten in well-
meaning measures aimed at changing attitudes towards black minority ethnic groups through awareness-raising, education and training. Approaches
identifying the historic role of racism in the British empire and slavery, tend
to neglect the possibilities that attitudes towards other ethnic groups are

continually been generated in constantly-changing power structures and patterns of interest (Chesler 1976).

6. Urban systems governing the distribution of life chances

A decade later in the study of Handsworth (Rex and Tomlinson 1979), the elements of social structure implicated in the study of ethnic conflict have been extended beyond the focus on housing allocation to include consideration of the City's employment, education, and political systems.

In regard to the labour market, one consideration is the extent to which, in comparison with others, members of an ethnic group can obtain a job in the first place, and then, of course, what kind of job they are able to obtain. Rex points to the possibility of the emergence of dual labour markets. One is open to candidates with contacts who, when approached, have regular hours, trade-union protection, welfare benefits, and good wages. The other has irregular hours, short-term or part-time employment, poor or non-existent trade union protection, few welfare benefits, low wages, and a relationship with the employer based on immediate utility. The work force is divided between an organised working class that has secured a contractual relationship with those running the economy, and an 'underclass' which has no economic security and views work merely as necessary to survival (Rex and Tomlinson 1979: 16).

The hypothesis is that a dual labour market of this kind, if it exists, also represents an ethnic division, with new migrants being either unemployed or part of an occupational underclass. Racial discrimination in employment is likely to operate systematically to confine ethnic minorities to lower and more poorly-paid positions, with a knock-on effect on their role as consumers, particularly of housing.

Jobs and housing are two important ways of allocating life chances in urban society. The other, of course, is education. Not only do schools provide for public socialisation of children into society, but they act as selection agencies, determining who knows what and who does what in later life. As Rex and Tomlinson put it, schools decide 'whether each particular child enters the ruling, the ruled, or intermediate sections of society' (ibid., 1979: 24).

No study of an urban area of Handsworth could be complete without an assessment of the role of education in the socialisation, and status and occupational allocation, of the children of black and minority ethnic groups. In Birmingham, however, the education system has become increasingly complex, with state comprehensive schools existing side by side with direct grant and grammar schools, together with a private sector. The authors point out that 'in the final quarter of the twentieth century in Great

Britain, education has a class-selective role more complex than ever before'
(ibid.: 27). Irrespective of its complexity, the role of the education system
for black and minority ethnic social mobility remains crucial (but see Tomlinson, chapter 11 in this volume).

To complete the picture, the Handsworth study also explores the politics of black and minority ethnic communities. Four related aspects are
mentioned: the existence or non-existence of a Civil Rights Movement
claiming equal rights in a shared value system, the development of pater-
nalistic initiatives by British political parties, the emergence of individual
ethnic group politics insisting on its own identity and campaigning for justice without assimilation, and the growth of white political organisations
hostile to ethnic minorities and immigration (ibid.: 30).

With these four parts – housing, employment, education and political
systems – in place, Rex and Tomlinson proceed to analyse their empirical
data, summarising their findings in a memorable chapter entitled 'Working Class, Underclass and Third World Revolution'. They conclude that it is
likely to take many years for the minorities to be absorbed into the white
working class and to achieve equal rights (ibid.: 275), a prediction that appears to have been justified some twenty-five years later.

7. Social integration

It may surprise some readers to learn that the reports on Bradford, Burnley
and Oldham (2001), the debates they triggered on the degree of community
fragmentation in northern towns, and subsequent government initiatives
to promote 'community cohesion' had been preceded twenty years earlier
by the findings of the Handsworth study which dealt in some degree of
sociological sophistication with the quality of the relationships developing
between West Indians, Asians and their white working-class neighbours. As
stated in the preceding section, the authors concluded that it was most unlikely that black and minority ethnic population would be absorbed within
a generation, or acquire equal rights with whites (Rex and Tomlinson 1979:
279).

The differences, it was pointed out, were not simply quantitative, but
qualitative and structural, with the immigrant situation being characterised
by a different kind of position in the labour market, a different housing situation, and a different form of schooling. Black and minority ethnic groups
had succeeded in gaining access to some employment, housing and schooling, but were, nevertheless, still stigmatised as a threat to the social stability
of the system.

In 1979, Rex and Tomlinson were pointing out that the question of the
absorption or integration of black and ethnic minorities had already been

settled negatively, with the white working class rejecting black immigrants and joining with other indigenous classes against them. In the same terms as those used more than twenty years later by the authors of the community cohesion reports (who were clearly oblivious of their work), they describe 'the increasing polarisation... between the West Indian and Asian minorities on the one hand and the British cultural, social and political organisations on the other' (ibid.: 276).

Sir Herman Ouseley's report on Bradford (Bradford Vision 2001) publicly identified what his Race Review team saw as growing racial, ethnic, religious and class divisions among the population of the district. White people apparently thought that their needs were neglected in favour of Muslims, in particular Pakistanis, who were given preference over them. Members of the Muslim community, on the other hand, believed that Islamophobia and racism were blighting their lives and that they were treated unfairly by decision-makers. According to Ouseley, different communities were seeking to protect their identities and cultures by discouraging and avoiding contact with other communities and institutions. This 'self-segregation' was driven by fear of others, the need for safety from harassment and violent crime, and the belief that it was the only way to retain cultural identity and faith. Different ethnic groups were segregating themselves and retreating into 'comfort zones' made up of people like themselves. Their children went to separate schools.

The report assumes from the start that Bradford is experiencing *increasing* polarisation, segregation and fragmentation along ethnic lines. Little solid empirical evidence, apart from the anecdotal views of local people, is gathered or presented in support of 'polarisation', or of it increasing. From a sociological point of view, the use of the diverse opinions of local people, who have 'spoken out', to underpin the report's more significant claims is methodologically unsatisfactory. Nor, of course, is there any deeper structural or processual explanation along the lines adopted in the earlier Birmingham studies of the phenomenon, or of why it is occurring. Indeed, as an indication of the failure to recognise the power of underlying social systems, the Ouseley report sees the solution to the fragmentation it identifies as lying merely in educational and attitudinal initiatives, rather than in government intervention in housing and employment markets. This softer approach, involving the adoption of 'British values', exemplified by, for example, citizenship ceremonies, has now become an integral part of government strategy.

The Sparkbrook study also provides another remarkably prescient comment on discussions relating to integration, especially in the light of recent government measures to promote citizenship through education, tests and ceremonies: '...the striking thing about discussions of integration in Birmingham was that it was discussed among white people and that it usually finished up with proposals for measures against the immigrants which at best had not been discussed with them and at worst were of a plainly punitive character'(Rex and Moore 1967: 267–8).

8. Social conflict

Emphasising as he does the role of class struggle and collective bargaining, Rex is clearly critical of a functionalist theory that relies on the sharing of values to explain social unity. He points out the differences between ruling class values, and other value systems coexisting in the 'lower reaches of the structure' of all advanced capitalist societies. The concept of agreed values will remain precarious without agreement on how social rewards are to be divided up, an agreement which might be undermined if the balance of power is disturbed by economic crisis or revolution. Racial conflict arises in societies where the system of reward is not agreed and where, for particular racial groups, social mobility, and the rewards associated with it, are restricted.

In policy terms, this is what makes the promotion of racial equality and opportunity the key to improving race relations. (I remain fascinated by the claim, often made by John, that there is no such thing as 'good race relations' and that we should be concerned only with situations in which 'conflict of aims exists and certain specific social processes are engendered as the parties pursue their conflict with one another' (Rex 1970: 124).

In *Social Conflict* (1981), Rex provides a more systematic exposition of his conflict theory, setting out a model of two-sided conflict, and going on to explore market and exchange-based conflict, the relation between group conflict and contradictions in the social system, and conflict of a national, ethnic and class kind. He is particularly preoccupied in his work with the conflict between immigrant labour, native-born labour, employers and governments in the advanced industrial societies, and draws attention to the fact that, in these situations, the established labour force will have won concessions from employees in regard both to wage levels and welfare.

The issue for race relations is whether these concessions are reserved for the established (white) workers, or granted equally to the immigrant workforce. If the latter is denied access, then it will find itself in the position of an 'underclass'. The social conflict, thus described, is multi-layered with multiple consequences, one of which is to strengthen the bonds between members of the underclass as they recognise their common interests and make their class 'for itself' (Rex 1981: 100–01). Ethnic groups and organisations, then, are engendered by market interaction, competition, conflict, and in maintaining a balance of power (ibid.: 116). The conflict envisaged here is not merely a product of employment relations, but can occur between parties in any of the major social institutions: employment, politics, education, local neighbourhood, leisure facilities, health care, etc.

In Birmingham, the course of race relations can be conceived as a series of conflicts, as workers from Ireland, Italy, the Caribbean, and the Indian subcontinent and, more recently, from places such as the Balkans, Iraq, Somalia, and Sierra Leone, compete with the established workforce and one another, to enter and improve their standing in the labour market, education, housing, and political systems. Occasionally, that conflict becomes violent.

Contributing to the analysis of British urban unrest in the 1980s under the heading 'life in the ghetto' (Benyon and Solomos 1987: 103–110), Rex drew attention to the warning contained in the Handsworth study (Rex and Tomlinson 1978) that, unless political progress was made, the future of Handsworth would be one of 'mindless violence and despair'. Handsworth, he declared, was a 'purpose built ghetto' partly brought about by the city's failure to intervene effectively in the housing market. As a result of intense racial clustering, the black and Asian populations had now become firmly segregated in inner-city schools, with black and Asian school leavers having very little chance of gaining employment. Unemployed young people on the streets then came into contact with the police who were expected to deal vigorously with incidents of street theft and robbery with violence, thus incurring the criticism that they were picking on black youth. This scenario helped to explain the violent anti-authority rioting that had taken place in Handsworth in September 1985.

Rex's contribution to analyses of ethnic conflict in metropolitan Britain helped Reeves and Allbrook (2006) to develop a typology of eight categories of British urban ethnic conflict and violence: inter-ethnic, anti-newcomer, anti-authority, anti-racist, loss of control, turf war, terror backlash, and anti-blasphemy, many of which arise directly or indirectly from competition between ethnic groups. The 22 October 2005 disturbances in Birmingham Lozells provide a telling example of inter-ethnic minority conflict, that is, violence between ethnic minority communities living in close proximity in the city.

In the weeks before the riot, a rumour was spread by private radio that a black girl of fourteen had been raped by a gang of between three and twenty-five Pakistani men in a suburban store selling black beauty products. The Jamaican girl, it was said, would not come forward because she was an illegal immigrant and would be reported. Despite strenuous efforts, the police were unable to find evidence of a rape or a victim.

Most of the shops in the Lozells Road and Handsworth Road were owned by Asians, largely of Pakistani ethnic origin. They decided to close their shops for an hour on a Saturday as a mark of respect and to affirm that, if the rape had occurred, they wholeheartedly condemned it. Most, however, thought the rumour had been circulated to discourage black people from trading with Asians and complained that their shops had been threatened and attacked by black youths, who had knocked goods from the shelves and used abusive language.

The Asian owner of a black beauty shop claimed that a gang of black men had entered his shop, called him a racist and threatened to shoot him and burn his shop. The police had merely told him to phone again if there was further trouble. Five hundred people then demonstrated outside of his shop, demanding that it be boycotted and the rapists brought to justice. The speakers asserted that black people were being exploited and driven out of the area by Asians.

In the evening, a meeting of the black community was arranged in the local New Testament Church of God, hosted by the pastor, with the police and local MP in attendance. The police announced that five people had been arrested in connection with the allegation and that another woman had made a complaint about sexual harassment in the same shop.

At the close of the meeting, a riot broke out between blacks and Asians, each party claiming the other had started it. The black community believed that Asians gathered outside the church shouting 'kill the niggers' and that black youths reacted to defend themselves. The Asian community were convinced that the crowd emerging from the church and neighbouring streets was armed with baseball bats and bricks to attack Asian shops, and the black gangs had approached a mosque which Asian youths took steps to protect.

Eyewitnesses reported that the violence was terrifying, with youths running up and down the road smashing things up and kicking things over. The rioters entered public houses and roughed up customers. A Pakistani taxi driver suffered serious head injuries when his vehicle was attacked with bricks. Petrol bombs were thrown and the night was punctured by gunfire. A 23-year-old black man was stabbed to death as his Asian attackers, wearing hoods and bandanas, hurled racist abuse that included the word 'nigger'. Twenty-five people were hospitalised, four with stab wounds, and at least a dozen homes and businesses were ransacked. Police said that more than 80 offences were committed in a 75-minute 'burst of extreme violence'.

9. Listening to and understanding social actors

Throughout Rex's work there is a Weberian insistence that the meanings given to behaviour by the various parties to a social transaction or context must be regarded as having equal validity and authenticity, and that the resultant 'social action' – that is, action carried out by an individual to which a person attaches a meaning – has to be the focus of the research exercise.

The account above of the 2005 Lozells riot highlights the importance of understanding the points of view of all the major participants.

Rex and Moore's Sparkbrook study is much preoccupied with the social action, individual and collective, of the people living in the area: the English, Irish, West Indians, Pakistanis and others (Europeans, Gujaratis, Punjabis, and so-called 'precipitants'), who were systematically interviewed in the course of the research. The results were translated into short case studies of family circumstances, often with telling quotes.

In the Handsworth study, structured interviews were conducted with 300 white British, 300 Asians, and 300 West Indians, a further sample of 100 white British and 100 black council tenants, and a small sample of Asian and West Indian young people to establish their views and experience of housing, employment and their own and children's education. Further unstructured interviews were held with local government officials, councillors, MPs, community activists, and representatives of official bodies.

An attempt is made to provide an understanding or insight, a *verstehen*, of their social actions, that is the meaningfulness of their behaviour, through systematic questioning and by directly observing what they do, and by entering into a dialogue with them. One noticeable feature of the resultant research texts is a surprisingly successful attempt to explain, rather than merely to classify or condemn, the political positions adopted by individuals, including those expressing racist views. It is, of course, possible to understand their often complex, even self-contradictory views without condoning them.

Today, quite rightly, the issue of consulting with black and minority ethnic groups, and taking into account what they have to say, is enshrined in the schedules to the Race Relations (Amendment) Act 2000. Unfortunately, there is little evidence that the public authorities themselves are able to understand or achieve an insight into the social actions of the communities with whom they are forced to consult.

Even when this is attempted, it is not always easy to distinguish between the different interests involved, or to formulate policies that serve the community collectively, rather than merely sections of it. In the case of public authorities, it is likely that their financial interests or constraints, or those of their work force, often make them impervious to the influence of the communities they have been set up to serve.

10. The possibility of rational action

Rex's sociology is not merely phenomenological. Just as Weber tried to explain the rise of capitalism, Rex explains how lack of access to the private housing market or rented council housing obliges newcomers to occupy lodging houses in 'the twilight zone', a consequence which is perceived by the white population as a matter of choice and suitability, and leads to the emergence of an accompanying justificatory racist ideology. There is an acknowledgment that individual perceptions rarely provide a satisfactory causal explanation of the totality of the social processes at work.

Indeed, most of the parties to the Sparkbrook study, including those with the power to affect outcomes, are dangerously unaware of the nature and impact of the housing market, its segmentation, the forces at work, and the way their behaviour and decisions are affecting the life and future state of Birmingham. A similar sense of the complexity of social relations between ethnic groups and the City Council, police and school authorities, and of the respective parties' general incomprehension of its implications emerges from the study of Handsworth.

The Handsworth study's success can be judged by the degree to which it throws light on the different views of Asians, West Indians and white people living in the Handsworth area and whether it makes sense of respective ethnic mindsets in relation to the varied experiences of housing, employment, education and racial discrimination. The young are also identified as having rising expectations, or new expectations, not shared by their parents, and as being frustrated by exposure to prejudice and discrimination (Rex and Tomlinson 1979: 208).

The aim as ever is to illuminate the views, values and actions of these populations from the point of view of their daily experiences of social structure and the decision fields in which they operate: something that the Handsworth analysis takes very seriously and succeeds to a large extent in achieving.

By making decision makers conscious of the effects of their action, there is an opportunity to engage in rational action. Rational action in Weberian terms is 'the methodical attainment of a definitely given and practical end by means of an increasingly precise calculation of means'. It is to be contrasted with traditional action, based on custom and practice, or affective action, based on an immediate emotional response.

Eleven proposals for 'rational action' are set out in the Sparkbrook study (Rex and Moore 1967: 270). They are seen as an alternative both to the traditional, long-standing housing, planning and public health policies of the Birmingham Corporation and to the ill-considered blaming of New Commonwealth immigrants for the housing shortages and dilapidation of the twilight zones.

11. Intervening to change the course of events

Much of John Rex's sociological writing sets out not only to provide an analysis and explanation of social relations, especially British race relations, but to suggest alternative courses of action and intervention that might benefit a greater number of groups and individuals, particularly those that are vulnerable. This is applied sociology in the weaker sense that it deals with immediately recognisable everyday, social, economic and political issues of practical relevance to all citizens and decision-makers, as well as in the stronger, that it provides both explicitly and implicitly- reasoned recommendations as to what action might be taken to bring about more desirable social outcomes.

Rex believes that 'the paradox of sociology lies precisely in this, that though we are compelled by forces external to ourselves, these forces are nonetheless made by men and can be changed by men' (Rex 1973a). Sociology, therefore, has the important capacity to make people aware of the nature of the forces that serve to oppress them.

Yet Rex insists that there is a distinction to be made between providing critical insight into the mechanism of oppression and the moral and political choices and actions that invariably arise from that insight. Put more starkly, 'to assume that our role as sociologists gives us an entitlement to political leadership is simple arrogance, which fails to recognise that political change is the task of these who suffer political oppression' (Rex and Tomlinson 1979: 320).

While moral choice of this kind should always be distinguished from the kind of sociological analysis that Rex has in mind, it is unlikely to be effective in changing the world – or Birmingham – for the better, unless it is based on knowledge of how existing structures operate to create or alleviate inequality and discriminatory relations.

Rex makes no secret of his view that the descriptive and analytical task of sociology is an essential prelude to successful intervention and very necessary if political action is to be pursued rationally: 'if it can be shown that certain ethnic and racial minorities suffer disadvantage, precise sociological descriptions of this disadvantage will enable political groups to take action to rectify it. If it is shown that there are conflicts of interests between minority and majority groups, sociological analysis will suggest ways in which conflict may be pursued or resolved. Objective sociological analysis by no means prevents political action: it prepares the way for it' (Rex and Tomlinson 1979: 1).

Conclusion

In conclusion, while the two Birmingham studies constitute only a small part of John Rex's work on sociological theory and research and were published respectively 39 and 27 years ago, they are still capable of providing a model for the investigation of the systems and processes governing race and ethnic relations in urban areas today. Indeed, as this chapter endeavours to show, without the theoretically-grounded and thoroughly-researched approach adopted in Sparkbrook and Handsworth, it is unlikely that the underlying processes by which contemporary race relations are fashioned, or integration, community cohesion, or social conflict and fragmentation occur, will ever sufficiently be understood.

Without a better understanding of the city systems determining its race relations, effective intervention to influence their peaceful development is unlikely. Any strategy devised by race equality practitioners must be underpinned with the kind of sociological study exemplified by the urban sociology of race relations developed by John Rex and his colleagues. On this, effective action to eliminate racial discrimination, increase racial equality and improve race relations depends.

11

Race and Education in Birmingham: Then and Now

SALLY TOMLINSON

O VER THIRTY YEARS AGO, in the spring and summer of 1974, John Rex and I made a series of visits to Birmingham, laying the foundations for a four-year study of race and community relations in the city of Birmingham. The research, eventually published in 1979 as *Colonial Immigrants in a British City: a class analysis* (Rex and Tomlinson 1979), analysed the relationship between West Indian and Asian immigrants from former colonial countries, and the class structure of a British City.[1]

The research had its history in the study in Sparkbrook, Birmingham, carried out in the 1960s (Rex and Moore 1967), which was conceived as the first of a series of urban sociological studies. The Sparkbrook study examined the conflicts which arose over the allocation of scarce resources – especially housing at that time. The 1970s study, concentrating on the Handsworth area, took as given that there was a conflict for resources in other areas, in employment, education, social and other services, and asked how far minorities, immigrant into the city in the 1960s and 1970s in the city were able to get access to these resources and to attain and keep their citizenship rights. The study was based theoretically on T H Marshall's study of citizenship and social class (Marshall 1950), and on Rex's own

studies to that date of 'race' and class in colonial and metropolitan societies (Rex 1970; 1973). We concentrated on employment, asking what sort
of conflicts and accommodations were generated over access to jobs, union
activity and immigrant workers organization; on housing, asking how immigrants into the city were faring in the housing market; and on education,
asking what were the educational and qualifications of immigrant workers
and how were their children faring in Birmingham schools. A key issue
for migrants in the 1970s was that the education of their children was crucial. It was regarded as the major route to social and economic security and
mobility, and the future integration of the next generation as full British
citizens.

Rex had noted earlier the complexity of stratification patterns in
economically-advanced metropolitan countries. People perceived as
racially or ethnically different settle into an established class system and a
status system, in which those from colonial backgrounds were deemed inferior to 'native' British, and into a system of political and economic power
to which immigrants in most cases lacked access (Rex 1970: 88). The
Handsworth study asked how far immigrant workers did enjoy the same
rights as their fellow workers in British cities, how far group attachment
of minorities was organised on an ethnic or country-of-origin basis, how
far it was possible for minorities to gain acceptance and equal treatment
while maintaining a cultural identity, and how far class-consciousness in
British society excluded immigrant minorities and their children (Rex and
Tomlinson 1979).

This chapter concentrates on the question as to how far the children and
grandchildren of those we interviewed in the 1970s have benefited from
some measure of equal treatment in the education system, and how far their
educational achievements allow them access to higher qualifications and
employment, and the social and economic security their parents desired
for them.

Birmingham then and now

It should be noted at the outset that any casual visit to the city will confirm
an impression of what Gilroy (2005: 131) called a 'convivial metropolitan
culture', where minority young people are visibly working in and managing what the city calls the 'visitor' sector – the consumerist, leisure
and entertainment industries,[2] and are enthusiastic participants in further
and higher education. But in the outer suburbs and surrounding countryside, what Gilroy also described as a 'discourse of imperilled Englishness'
(p. 130) can easily be found, and the impression is of a multiracial city
and a white countryside. Nevertheless, over thirty years, there has been

movement of some minorities to the outer suburbs, as black and Asian middle classes have slowly developed alongside white middle classes. Census data on Birmingham wards in the 1970s show that people migrant from what was then termed the 'New Commonwealth' – the Caribbean, India, Pakistan and (from 1973) Bangladesh, were concentrated around the city centre. The Soho, Handsworth and Aston wards to the north having respectively 48%, 32% and 30% of New Commonwealth citizens, with more Caribbean and Indian residents. The Sparkbrook, Deritend and Small Heath wards to the south had some 30%, 27% and 21%, with more Pakistani migrants. In the suburbs, Northfield, then home to the large employer British Leyland[3] had only 0.7% resident New Commonwealth migrants. Perry Barr, the ward next to Handsworth, had some 2%. Family size of the migrant groups was larger than white, and in inner wards 'white flight' of younger people had already occurred, with older white people remaining.

After the 2001 census analysts were predicting that by 2010, Birmingham, would become a city with more minorities than a 'white majority', The higher birth-rates among younger minority people, and other migrations – especially the arrival of refugee and asylum-seeking groups, partly accounted for this.[4] Although ward boundaries were changed somewhat in 2004, census data showed that there had been some outward movement of migrant families and their children to suburban areas, but the proportions of black and Asian families in the inner city wards was considerably higher by the early twenty-first century. The old Handsworth and part of Soho and Aston wards, were now 80% 'non-white', the Soho ward 63% and Sparkbrook almost 80%, with 44% of residents being of Pakistani origin. More Indian families had moved to the suburbs, Quinton ward, which had virtually no minorities in the 1970s, had 7% Indian families and 4% black families by 2001. Perry Barr, next to Handsworth, was 98% white in 1971 but only 72% white in 2001. Chinese families were more dispersed around the city (Birmingham City Council 2005). The 2001 census included a question on religion, and over 14% of the city population identified as Muslim – 9% of all British Muslims (and 16% of Britain's Pakistani population) were living in Birmingham. Politically, minorities in Birmingham had made inroads into mainstream politics. By 2005, there were some 20 out of 120 city councillors from minority groups, an Asian lord mayor had served a term, and the parliamentary seat in Perry Barr was won for New Labour in the 2005 election by Khalid Mahmood. In Sparkbrook all the city councillors were of Pakistani origin, as were four out of seven candidates for the 2005 general election.

Changing employment patterns influenced a changing class structure. The immigrant population in the 1970s had come to take the less attractive jobs in factories and the service sector, and union activity and migrant workers organizations were a feature. By 2005, 80% of all those in employment in the city were in an expanded and changed service sector, education, health, banking, finance, retail and leisure. Some 15% were still employed in manufacturing, mainly white and Indian workers, Pakistanis were mainly in whole-sale and retail trades, Bangladeshis in the hotel and restaurant trade, and black workers in health and social care (Birmingham City Council/economy 2005). Union activities had become more low key and consensual. Unemployment in areas with high numbers of minorities was, as in the 1970s, disproportionately high. In the Handsworth-Lozells ward in 2004 the unemployment rate was 26%, compared to 6% in Quinton ward. The areas with the highest number of minority children under 15 were those with higher unemployment, single parentage and other indicators of disadvantage.

Equality and diversity

Among many changes in the city over thirty years has been an acceptance by local political leadership that overt racialist practices and theories are no longer acceptable. It may still be true, on a societal level, that 'discriminatory treatment depends ... upon tides in public opinion, and although these tides flow in a racist direction, they rarely ebb' (Rex and Tomlinson 1979: 47) but the practices and attitudes of the 1970s in the city have changed considerably. It was possible to document then, for example, overt discrimination against minorities in the housing department (ibid.: 142). In the area of special education, (Tomlinson 1981), there were some local political leaders who worked to minimise the effects of a minority presence in the city, and there was sensationalist local media reporting of race issues. There was also an atmosphere of defensiveness and suspicion of academic attempts to research race issues. Although Birmingham had pioneered a response to the education of migrant children by setting up a Department for Teaching English as a Second Language in 1960, the Education Department in the 1970s became embroiled in arguments over the collection of 'immigrant' statistics, preferred to regard minority children as part of the disadvantaged, and was not enthusiastic about research which was overtly concerned with 'race'. Our initial contact with the Labour Chair of the Education Committee in 1974 was disappointing in that we were not offered 'general authorization to enter schools' (Rex and Tomlinson 1979: 172), although the response of Heads and teachers was more welcoming. The defensiveness of officials in the 1970s was partly due to the activities of some black radical organisations, particularly in the Handsworth area, although it was ironic that several of the most 'suspect' groups were in fact supporting the African National Congress and anti-apartheid movements in South Africa. There was a fear of the popularity of the Rastafari movement at that time, which was perceived as a threat linked to crime and conflict, and given much police attention. A Midlands school inspector (HMI) noted in an interview that 'heads are wary of black power people' (Rex and Tomlinson 1979: 187) In 1985, frustration with lack of education and employment opportunities were a prime cause of riots in Handsworth, and galvanized the city into action in these areas.. Although by the 2000s the emergence of drug-dealing, 'gangs and guns' (McLagan 2005) still gave rise to sensationalist reporting and police attention, and the 'Islamic fundamentalist' (see Rex 1996) had replaced the dread-locked Rastafarian as a demon figure, the city response to its minority citizens had become more open, positive and measured than thirty years ago.

A report on race equality and education published in 2002 noted that 'Birmingham has been identified nationally as a leading authority in the field of race equality. Our findings on the progress made and the problems that persist, have significance beyond the city itself (Warren and Gillborn 2002: ii). The City Council vision, published on its web-site, declares that 'Birmingham Council believes that the diversity of the local community enriches the city and contributes to its social and economic prosperity ... and is committed to the principle that all people have a right to equality of opportunity and equity in the way they are treated and in the services they need, want and receive' (Birmingham City Council 2005). There is a Corporate Equality Scheme (CES) which provides a strategic framework for the provision of equitable services – 'irrespective of age, disability, gender, race, religion and belief, and sexual orientation.' There is an Equalities Division in the city administration, and Equity and Diversity teams have been developed, to take a lead in Social and Health Care, Learning and Culture, Local Services, Housing and Development and Resources. Each team has a manager, and high numbers of minorities are employed and involved in the teams. Birmingham Race Action Partnership (BRAP) is one of a number of community-based projects seeking to advance race equality.

Race and Education – National

From the 1960s to the 1980s, the children of minority parentage entered a school system where overt selection was disappearing and comprehensive education becoming the norm. Where selection for grammar schools remained, minorities were less likely to be successful. In Birmingham in the early 1970s, the system was still based on selection, with 21 grammar schools, and the rest 'comprehensive' or bilateral. By 1974 the city was divided into 18 consortia, with parents able to 'choose' between several non-selective schools in their area, with attempts to equalise funding and resources. At this time only 1% of immigrant children were successful in selective examinations. Policies to initiate fair admissions in comprehensive schools led to some grammar schools privatising, and, by 2004, 164 remained in England overall. These schools however, did affect the intakes of over five hundred 'comprehensives' in some thirty-six local authorities, including Birmingham. In the 1970s it was official policy to subsume minority issues under disadvantage (DES 1974), a view that persisted into the 1990s, despite evidence that minorities experienced problems in health, housing, education and employment, in excess of the majority. The out-going Prime Minister John Major asserted in 1997 that 'policies must be colour blind ... they must just tackle disadvantage' (Major 1997). The issue of the 'underachievement' of minority children, especially African-Caribbean and Pakistani boys, became from the 1960s, a forty-five year saga of accumulating evidence that an unchanged education system could not successfully educate many young minority people, and a good deal of political hand-wringing and 'blaming the victim' ensued (Mirza 1992; Gillborn 1995; Tomlinson 1984, 2005a, 2005b). From the 1980s, many local authorities, notably the Inner London Education Authority (abolished in 1988) and Birmingham, made serious attempts to tackle low achievement, developed equal opportunity policies, appointed multicultural advisers and set up curriculum projects. Race legislation, raised awareness among practitioners, and pressure from minority parents and community groups and national and international groups concerned with equity were all factors leading to the improved treatment and raised achievements of minorities.

Post-1988, however, the slow but steady progress towards a more equitable incorporation of minorities in the education system was considerably impeded by a new framework for funding and administering all aspects of education, based on 'parental choice'. Although almost all minority parents held values about the worth of education that were distinctly middle-class the location of most minorities in inner cities created new disadvantages. Schools with minority students had higher working-class intakes (Benn and Chitty 1996) and choice legislation enabled privileged choosers to avoid schools with higher numbers of minority students (Gerwirtz et al. 1995). The New Labour government post-1997 attempted to tackle a number of long standing inequalities, notably making a positive decision to offer Muslim schools similar state funding to that given to other faiths, replacing the old funding for 'new commonwealth children' with an Ethnic Minorities Achievement Grant, and setting up a Social Exclusion unit with a first brief to inquire into school exclusion - black boys being four times more likely to be excluded from school than others. By 2004, there was evidence that even middle-class black parents were concerned about the possible exclusion of their boys, and some were sending children back to the Caribbean for secondary education (Goring 2004). The government also set up an inquiry into the 1993 murder of black student Stephen Lawrence (Macpherson 1999), the outcome of which partly influenced strengthened race relations legislation in 2000. The Race Relations (Amendment) Act required local authorities to prepare Race Equality Schemes and all schools to have Race Equality Policies.

But the new Labour government in 1997 also committed to continuing policies creating a diversity of schools, with market competition between schools fuelled by league table publication, the extension of a specialist schools programme,[5] retention of the remaining grammar schools and an Academies programme whereby sponsors from private, voluntary and faith groups could establish new schools A policy of labelling schools as 'failing' also affected many schools attended by minorities and refugees. All this was underpinned by an ideology of meritocracy – the view that the successful were deserving due to merit. The naming of schools as foundation, voluntary aided, community, specialist, city technology colleges, special schools (for children with learning difficulties and disabilities), beacon schools and academies, reforms to the further education colleges, and complex funding arrangements for post-16 students, were confusing for all parents, especially minorities who lacked knowledge and information about the school system (Tomlinson 2005b). However, minorities, as with majority parents, soon worked out the developing hierarchies of schools into those more or less desirable in the ability to equip their children with the necessary qualifications. Educational 'Initiatives' produced regularly by central government required local education authorities constantly to produce responses, and failed 'reforms' were quietly abandoned. Although little research information on how minorities were faring in this diverse and reformed system has been available, the evidence so far is that white parents have continued to move their children away from schools with large numbers of minorities, and the emerging black and Asian middle class adopt similar strategies, with expressed preference for selective state schools or private schooling (Noden et al. 1998; Abbas 2004).

The issue of the lower educational achievements of some groups – especially African-Caribbean and Pakistani pupils performance in public examinations at 16, had become a source of much bitterness and frustration for minority parents over the years. The issue was viewed with concern by the New Labour government, and every White Paper and document introducing new legislation from 1997 included a section on raising standards and achievements of minorities. By 2003, the government was acknowledging that 'opportunities are unequal for many of the one in eight pupils who come from a minority ethnic background' (DfES 2003), speculating on the reasons for differential performance between groups. Proposals for improvement, including a more comprehensive programme for English as an Additional Language were somewhat ironic, given that teaching migrant children English was a priority from the 1960s, especially in Birmingham, and it was later government policies that dispersed expert bilingual teachers and cut funding. The paper also included a warning that if African-Caribbean boys continued to be 'failed by the system' they would end up in the criminal justice system (ibid.: 32) However, in attempting to explain the overall differential performance of different groups, especially Indian and Chinese pupils, who on a national level achieve higher at GCSE level and in university entry, some facile comparisons were made, which had the effect, long noted in research, of pathologising black and Muslim students and families. The 2003 White paper commented that 'many African-Asian and Chinese communities developed after the Pakistani community, yet these young people have significantly better exam results' (DfES 2003: 10). There is no recognition that the majority of Pakistani settlers came from rural backgrounds and parents undertook low-skill jobs, whereas East African Asians (mainly Indian) settling after expulsion from Kenya and Uganda had higher educational backgrounds and rapidly achieved middle class status. Patterns of settlement have ensured that overall Chinese children are more likely to attend schools with fewer minorities, (Burgess and Wilson 2003) and both Indian and Chinese groups, as many white parents do, make much use of private tutoring. There is a long history of misunderstandings between homes and schools and low expectations of black children which has persisted into the 2000s (Shotte 2002), and even when black pupils do achieve well in suburban schools they can report low expectations and negative stereotyping (Smith 2004). Reasons for this undoubtedly lie in the refusal of successive governments to address the Anglocentric nature of the national curriculum, despite the assurance by the Qualifications and Curriculum Authority (in response to the Macpherson Report 1999) that from 2000 the curriculum would develop 'lively enquiring individuals capable of rational thought and positive participation in our ethnically diverse society' (QCA 1999). Neither is there adequate training of teachers to work in such a society.

However one well-publicised policy intended to improve the education of all children in cities was the Education Action Zone programme (EAZs) initiated in 1998 with 73 zones in operation before their amalgamation into an *Excellence on Cities* programme (DfEE 1999) Aspects of this programme were aimed at minority parents concerned about their children's education.

In particular the programme offered special chances for the gifted and talented, provided more learning support units and learning mentors for the slower learners and the disaffected. The government also gave more attention to child-care and children's services. In 2000 the torture and death of Victoria Climbie, an eight year old child of West African origin, led to a public inquiry into the failure of children's services and the publication of a green Paper *Every Child Matters* (Treasury 2003), which required school, health and social services to work more closely together. As with other initiatives, local authorities differed in the extent to which they developed and funded new requirements, but the evidence is that Birmingham responded very positively to the Every Child Matters agenda.

Race and education in Birmingham – then

Our study of the response of the education system in Birmingham to the absorption of the children of immigrant parentage in the 1970s noted at the outset that the lack of central planning was reflected at local level. We commented that, in a society that really valued equality of opportunity and outcome, the manifest disadvantages of the children would have been noted and consideration given to the problems the children might face in migrating and living in different cultural and class milieux, within a society that fostered racism (Rex and Tomlinson 1979: 163). Apart from the activities of overt racist groups[6] there was considerable liberal unease at that time about racial counting and collection of statistics, about dispersing children to prevent 'racial enclaves', about the language problems of non-English speakers, and whether the 'lower' performance of minorities might affect indigenous children's education. But there was also considerable activity by minority parents and community groups who were anxious that their children were being educated in former secondary modern schools where there was little academic tradition, and within a curriculum that gave no recognition to African and Asian history and identity. In response to this, black holiday and supplementary schools had been set up by parents and teachers to improve achievement, and, at one Handsworth comprehensive school, a Black Studies course, set up by white radical teachers, was incorporated into social studies, which caused the Chief Education Officer to visit the school and close the course. The City did produce, in 1974, a religious education syllabus which included study of all major world religions, humanism, and communism. This was eventually ruled to be illegal and Influenced by left-wing theologians!

In the early 1970s, Birmingham secondary education was still largely based on selection, with political battles fought over the future of the grammar schools. especially the prestigious King Edwards Foundation schools.

By the later 1970s only eight state grammar schools remained for which optional tests could be taken. The Labour-supported consortium system of grouping schools together, encouraging cooperation and shared resources could have been an excellent solution to spreading equitable education, but was ended in 1979 when the Conservatives won power at central and local level.[7] Thereafter, the city responded over the next twenty-five years to constant 'reform' of the education system, which included adjusting to some forty Education Acts, hundreds of accompanying regulations, and dozens of initiatives.

In the 1970s, the majority of immigrants from the Caribbean had left school by 15 and the few who had had some education in Britain had mainly left school without any qualification, although many went into further education colleges to try to obtain a skill or qualification. Asian migrant groups had more diverse education backgrounds, some had no education at all, and some had degrees and professional qualifications. In the Handsworth study 38% of Asians had educational qualifications against 8% from the Caribbean. We forecast that 'It could well be that in a generation, class divisions within the Asian community will begin to open up, partly influenced by the educational differences within this population' (Rex and Tomlinson 1979: 190) There was evidence that, contrary to teachers beliefs, minority parents did take an interest in their children's education and many were happy that their children were actually in school and receiving an education. Those who were dissatisfied complained of poor discipline and different teaching methods, often related to the expectations of schools shaped under the colonial education systems the parents had experienced. Teachers at this time did tend to operate within a framework of stereotypes about minority pupils, having themselves received little information or training about the backgrounds of their pupils, and it could clearly be seen that parental expectations of what schools could do for their children and schools definitions of the children as problems, would create misunderstanding and conflicts. A small group of minority young people aged 16–24 who had come with their parents and entered schools, were interviewed. They were already dissatisfied with their educational opportunities and the lack of preparation for desirable jobs, and had ambitions beyond the expectations of their schools, teachers and careers officers.

Race and education in Birmingham: now

Clearly, over thirty years later, there have been enormous changes in attitude towards, and planning for, the education of minority young people in Birmingham, a public commitment to offering equal educational opportunity and treatment, and to 'closing the gap' in educational achievements.

The previous Chief Education Officer from 1995, the highly respected Tim Brighouse, was committed to equity and raising achievement, as is the current Director Tony Howells. The 2002 report by Ofsted, the schools inspectorate, noted that 'Birmingham LEA is one of a small number of LEAs which stand as an example of what can be done, even in a challenging urban environment' (Ofsted 2002) An 'Aiming Higher' Partnership, bringing together schools, Colleges, higher education institutions and Connexions (the renewed careers service) has been in operation since 2001 as part of a national initiative to raise the attainment of the 'disadvantaged', and the city has adapted the *Excellence in Cities* initiative to raise standards and achieve race equality. There is, as noted, a Learning and Culture team among the seven Equity and Diversity teams in the city Equalities Division, within this the School Effectiveness group is particularly concerned with race and attainment.[8] However, despite greatly improved achievements among all minority groups and much more successful incorporation of young people into the education system many old problems remain and new issues and disadvantages have surfaced.

After the break up of the inner London Education Authority in 1988, Birmingham became the largest education authority in the country. In 2003 the authority was responsible for some 500 schools, 321 primary schools, (161 with nursery classes), 76 secondary schools, (40 with sixth forms including the 8 selective schools), and 36 without sixth forms, plus 31 special schools (learning difficulties) and 38 special units in mainstream schools. Some 71 of the schools were voluntary aided, mainly Catholic, 'faith' schools, with one Church of England secondary-in charge of their own admissions. One Muslim state-aided school had been set up. Some sixteen thousand students were studying in the colleges of further education, a majority of them from minority groups. Over nine thousand teachers were employed and the total educational revenue expenditure for that year was some £673 million. By 2005 the city still had no 'Academy' and little enthusiasm for that kind of business-sponsored school. As in other authorities, there was some anxiety that the local authority might be pressured into supporting an academy by the withholding of grants for new schools Under Brighouse, the city schools were divided into networks of 'Collegiate' schools, the intention, as in the 1970s consortium system, being that schools would cooperate and assist each other, more 'successful' schools supporting the less successful. The good intentions, however, were in contradiction to national policies encouraging competition between schools, fuelled by the publication of league table results in public examinations, and could not overcome the effects of an hierarchical 'diversity' of schools becoming known. The more schools gained reputations for being the most desirable, the more frustrated some parents became at what they perceived to be a second class schooling for their children. Media attention focused on charismatic head teachers with formulae for improvement, the head of one local federation of three schools, Sir Dexter Hutt, knighted for his educational efforts, being regularly praised by central government for his approaches to school discipline (Smithers 2005), his own school being nearly 70% white. Birmingham had adhered to national government policies to provide a 'diversity' of schools, and as in other cities, in so doing had created a more subtle system of selection by schools than the overt system of the 1970s. The moves towards comprehensive schools taking all abilities and with a fairer spread by social class and race, have given way to a market-oriented system in which neither schools nor parents could be blamed for attempting to maximise their own self-interest, but which does not work towards social and racial cohesion (see West et al. 2004).

The ethnic origin of school pupils in the city schools in 2004 was some 52.4% white, 18.4% Pakistani, 8.8% African-Caribbean, 6% Indian, 5.9% mixed race, 3.9% Bangladeshi 0.4% Chinese, 1.3% other Asian, and 2.8% other or unknown origin. As expected, minority children and young people were heavily concentrated in particular wards of the city, the Handsworth-Lozells ward having almost 48% of its population under nineteen, the Sparkbrook ward 41% under nineteen. In a number of wards schools were virtually 'all-minority'. As in the 1970s important questions centred on how minorities were faring within the diverse system. John Rex had continued to point out that in a highly competitive system it is incumbent on the authorities to provide equality of opportunity for all groups to achieve equally (Rex 1988, 1996). In Birmingham the authority was especially concerned to collect information on how different groups performed at key stages through their schooling, at GCSE level at 16, and in selection for the grammar schools. Selection by 'faith' is still a relatively under-researched issue, but it could be noted that one RC school was over 90% white and several others over 85% white. In contrast, the C of E School recorded only 23% white, 26% 'other' and 18% African and Caribbean students.

The study by Warren and Gillborn (2002), using information provided by the Education department and the city statistics office, provided the good news that while attainment at GCSE from 1993 to 2001 improved nationally, in Birmingham improvement was significantly greater than the national pattern. The pattern of improvement by gender mirrored national trends, girls in Birmingham achieving better results than boys in each ethnic group, Indian girls being the highest achievers of all.[9] African Caribbean boys were least likely to achieve the benchmark five higher grades at GCSE, only 17% achieving these in 2001. As with previous research findings (Gillborn and Mirza 2000) the performance of black children was shown to deteriorate as they moved through the school system, and in Birmingham, although at five years old, black pupils entered with assessments in advance of the LEA average, there was a decline in progress during their time in school. The 'black-white gap' increased during schooling for black boys and girls. African-Caribbean pupils are twice as likely to be excluded from school as white pupils, and, as in the 1970s, are over-represented in special schools and units. Pakistani pupils were also heavily over-represented in special education. In 2004, 17.7% of special school pupils were of Pakistani origin. Thus the overall pattern of educational achievement, although much improved over the years, still demonstrated the national pattern of lower school achievements of a majority of black African-Caribbean, Pakistani and Bangladeshi Muslim boys. White boys on free school meals-still the official sign of poverty, performed similarly to black boys. Since (in 2001) over 50% of Indian boys and nearly 60% of white boys failed to achieve the benchmark five A–Cs, the city demonstrably has an uphill task to improve performance of all groups in the current examination system. There is evidence, however, that the city is taking a lead in developing a curriculum and qualifications post-14 that may be more suitable for the twenty-first century for all pupils. After the swift government dismissal of the Tomlinson report (DfES 2004) advocating an overarching Diploma at 18, Birmingham heads and officials are working towards the development of a Birmingham Diploma.

Given the clear anxiety of parents in all minority groups for their children to succeed in school (Warren and Gillborn 2002; Abbas 2004) it is unsurprising that many parents enter their children for selective tests both for the state grammar schools and fee-paying private schools. High numbers of Birmingham college student interviewed by Abbas reported that they had taken selective tests, Indians being most and Bangladeshis least likely to have done so. They also reported home tutoring and help from parents and peers. The three grammar schools in the suburbs remained predominantly white. The five located in high minority wards (Handsworth has two grammar schools) were by 2004 taking almost half their pupils from minority, mainly Indian, communities. The King Edwards Handsworth school took in some 32% Indian, 6% Pakistani and 2.4% Chinese that year.[10] The entry, however, was predominantly middle class, only 2% being on free school meals, compared to 37% in the city overall. As Abbas indicated, it is middle-class Asian parents who prepare and enter their children for selective tests, believing that other schools could not provide the necessary academic education. 'Middle-class South Asian parents in petty bourgeoisie and professional employment are better able to condition their children for selective school entry' (Abbas 2004: 51). These parents considered those who did not prepare their children for entry to be ill-informed and lacking in prudence, although it also appeared that even working class Muslim parents considered not only selective schools but all those schools with larger numbers of white children to have higher standards.

Class, race and the younger generation

From a long-term perspective it certainly appears that those responsible for education in Birmingham have over the years taken their responsibilities to educate all young people seriously, and many of the children and grandchildren of those interviewed by Rex and Tomlinson in the 1970s have achieved a good deal more in terms of educational qualifications within what perforce is an unequal and selective system, than the older generations. However, dissatisfaction with the system among many parents and students is also evident, as minority parents and students continue to expect schools to provide them with an education that will enable them to enter higher education, professional jobs, or at least secure employment, and this is manifestly not happening for a large number. Minority young people, particularly South Asians, are also conscious of the need for preparation for work in a global technological economy, keeping in touch with relatives in the subcontinent via the internet and satellite phone and aware of global diaspora as family members move between countries to work. Education is still regarded as a major route to social and economic mobility, and economic security, by all groups, and there is more evident disappointment and anxiety if children do not succeed in the competition for the 'best' schools or obtain the necessary qualifications, than there was in the 1970s. Despite the movement of some middle-class minority groups to the suburbs, there is increasing locational separation of ethnic white and minority groups in the city and the problems of many schools are problems of ethnic and class differences and disadvantages.

It certainly appeared that thirty years after the Handsworth study, the forecast by Rex and Tomlinson that class divisions would open up between minority groups, especially Asians, has come about, although the nature of minority class divisions is complex and little studied. The background of Asian students continues to influence their chances of success or otherwise, in absorption into the economic and political mainstream, and their success in negotiating the diverse and selective education system. For example, many Gujerati Hindus, Punjabi Sikhs and Muslim Ismaelis, who settled in East Africa and were ejected in the late 1960s and early 1970s, have become successful entrepreneurs and professionals and are able to encourage their children in education, via economic and cultural capital, as can many Hindu and Sikh settlers from the Asian sub-continent. Poorer and less skilled Pakistani and Bangladeshi Muslim migrants still occupy marginal positions in Birmingham society, and although they want their children to succeed in education, have less knowledge about the system, few economic resources, and are frustrated by what they see as an unresponsive system. The relatively small number of Chinese children, to be found disproportionately in selective schools are held as a 'success story' by government, although the parents of the children currently in schools include business and professional migrants who came to Britain during the 1970s and are in a better position to encourage their children (Chen 2004). The Asian young people interviewed by Abbas and Warren and Gillborn felt reasonably secure with their religious and cultural identity, which they felt assisted their educational endeavours. However the extent of religious cohesion or antagonisms, especially between the various Muslim minority groups, and how far any groups influence schools and education, is still unknown. Likewise, how far white majority – often distorted – perceptions of Muslims influences their school choice decisions is also unknown.

The role of education, or lack of it, in determining the class position of young African-Caribbeans does accord to some extent with Rex and Tomlinson's conclusions of thirty years ago (1979: 281), that the odds are stacked against the young people in terms of social and economic mobility or secure employment. There has been some success among young African-Caribbeans in obtaining educational qualifications and employment, and there are numbers of successful young black students going into higher education. But it appears that the entry qualifications are more often acquired at further education college rather than school. Schools, despite help and advice from the various teams, initiatives and organisations, still appear to have lower expectations of young black people, continue to stereotype them and are not able to offer a curriculum that reflects the history, background and current experiences of black people in Britain. It is still the case that 'the West Indian (sic) child is always called ... to celebrate a culture in which s/he is systematically downgraded' and although there are initiatives against racial bullying and harassment, there are no serious and long term plans to tackle racism via the curriculum. It is of concern that (in 2001) 66% of black girls did not achieve the five essential A–C grades, but more worrying is the 83% of black boys who were not prepared by schools to do well in their school education. Although the media and police attention give publicity to the small numbers of young black men drawn into criminal activity, there are larger numbers who wish to join a mainstream 'working' class, but who slip into unemployment and temporary work, largely because of lack of educational and training opportunities, and others who try to respond to exhortations to invest in their own human capital, often at their own expense. As John Rex has pointed out, this need not be the case, 'ours is a society which has produced institutions to deal with the injustices of capitalism' (1996: 28) and it is not impossible to envisage setting right the injustices of the past for black people. The incorporation of all minorities as equal citizens in Birmingham and Britain depends on many factors other than education. But the potential for disadvantages and new forms of exclusion in national education systems, which affects placement in national and global economies, is becoming very obvious.

Thanks to John Hill, City Statistics Office and Sylvia MacNamara, Learning and Culture Team, Brimingham City Council.

Notes

Chapter 1

1. One consequence of writing this piece, and the re-reading of John Rex's work that it has required, has been to realise just how much I learned, particularly from *Key Problems*. If, for example, I were writing *Foundations of Sociology* (Palgrave 2002) today, I would be obliged to acknowledge that debt explicitly.
2. Bringing these two things together, John Rex's belief in the need to approach 'race' and ethnic relations from a social theoretical point of view – and the balance that he has tried to strike between his own *very* definite theoretical position and his equally definite understanding of the need for theoretical pluralism – is exemplified by the edited collection *Theories of Race and Ethnic Relations* (Rex and Mason 1986).
3. I do not have the reference for this review because I have taken it from the cover of the paperback edition (and therefore have to trust that the quotation is accurate).

Chapter 3

1. Rex's book was first published in 1961 as *Key Problems of Sociological Theory* (Routledge and Kegan Paul, London). It was translated into Spanish, German, Japanese, and Portuguese in 1970.
2. See José Luis Reyna, 'La investigación sociológica en México' in *Ciencias Sociales en México. Desarrollo y Perspectivas*, edited by José Luis Reyna (Mexico City: COLMEX, 1979), 49–72; Fernando Castañeda, 'La Constitución de la sociología en México' in *Desarrollo y Organización de las Ciencias Sociales en México*, edited by Francisco José Paoli Bolio (Mexico City: CRIM-Porrúa, 1990), 397–430.
3. Herminio Martins, ed., *Knowledge and Passion. Essays in Honour of John Rex* (London and New York: I.B. Tauris, 1993).

4. Martin Albrow, 'Reflections on the World Reception of Max Weber' in Martins, *Knowledge and Passion*, 79–98.

5. Jenkins, Richard, 'The Place of Theory: John Rex's Contribution to the Sociological Study of Ethnicity and 'Race' ', *Ethnic and Racial Studies* 28 (2), March (2005): 201–11.

6. Robin Cohen, 'Race and Ethnicity in a Post-Apartheid Society: Pluralism Revisited,' in Martins, *Knowledge and Passion*, 1–22

7. John Rex and David Mason, *Theories of Race and Ethnic Relations* (Cambridge: Cambridge University Press, 1986).

8. See Burton R. Clark, *Creando universidades innovadoras. Estrategias organizacionales para la transformación* (Mexico City: Editorial Porrúa y Coordinación de Humanidades, UNAM 2000).

9. A Spanish version of this text has been sent to the *Revista Mexicana de Sociología* (Mexican Journal of Sociology).

10. Nancy Utley and Oscar Fernando Contreras Velasco transcribed the tapes. That transcript was the basis for a first draft in English in the form of an interview. Professor Rex reviewed that version. Laura Velasco and Oscar Contreras then translated that text into Spanish, further refining details and adding some information based on e-mail correspondence with Professor Rex. From the Spanish version, Patricia Rosas translated the essay and edited all the text in English.

11. Nkrumah, with his proposal for Pan-Africanism based on a consciousness-raising philosophy, was one of the most important actors in the African nationalist movement. In 1950, Ghana was the first African nation to achieve independence.

12. Stuart Hall is an exception since he was born in Kingston, Jamaica, a British colony that only achieved independence in 1962. As a citizen of the British Commonwealth, he received a Rhodes Scholarship to study at Oxford.

13. In the 1960s and 1970s, Nicos Poulantzas was a major influence on the group at the *New Left Review*, where he was involved in several debates on state capitalism.

14. Andre Gunder Frank was born in Germany, emigrated to Switzerland, and studied at the University of Chicago. He worked in the administration of Salvador Allende in Chile.

15. *Sociology and the Demystification of the Modern World* (London: Routledge and Kegan Paul, 1973).

16. *Race Relations and Sociological Theory* (London: Weidenfeld and Nicolson, 1970). This book was revised and new material added in 1983, and it was then translated into Malaysian and Japanese.

17. John Rex and David Mason, editors. *Theories of Race and Ethnic Relations* (London: Cambridge University Press, 1986).

18. Mike Featherstone is the founder and current editor of journal *Theory, Culture and Society*, which has a post-modern orientation and is produced by the centre of the same name at the University of Durham.

19. In 1973, Robert Miles was part of the research team for the National Research Unit on Ethnic Relations of England's Social Science Research Council. His work has focused on the history and theory of racism and on the relationship between international migration and capitalism. In 2000, Miles was appointed professor at the University of North Carolina, Chapel Hill.

20. Chris Pickvance is the head of the department of Urban Studies at the University of Kent in England. Pickvance can be classified as a Marxist sociologist focusing on urban studies, and as Castells himself notes, Pickvance is the principal disseminator of Castells' ideas.

21. *Social Justice and the City* (Baltimore: Johns Hopkins University Press, 1973. Harvey is currently professor in the Department of Geography and Environmental Engineering, Johns

Hopkins University.

22. *The Urban Question: A Marxist Approach* (Boston, MA: MIT Press, 1977). – castelles

23. Manuel Castells, *The Information Age: Economy, Society, and Culture* (three volumes). (Oxford: Blackwell, 1996–1998; 2nd edition 2000).

24. Will Kymlicka is professor of Philosophy at Queens University in Ontario, Canada. In 2002, he taught a course called, 'Can Western Models of Minority Rights Be Applied in Eastern Europe?' His liberal position has been very influential in policies on ethnic relations in Canada.

25. Sam Whimster, a specialist on Max Weber, is a Reader in Sociology, London Metropolitan University.

Chapter 5

1. A term first coined by Walter Buckley, *Sociology and Modern Systems Theory*, Prentice Hall, New Jersey, 1967. Morphogenesis refers 'to those processes which tend to elaborate or change a system's given form, structure or state' (p. 58). It is contrasted to morphostasis which refers to those processes in a complex system that tend to preserve the above unchanged.

2. As distinct from 'action'. This distinction, insisted upon by Max Weber, is properly defended by Colin Campbell, *The Myth of Social Action*, Cambridge University Press, 1996.

3. John Rex has always opposed the Humean account. See *Key Problems* (Rex 1961: ch. 1).

4. This shows that I do not follow Weber in representing 'affectual action' as a separate form.

5. The 'epistemic fallacy' is the substitution of how matters are taken to be for how they in fact are, even if we cannot or do not know the latter. See Andrew Collier (1994), *Critical Realism*, London: London: 76–85.

Chapter 6

1. The support of the Office for National Statistics, CCSR and ESRC/JISC Census of Population Programme is gratefully acknowledged. The author alone is responsible for the interpretation of the data.

2. It is important to note that we are using the categories assigned by the census. Most of the children are UK citizens and not citizens of Bangladesh or India *etc*. Strictly one should refer to these children as 'attributed a Bangladeshi ethnic background in the 2001 Census'. The use of 'ethnic' labels in the census is not unproblematic, see Moore (1983).

3. Because of small numbers, the North East was excluded from this particular analysis.

Chapter 7

1. The university discipline 'International Migration and Ethnic Relations' is now being taught in some universities both at undergraduate and graduate levels. It is in Scandinavia often abbreviated IMER.

2. Early examples are the Centre for Research in Ethnic Relations at the University of Warwick, UK, and the Stockholm University Centre for IMER Research in Sweden.

3. The connotation of the term 'immigration policy' varies. It will in this article be used to sum up both control and integration policy.

4. Hammar, T. (1985, edit.) *European Immigration Policy, a Comparative Study*, Cambridge: University Press. A highly qualified team of scholars from six countries was invited and given full freedom to elaborate a scheme for evaluation and comparison of Sweden and five countries, of which three had a colonial past (Britain, France and the Netherlands), and two were 'guest-worker' countries (Germany and Switzerland).– I am grateful to John Rex, who

gave me a most valuable assistance, both in finding the most competent participants in the project, and for publication of the book in the ESRC comparative ethnic and race relations series, Cambridge University Press.

Chapter 11

1. West Indian and Asian was the terminology used in the 1970s. In the household survey for the research 1,100 heads of households were interviewed. This included 400 black men and women born in ex-British Caribbean territory, 331 from Jamaica, 300 (mainly) men from the Asian sub-continent, 243 from Indian and 42 from Pakistan, and 400 'white' British. Three hundred unstructured interviews were carried out with councillors, local government officials, teachers, social workers, community activists (from all groups) employers, High Commissioners, church, temple and mosque leaders, and others.

2. The Birmingham city centre shopping precinct, alleged to be one of the largest in Europe, employs younger minority people than white.

3. In 1976 there was discrimination against the relatively few black workers at the Longbridge plant via an aptitude test for promotion (Rex and Tomlinson 1979, 125). The Longbridge-Rover car plant eventually closed in 2005, its closure affecting many other industries and services in the city.

4. Civil wars in the 1990s have brought in refugees and asylum seekers from Somalia, Sudan, Nigeria, Sri Lanka, Turkey, Bosnia, Kosova, Sierra Leone, Afghanistan and other places. The single European Act entitles more movement of EU nationals and migrant labour has been encouraged by the formalization of work permits.

5. The Conservative government in the early 1990s built on their city technology college programme to encourage secondary schools to develop a specialism in the curriculum, with funding from business and communities to be matched by government. The New Labour government post 1997 continued this policy and by 2004 over half secondary schools had a specialism, notably technology, languages, arts and sports, with a few in business, engineering science and maths. Sports schools tended to be located in inner cities.

6. Tomlinson's children were in Birmingham schools in the 1970s and during the 1977 general election, at which the National Front put up several candidates, were handed NF literature at the school gates. There were demonstrations against racist groups and attacks in 1976 and 1977.

7. Tim Brighouse, Chief Education officer in Birmingham in the 1990s, was appointed in 2003 as a Commissioner with a brief to improve London schools. He has suggested a 'collegiate' system similar to the Birmingham system.

8. The Director of the School Effectiveness team has a staff of six who are particularly concerned with race and attainment research. There are currently studies of attainment of minorities from the Key Stages (KS) 1 to 4, a study of the attainments of African-Caribbean children in primary school, a study of mainly Irish underachieving children, and a study of Somali children. This large group, mainly entering as refugees from civil wars in Somalia in the 1990s (see Lewis 2004) have particular language problems, some having migrated via Sweden and Holland.

9. GCSE performance (A–C level) by gender and ethnicity in 2001 were: Indian girls 65%, White and Bangladeshi girls 50%, Indian boys 49%, Pakistani girls 42%, White boys 39%, African-Caribbean girls 34%, Pakistani boys 31%, Bangladeshi boys 27%, African-Caribbean boys 17%. All groups except Bangladeshi boys improved over three years (Warren and Gillborn 2002: 9).

10. Adapted from Birmingham Education Department statistics, 2004.

References

Chapter 1

Bourne, J., and A. Sivanandan(1980), 'Cheer-leaders and Ombudsmen: The Sociology of Race Relations in Britain', *Race and Class*, 21(4): 331–352.

Gilroy, P. (1980), 'Managing the 'Underclass': A Further Note on the Sociology of Race Relations in Britain', *Race and Class*, vol. xxii, no. 1, pp. 47–62.

Lawrence, E. (1982), 'In the abundance of water the fool is thirsty: sociology and black 'pathology', in Centre for Contemporary Cultural Studies, *The Empire Strikes Back: Race and racism in 70s Britain*, London: Hutchinson.

Martins, H. (1993) (ed.), *Knowledge and Passion: Essays in Honour of John Rex*. London: I. B. Tauris.

Moore, R. (1977), 'Becoming a Sociologist in Sparkbrook', in C. Bell and H. Newby (eds.) *Doing Sociological Research*, London: George Allen and Unwin.

Rex, John (1961), *Key Problems of Sociological Theory*. London: Routledge and Kegan Paul.

—— (1970), *Race Relations in Sociological Theory*. London: Routledge and Kegan Paul.

—— (1981), *Social Conflict*. London: Longman.

—— (1983), *Race Relations in Sociological Theory*, second edition. London: Routledge and Kegan Paul.

—— (1986), *Race and Ethnicity*. Milton Keynes: Open University Press.

—— (1991), *Ethnic Identity and Ethnic Mobilisation in Britain*. Warwick: Centre for Research in Ethnic Relations.

—— (1996), *Ethnic Minorities in the Modern Nation State*, Basingstoke: Macmillan.

———— and D. Mason (1986) (eds.), *Theories of Race and Ethnic Relations*, Cambridge: Cambridge University Press.

———— and Robert Moore (1967), *Race, Community and Conflict: A Study of Sparkbrook*. Oxford: Oxford University Press.

———— and Sally Tomlinson (1979), *Colonial Immigrants in a British City: A Class Analysis*. London: Routledge and Kegan Paul.

Chapter 4

Bartov, O. (1997), 'Of past wrongs – and their redressing' (Review of Karsh 1997), *Times Literary Supplement* no. 4935, 31 October, p. 13–14.

Bulmer, M. (1993), 'The apotheosis of liberalism ? *An American Dilemma* after fifty years in the context of the lives of Gunnar and Alva Myrdal', *Ethnic and Racial Studies*, vol. 16 no. 2, April: 345–57.

———— (1998), 'Conceptualising fractured societies' [introduction to special issue on *Aspects of ethnic division in contemporary Israel]* *Ethnic and Racial Studies* vol. 21, no. 3, May: 383–407.

———— (2005), 'Sociology in Britain in the Twentieth Century: differentiation and establishment', in A H Halsey and W G Runciman (eds) *British Sociology seen from within and without*. Oxford: Oxford University Press for the British Academy: 36–53.

Glaser, Daryl J. (2003), 'Zionism and Apartheid: A Moral Comparison.' *Ethnic and Racial Studies* vol. 26, no. 3: pp. 403–421.

Guibernau, M. and J. Rex (1997) (eds.), *The Ethnicity Reader: nationalism, multiculturalism and migration*. Cambridge: Polity.

Halsey, A. H. (2004), *A History of Sociology in Britain: Science, Literature and Society*. Oxford: Oxford University Press.

Karsh, E. (1997), *Fabricating Israeli History: the 'New Historians'*. London: Frank Cass.

Mannheim, K. (1940), *Ideology and Utopia*. London: Routledge and Kegan Paul.

Morris, A. J. A. (1977), *C P Trevelyan 1870–1958: portrait of a radical*. Belfast: Blackstaff Press.

Myrdal, G. (1953), *The Political Element in the Development of Economic Theory*. London: Routledge and Kegan Paul.

———— (1958), *Value in Social Theory: a selection of essays on methodology edited by P Streeten*. London: Routledge and Kegan Paul.

———— with R. Sterner and A. Rose (1944), *An American Dilemma: the Negro Problem and Modern Democracy*. New York: Harper and Row.

Oakes, G. (1988), *Weber and Rickert: Concept Formation in the Cultural Sciences*. Cambridge, MA: MIT Press.

Platt, J. (2003), *The British Sociological Association: a sociological history*. Durham: Sociologypress.

———— (1959), 'The Plural Society in Sociological Theory', *British Journal of Sociology*, vol. 10, No.2, June, 114–124.

———— (1961), *Key Problems in Sociological Theory*. London: Routledge and Kegan Paul.

———— (1970), *Race Relations in Sociological Theory*. London: Weidenfeld and Nicolson.

——— (1974), *Sociology and the Demystification of the Modern World*. London: Routledge and Kegan Paul.

——— (1997), 'The concept of a multicultural society', in Guibernau and Rex (1997) (eds.): 205–220.

——— and D. Mason (1986) (eds.), *Theories of Race and Ethnic Relations*. Cambridge: Cambridge University Press.

——— and R. Moore (1967), *Race, Community and Conflict: a study of Sparkbrook*. Oxford: Oxford University Press, for the Institute of Race Relations.

Rouhana, N. N. (1997), *Palestinian Citizens in an Ethnic Jewish State*. New Haven, CT: Yale University Press.

Samuel, Herbert (Viscount) (1945), *Memoirs*. London: Cresset Press.

Trevelyan, Laura (2006), *A very British family: the Trevelyans and their world*, London: I B Tauris

Wasserstein, B. (1992), *Herbert Samuel: a political life*. Oxford: Clarendon Press.

Weber, M. (1949), *The Methodology of the Social Sciences* [translated and edited by E. A. Shils and H. A. Finch] Glencoe, IL: The Free Press.

Web site: <http://www.john-rex.com/> visited on January 15 2006.

Chapter 5

Archer, Margaret S. (1979), *Social Origins of Educational Systems*, London and Beverly Hills: Sage.

——— (1988), *Culture and Agency: The Place of Culture in Social Theory*, Cambridge: Cambridge University Press.

——— (2001), *Being Human: The Problem of Agency*, Cambridge: Cambridge University Press.

——— (2003), *Structure, Agency and the Internal Conversation*, Cambridge: Cambridge University Press.

——— (2004), 'Emotions as Commentaries on Human Concerns', in Jonathan Turner (ed.) *Advances in Group Processes*, Elsevier: Elsevier Science: 327–356.

——— and Jonathan Q. Tritter (2001) (eds.), *Rational Choice Theory: Resisting Colonisation*, London: Routledge and Taylor and Francis.

Bhaskar, Roy (1989a), *Reclaiming Reality*, London: Verso.

——— (1989b), *The Possibility of Naturalism*, London: Harvester Wheatsheaf.

Bourdieu, Pierre (1977), *Outline of a Theory of Practice*, Cambridge: Cambridge University Press.

——— (1990), *The Logic of Practice*, Oxford: Polity Press.

Frankfurter, Harry G. (1988), *The Importance of What We Care About*, Cambridge: Cambridge University Press.

Hollis, Martin (1977), *Models of Man; Philosophical Thoughts on Social Action*, Cambridge: Cambridge University Press.

——— (1989), 'Honour Among Thieves', *Proceedings of the British Academy*, LXXV: 163–180.

———— and Steve Smith (1990), *Explaining and Understanding International Relations*, Oxford: Clarendon Press.

———— ———— (1991), *Explaining and Understanding International Relations*, Oxford: Clarendon Press.

———— ———— (1994), 'Two Stories about Structure and Agency', *Review of International Studies*, 20(4): 241–251.

James, William (1890), *The Principles of Psychology*, vol. 1, London: Macmillan.

Jenkins, Richard (2005), 'The place of theory: John Rex's contribution to the study of ethnicity and 'race' ", *Ethnic and Racial Studies*, 28(2): 201–211.

Mills, C. Wright (1959), *The Sociological Imagination*, Oxford: Oxford University Press.

Rex, J. (1961), *1961 Key Problems in Sociological Theory*, London: Routledge and Kegan Paul.

Searle, John (1990), *Mind, Language and Society*, London: Weidenfeld and Nicolson.

Chapter 6

Bell, Colin and Howard Newby (1977) (eds.), *Doing Sociological Research*, London: Allen and Unwin.

Bradshaw, Jonathon and Roy Sainsbury (2000), *Experiencing Poverty*, Aldershot: Ashgate.

Hancock, L. (1995), 'Tenant Participation and the Housing Classes Debate', PhD Thesis, University of Liverpool (unpublished).

Moore, Robert (1983), *The Question of Race in the 1986 Census* The Home Affairs Committee of the House of Commons, 1982 – 3 HC33-II 138 – 146

———— and Tina Wallace (1975), *Slamming the Door: the administration of immigration control*, London: Martin Robertson.

———— (1993), 'Citizenship and the Sociological Agenda', in Martins, H. (ed) *Knowledge and Passion: essays in Honour of John Rex*, London and New York: I B Tauris.

———— (2000), 'The Debris of Empire: the 1981 Nationality Act and the Oceanic Territories', *Immigrants and Minorities*, 19(1): 1–24.

Office of the Deputy Prime Minister (2004), <www.odpm.gov.uk/odpm/SOA/ LASummaries2004.xls>. Accessed 7 January 2007.

Rex, John and Robert Moore (1967), *Race Community and Conflict*, Oxford: Oxford University Press.

Wathan, Jo, Claire Holdsworth and Rachel Leeser (2001), *A Rule-Based Definition for Census Family and Household Reference Persons: Choices and Impacts*, CCSR Occasional Paper no. 21.

Chapter 7

Bauböck, R. (1999), 'Immigration Control without Integration Policy: An Austrian Dilemma', in G. Brochmann and T. Hammar (eds.) *Mechanisms of Immigration Control, A Comparative Analysis of European Regulation Policies*, Oxford: Berg: 97–134.

Cornelius, W. A., T. Tsuda, P. L. Martin and J. A. Hollifield (1994) (eds.), *Controlling Immigration, A Global Perspective*, first edition, Stanford, CA: Stanford University Press.

——— ——— — — (2004) (eds.), *Controlling Immigration, A Global Perspective*, second edition, Stanford, CA: Stanford University Press.

Fenger-Grön, C. et al. (2003), *Når du strammer garnet, et opgör med mobning af mindretal og ansvarslös asylpolitik* (Restrictions – a Critical Account of the Mobbing of Minorities and of a Reckless Asylum Policy), Denmark, Aarhus: Universitetsforlag.

Freeman, G. P. (1995), 'Modes of Immigration Politics in Liberal Democratic States', *International Migration Review*, 29(4): 881–902.

——— (2002), 'Winners and Losers: Politics and the Costs and Benefits of Migration', in A. M. Messina (ed.) *West European Immigration and Immigrant Policy in the New Century*. Westport: Praeger Publishers.

Hammar, T. (2001), 'Politics of Immigration Control and Politicisation of International Migration', in M. A. B. Siddique (ed.) *International Migration into the 21st Century, Essays in Honour of Professor Reginald Appleyard*, Cheltenham: Edward Elgar, 15–28.

——— (1999), 'Closing the Doors to the Swedish Welfare State', in G. Brochmann and T. Hammar (eds.) *Mechanisms of Immigration Control: A Comparative Analysis of European Regulation Policies*, Oxford: Berg, 169–202.

Layton-Henry, Z. (1992), *The Politics of Immigration: Immigration, 'Race' and 'Race' Relations in Post-War Britain*, Oxford: Blackwell.

Martins, H. (1993) (ed.), *Knowledge and Passion, Essays in Honour of John Rex*, London: I B Tauris and Co Ltd Publishers.

Messina, A. M. and C. V. Thouez (2002), 'The Logics and Politics of a European Immigration Regime', in Anthony M. Messina (ed.) *West European Immigration and Immigrant Policy in the New Century*, Westport: Praeger Publishers, 97–120.

Oriol, M. (1981), *Report on Studies of the Human and Cultural Aspects of Migrations in Western Europe 1918–1979*. Strasbourg: European Science Foundation, ESF.

Rex, J., D. Joly and C. Wilpert (1987), *Immigrant Associations in Europe*, Aldershot: Gower.

Spencer, S. (2003), 'Introduction' in S. Spencer (ed.) *The Politics of Migration, Managing, Opportunity, Conflict and Change*, Oxford: Blackwell.

Westin, C. (1993), 'Xenophobic Activation, Public Opinion and Integration Policies in Europe', in Charles Westin (ed.) *Racism, Ideology and Political Organisation*, Stockholm: Ceifo, 167–181.

Chapter 9

Abbas, T. (1997), 'British South Asian Youth: A New Diaspora', *Dialogue*, December: 4–5.

——— (2002), 'A retrospective study of South Asian further education college students and their experiences of secondary school', *Cambridge Journal of Education* 32(1): 73–90.

——— and M. Anwar (2005), 'An analysis of race equality policy and practice in the city of Birmingham, UK', *Local Government Studies* 31(1): 53–68.

Ahmed, A. S. (1995), ' 'Ethnic cleansing': a metaphor for our time?', *Ethnic and Racial Studies* 18(2): 1–25.

Althusser, L. (1977), *For Marx*, Translated by Ben Brewster, London: NLB.

Anwar, M. (1979), *The Myth of Return: Pakistanis in Britain*, London: Heinemman.

Castles, S. and G. Kosack (1973), *Immigrant Workers and Class Structure in Western Europe*, London: Oxford University Press.

Dayha, B. (1974), 'The nature of Pakistani ethnicity in industrial cities in Britain', in A. Cohen (ed.) *Urban Ethnicity*, Tavistock, London.

Giddens, A. (1982), *Profiles and Critiques in Social Theory*, Berkeley and Los Angeles: University of California Press.

Gilory, P. (1980), 'Managing the 'Underclass': A Further Note on the Sociology of Race Relations in Britain', *Race and Class*, 22(1):47–62.

———— (1987), *There Ain't Black in the Union Jack*, London: Hutchinson.

Lawrence, E. (1982), 'Just plain common sense: the 'roots' of racism', in Centre for Contemporary Cultural Studies (ed.) *The Empire Strikes Back*, London: Hutchinson.

Mattausch, J. (1998), 'From subjects to citizens: British 'East African Asians'', *Journal of Ethnic and Migration Studies* 24(1): 121–141.

Miles, R. (1982), *Racism and Migrant Labour*, London: Routledge and Kegan Paul

———— and M. Brown (2003) (eds.) *Racism*, second edition, London: Routledge

Office for National Statistics (2001), *2001 Census*. <http://www.statistics.gov.uk>. Accessed 7 January 2007

Park, R., E. W. Burgess and R. D. McKenzie (1925), *The City*, Chicago: University of Chicago Press.

Parkin, F. (1979), *Marxism and Class Theory: a Bourgeois Critique*, London: Tavistock

Peach, C. (2000), 'The consequences of segregation' in F. W. Boal (ed) *Ethnicity and Housing. Accommodating Differences*, Aldershot: Ashgate.

Phizacklea, A. and R. Miles (1980), *Labour and Racism*, London: Routledge.

Ratcliffe, P. (1999), 'Housing inequality and 'race': some critical reflections on the concept of 'social exclusion'', *Ethnic and Racial Studies* 21(1): 1–22.

Rex, J. (1994), 'Ethnic Mobilisation in a Multi-Cultural Europe: Introduction: the Problem Stated', and 'Conclusion: The Future of Multi-Culturalism in Europe', in J. Rex and B. Drury (eds.) *Ethnic Mobilisation in a Multi-Cultural Europe*, Aldershot: Avebury.

———— (1996), *Ethnic Minorities in the Modern Nation State – Working Papers in the Theory of Multi-Culturalism and Political Integration in European Cities*, MacMillan: Basingstoke.

———— and R. Moore (1967), *Race, Community and Conflict*, Oxford: Oxford University Press.

Sarre, P., D. Phillips and R. Skellington (1989), *Ethnic Minority Housing: Explanations and Policies*, Aldershot, Avebury.

Shaw, A. (2000), *Kinship and Continuity. Pakistani families in Britain*, Amsterdam: Harwood Academic Publishers.

Solomos, J. (1982), 'The organic crisis of British capitalism: the experience of the seventies', in Centre for Contemporary Cultural Studies (ed.) *The Empire Strikes Back*, London: Hutchinson.

Ward, R. (1983), 'Race relations in Britain', in A. Stewart (ed.) *Contemporary Britain*, London: Routledge and Kegan Paul.

Weber, M. (1968), *Economy and Society*, New York: Bedminster Press.

Whitehand, J. W. R. and C. Carr (2001), *Twentieth Century Suburbs: A Morphological Approach*, London: Routledge.

Chapter 10

Adorno, T. W., E. Frenkel-Brunswick, D. J. Levinson, R. N. Sanford (1950), *The Authoritarian Personality*, New York, Harper and Row.

Bagley, C. (1970), *Social Structure and Prejudice in Five Boroughs*, London, Institute of Race Relations.

Banton, M. (1955), *The Coloured Quarter: Negro Immigrants in an English City*, London, Cape.

Benyon, J. and J. Solomos (1987) (eds.), *The Roots of Urban Unrest*, Oxford, Pergamon.

Blackstone, T., B. Parekh and P. Sanders (1998) (eds.), *Race Relations in Britain, A developing agenda*, London, Routledge.

Bradford Vision (July 2001), *Community Pride not Prejudice, Making Diversity work in Bradford*, (Chair: Sir Herman Ouseley), Bradford, Bradford Vision.

Burney, E. (1967), *Housing on Trial*, London, London: Institute of Race Relations Report and Oxford University Press.

Burnley Borough Council (December 2001), *Burnley Task Force* (Chair: Lord Tony Clarke), Burnley, Borough Council.

Cabinet Office (February 2002), *Ethnic Minorities and the Labour Market. Interim Analytical Report by the Performance and Innovation Unit*, London, Cabinet Office.

Chesler, M. A. (1976), 'Contemporary sociological theories of racism', in P. A. Katz, op. cit.

Commission for Racial Equality (1997), *A Fundamental Review of the Public Service Role of Racial Equality Councils*, report produced by KPMG for the CRE, London: CRE.

——— (2002), *A Place for Us All. Learning from Bradford, Oldham and Burnley*, CRE: London.

——— (August 2004), *Fairness for All: A New Commission for Equality and Human Rights, a response*, London: CRE.

Deakin, N. (1969), *Colour, Citizenship and British Society*, Institute of Race Relations report, Oxford: Oxford University Press.

Department for Trade and Industry (May 2004), *Fairness for All: a New Commission for Equality and Human Rights, cmnd. 6185*, London: DTI and DCA.

ECOTEC Research and Consulting Ltd/EKOS Consulting Ltd (2005), *Soho and Handsworth Area Investment Plan, Birmingham Sandwell Housing Market Renewal Area Pathfinder*, Birmingham: ECOTEC.

Foot, P. (1965), *Immigration and Race in British Politics*, Harmondsworth: Penguin.

Hall, S. (6 August 2003), 'New Labour has picked up where Thatcherism left off', *The Guardian*.

Her Majesty's Stationery Office (1965), *Race Relation Act, 1965*, London: HMSO.

——— (1968), *Race Relation Act, 1968*, London: HMSO.

——— (1987), *Race Relation Act, 1976*, London: HMSO.

——— (1998), *The Human Rights Act, 1998*, London: HMSO.

———— (2001), *Race Relation (Amendment) Act 2002*, London: HMSO.

Hill, M. and R. Issacharoff (1971), *Community Action and Race Relations: A Study of Community Relations Committees in Britain*, Oxford: Oxford University Press.

Home Office (2002), *Building Cohesive Communities: A report of the Ministerial Group on Public Order and Community Cohesion* (Chair: John Denham), London: Home Office.

———— (2005), *Improving Opportunities, Strengthening Society: the Government's strategy to increase race equality and community cohesion*, Race Cohesion, Equality and Faith Directorate, London: Home Office.

———— (June 2003), *Building a picture of community cohesion: A guide for Local Authorities and their Partners*, London: Home Office Community Cohesion Unit.

———— (November 2001), *Community Cohesion: A Report of the Independent Review Team* (Chair: Ted Cantle), London: Home Office.

Katz, P. A. (1976) (ed.), *Towards the elimination of racism*, New York: Pergamon.

Local Government Association (May 2002), *Guidance on Community Cohesion*, London: LGA.

Oldham Independent Review (December 2001), *One Oldham, One Future* (Chair: David Ritchie), Oldham: Metropolitan Borough Council.

Palmer, C. et al. (2002), *Discrimination Law Handbook*, London: Legal Action Group.

Peach, C. (1996), *Ethnicity in the 1991 Census. Volume Two: The ethnic minority populations of Great Britain*, London: HMSO.

Phillips, T. (September 2005), 'After 7/7: sleepwalking to segregation?'. Speech given to Manchester Council for Community Relations, London: CRE.

Policy Studies Institute (1988), *Review of the role and objectives of Community Relations Councils*, London: PSI/CRE.

Race Equality West Midlands (2003), *Community cohesion: concept, policy, implementation and theory. An introduction to recent community cohesion initiatives with reference to West Midlands Pathfinder programmes*, Birmingham: REWM, in association with the Government Office for the West Midlands, the Commission for Racial Equality, and West Midlands Race Equality Councils.

———— (2006), *British urban ethnic group Conflict and violence*, Birmingham: REWM.

———— (February 2005), *Confronting the racist activities of political parties. A guide for local authorities*, Race Equality Digest 12, Birmingham: REWM.

———— (June 2005), *What happened to far-right political parties in the West Midlands. An analysis of the 2005 General Election results*, Race Equality Digest 13, Birmingham: REWM.

———— (November 2005), *Opinion of ethnic communities in the immediate aftermath of the 22 October 2005 disturbances in Birmingham Lozells*. Birmingham: REWM Rapid Research Response.

———— (September 2005), *How to make the government strategy on community cohesion smarter (specific, measurable, agreed, realistic, targeted ethnically, and reciprocal)*, Race Equality Digest 16, Birmingham: REWM.

Ratcliffe, P. (1981), *Racism and reaction: A profile of Handsworth*, London: Routledge and Kegan Paul.

Reeves, F. (1981), *Race and Borough Politics*, Aldershot: Avebury.

———— and A. Allbrook (2006), *British urban ethnic group conflict and violence.* Working Paper I, Birmingham: Race Equality West Midlands.

Rex, J. (1961), *Key Problems of Sociological Theory*, London: Routledge and Kegan Paul.

———— (1970), *Race Relations in Sociological Theory*, London: Weidenfield and Nicholson.

———— (1973a), *Discovering Sociology*, London: Routledge and Kegan Paul.

———— (1973b), *Race, Colonialism and the City*, London: Routledge and Kegan Paul.

———— (1981), *Social conflict, a conceptual and theoretical analysis, London*: Longman.

———— (1986), *Race and Ethnicity*, Milton Keynes: Open University Press.

———— (1987), *'Life in the Ghetto'*, chapter 11, pp. 103–110, in J. Benyon and J. Solomos, *op. it.*

———— and R. Moore (1967), *Race, Community and Conflict: A study of Sparkbrook,* London: Institute of Race relations and Oxford University Press.

———— and S. Tomlinson (1979), *Colonial immigrants in a British city: A class analysis.* London: Routledge and Kegan Paul.

Rose, E. J. B. in association with N. Deakin et al. (1969), *Colour and Citizenship: A report on British Race Relations.* London: Institute of Race Relations and Oxford University Press.

Senior, C. and D. Manley (1955), *A Report on Jamaican Migration to Great Britain*, Duke Street, Kingston: Government Printer.

Smith, D. (1977), *Racial Disadvantage in Britain*, Handsworth: Penguin.

The Guardian (23 November 2005), 'Cities of Dreams', *Society Guardian.*

———— (23 November 2005), 'Middle Class flight and poor design damaging cities, warns Rogers', p. 11, *The Guardian.*

The Observer (20 November 2005), 'Message to the middle class: cities need you': 10, *The Observer.*

The Runnymede Trust (2002), *The Future of Multi-Ethnic Britain* (the Parekh report), London: Profile Books.

Weber, M. (1968), *Economy and Society*, three volumes, New York: Bedminster Press.

Chapter 11

Abbas, T. (2004), *The Education of British South Asians* London: Palgrave-MacMillan.

Benn, C. and C. Chitty (1996), *Thirty years On*, London: David Fulton.

Birmingham City Council (2005), <www.Birmingham.gov.uk>. Accessed 7 January 2007.

Birmingham City Council/economy (2005), <www.Birminghameconomy.org.uk>. Accessed 7 January 2007.

Burgess, S. and D. Wilson (2003), *Ethnic Segregation in England's schools*, CMPO working paper 03/86, Bristol: University of Bristol.

Chen Yuanngang (2004), *The negotiation of equality of opportunity for emergent bilingual children in English mainstream classes*, Unpublished PhD study, Goldsmiths College, University of London.

DES (1974), *Educational Disadvantage and the Needs of Immigrants* cm 5720, London: HMSO.

DfEE (1999), *Excellence in Cities*, London: The Stationary Office.

DfES (2003), *Aiming High: Raising the achievement of minority ethnic pupils*, London: Department for Education and Skills.

Gerwirtz, S., S. J. Ball and R. Bowe (1995), *Markets Equity and Choice in Education*, Buckingham: Open University Press.

Gillborn, D. and H. S. Mirza (2000), *Educational Inequalities: Mapping race, class and gender*, London: Office for Standards in Education.

Gilroy, P. (2005), *After Empire*, London: Routledge.

Goring, B. (2004), *The perspectives of Caribbean Parents on schooling and Education: Continuity and Change*, unpublished PhD, London South Bank University.

Lewis, I. M. (2004), *A Modern history of Somalia*, Oxford: James Curry.

MacPherson Sir William (1999), *The Stephen Lawrence Enquiry* cm 4262, London: The Stationary Office.

Major, J. (1997), Speech at Commonwealth Institute, London, 18 January.

Marshal, T. H. (1950), *Citizenship and Social Class*, Camdridge: Cambridge University Press.

McLagan, G. (2005), *Guns and Gangs: Inside Black Gun Crime*, London: Allison and Bushy.

Mirza, H. S. (1992), *Young Female and Black*, London: Routledge.

Noden P., A. West, M. David and A. Edge (1998), 'Choices and Destinations: transfer to secondary schools in London', *Journal of Educational Policy*, 13: 221–36.

Qualifications and Curriculum Authority (1999), *Review of the National Curriculum in England*, London: QCA.

Rex, J. (1970), *Race Relations in Sociological Theory*, London: Weidenfield and Nicolson.

——— (1973), *Race, Colonialism and the City*, London: Routldge and Kegan Paul.

——— (1986), *Race and Ethnicity*, Buckingham Open University press.

——— (1988), *The Ghetto and the Underclass*, Aldershot: Avebury.

——— (1996), *Ethnic Minorities and the Modern Nation state*, London: Macmillan.

——— and R. Moore (1967), *Race Community and Conflict*, Oxford: Oxford University Press and Institute of Race Relations.

——— and S. Tomlinson (1979), *Colonial Immigrants in a British City: A Class Analysis*, London: Routledge.

Shotte, G. (2002), *Education, Migration and Identities: relocated Montserratian children in London schools*, unpublished PhD London, Institute of Education.

Smith, Z. (2004), 'My Smart School Still failed me', *The Observer*, 12 September.

Smithers, R. (2005), 'Tough love', *Education Guardian*, 21 June.

Tomlinson, S. (1981), *Educational Subnormality*, London: Routledge

——— (1984), *Ethnic Minorities in British Schools*, London: Heinemann

——— (2005a), 'Race, ethnicity and education under New Labour', *Oxford Review of Education*, 31: 153–171.

——— (2005b), *Education in a Post-Welfare Society*, second edition, Abingdon: McGraw-Hill Open University Press.

Treasury, H. M. (2003), *Every Child Matters* cm 5860, London: The Stationary office.

Warren, S. and D. Gillborn (2002), *Race Equality and Education in Birmingham*, Birmingham: Birmingham Race Equality Partnership.

West, A., A. Hind and H. Pennell (2004), 'School Admissions and selection in comprehensive schools Policy and practice', *Oxford Review of Education*, 3: 47–369.

Index

Abbas, Tahir, 122, 132, 165, 173
affirmative action, 116
African National Congress, 14, 163
African-Americans, 48
Afshar, Haleh, 55
Ahmed, A.S., 123
Albrow, Martin, 32
Allbrook, A., 152
Allenby, Lord Edmund, 59
Althusser, L., 125
Amnesty International, 108
Anderson, Perry, 38
Anwar, M., 131, 132
apartheid, 57, 62, 163
Archer, Margaret S., 66, 69–74
Aston University, 42
asylum, 104, 107, 138
Austria, 106

Balfour Declaration, 58
Balfour, Lord Arthur James, 59
Banton, M., 6
Bartov, Omer, 58
Bauböck, R., 106
Benn, Tony, 75, 164
Benyon, J., 152

Bhaskar, Roy, 64, 66, 67
Birmingham, *see* Handsworth, *see*
    Sparkbrook, 9, 12, 18–21,
    40–41, 84, 87, 89, 90, 92, 93,
    121, 126, 132, 133, 135–139,
    142, 143, 146, 150–155,
    159–174
    Corporate Equality Scheme (CES),
        163
    education, 148, 162, 163, 166–174
    Muslims, 132, 133, 138, 161, 166,
        173
    New Commonwealth immigrants,
        136–139, 146, 147, 155, 161
    race, 141, 145, 152, 162, 163
    Race Action Partnership (BRAP),
        163
    race relations, 159
Birmingham Corporation, 155
Birnbaum, Norman, 37
Blackburn, Robin, 4
Blair, Tony, 142
Blauner, Bob, 113, 114
Bourdieu, Pierre, 7, 71
Bourne, J., 7

Bowles, S., 7
Bradford, 138, 149, 150
Bradshaw, Jonathan, 79
BRAP, *see* Birmingham, Race Action
        Partnership
Breyner, Sidney, 16
Brighouse, Tim, 169
Britain, 20, 41, 75, 79, 80, 95, 123, 126,
        137–139, 143, 146, 152–154,
        161, 163–166, 168, 169
    census data, *see* Sample of
        Anonymised Records,
        81–95, 133, 161
    Civil Rights Movement, 149
    'community cohesion' policy, 139
    ECOTEC/EKOS report, 146
    education, 163–169
    Education Action Zone (EAZ),
        166
    Human Rights Act of 1968, 137
    immigration, 102, 105, 131, 149
    Islamophobia, 150
    Muslims, *see* Birmingham, 122,
        133, 134, 150, 164, 169
    nationalism, 133
    New Commonwealth immigrants,
        127, 164
    race relations, 143, 147, 155, 159,
        164
    Race Relations Acts, 128, 137, 138,
        142, 154, 165
    racism, 150
    riots, 134, 152
    segregation, 150
British National Party, 138, 139, 143
British Sociological Association, 18
Brown, M., 125
Bulmer, M., 56
Burgess, S., 40, 126, 143, 166
Burnley, 138, 149

Campbell, Colin, 177
CAMS, 80–82, 84, 86, 95
Cantle, Ted, 139
capitalism, 123, 176
Cardoso, Fernando Enrique, 39
Carmichael, Stokely, 114
Carnegie Corporation, 51
Carr, C., 131

Castells, Manuel, 43
Castles, S., 124, 126, 128
Centre for Contemporary Cultural
        Studies, 129
CES, *see* Birmingham, Corportate
        Equality Scheme
Chen, Yuanngang, 173
Chesler, M.A., 148
Chitty, C., 164
Christians, 15, 84, 169
Church of England, 169
civil rights, 115, 116, 149
Clarke, Lord Tony, 139
class, 23, 24, 142, 143
Climbie, Victoria, 167
Clinton, President Bill, 115, 116
Cohen, Percy, 33
Cohen, Robin, 33
Collier, Andrew, 177
colonialism, 26, 28, 29, 33, 39, 53, 59
        'internal', 33, 114
colonisation, 41
Commission for Equality and Human
        Rights, 137
Commission for Racial Equality, 137
Commission of Racial Equality, 139
Commonwealth Property Owners
        Association, 40
Communist Party, 14
conditioning, 67–69
conflict, 4, 7–12, 19–22, 28, 32, 37, 48,
        54, 116, 123, 127, 129, 138,
        140, 142–144, 151, 152, 156,
        159, 163
    class, 10, 18, 19, 21–24, 128
    ethnic, 21, 23, 32, 54, 135, 138,
        139, 148, 152
    race, 21–23, 27, 116, 127, 151
    social, 34, 40, 123, 140, 151–153,
        157
    theory of, 18, 31, 39, 40, 151
Cornelius, Wayne, 103
Coser, Lewis, 7, 8
Cox, Oliver, 114, 115
CRER, 34
culture, 7, 43, 50, 66, 129

Dadoo, Dr. Yusuf Mohamed, 16
Dahrendorf, Ralf, 39

Daly, Lawrence, 38
Dayha, B., 130, 132
De Klerk, Frederik Willem, 16
Denham, John, 139
Denmark, 106
dependency theory, *see* Marxism, 31, 33
deprivation, 79–81, 86–92, 94–97
determinism, 68
DfEE, 166
DfES, 166, 171
Dilthey, Wilhelm, 49, 51
Disability Rights Commission, 137
Discourse Theory, 71
discrimination, 43, 114, 123, 126, 137,
      138, 140, 145, 147, 148
diversity, 43, 115
Du Bois, W.E.B., 115
Dudley, 138
Duff, Peggy, 37
Durham University, 47, 99
Durkheim, Émile, 5, 41, 117

EAZ, *see* Britain, Education Action
      Zone
empiricism, 48, 57, 141
Engels, Friedrich, 35
epistemology, 43, 65, 73
Equal Opportunities Commission, 137
equality, 141, 151, 157, 169
Erklaren, 63
ESF, *see* European Science Foundation,
      99
ESRC Centre for Research on Ethnic
      Relations, 4
ethnic cleansing, 123
Ethnic Minorities Achievement Grant,
      164
ethnicity, 6, 7, 9, 10, 12, 22, 41–44, 48,
      53, 60, 80, 84, 100, 115,
      121–125, 134, 140–143, 160,
      166, 178
ethnomethodology, 39, 41
European Science Foundation (ESF), 99
European Union, 138
      European Convention of Human
        Rights, 137
      European Race Directive, 137
exploitation, 9, 23, 26, 27, 123, 131, 140

Featherstone, Mike, 42
Fenger-Grön, C., 106
Forrest, 80
Frank, Andre Gunder, 38
Frankfurt University, 50
Franklin Report, 116, 117
Frankurter, H., 73
Frazier, Franklin, 112
Freeman, Gary, 104, 105
Friedan, Betty, 111, 112
Fukuyama, Francis, 25
functionalism, 5, 7, 18, 31, 32, 39, 151
Furnival, J.S., 18, 26, 32

Gale, Dr. Richard T., 134
Gandhi, Mohandas, 15, 16
Gellner, Ernest André, 9
George, Lloyd, 58
Gerwirtz, S., 164
Giddens, Anthony, 40, 125
Gillborn, Paul, 163, 164, 170, 171, 173
Gilroy, Paul, 4, 7, 129, 130, 160
Gintis, H., 7
Glass, David, 5, 39
Glazer, 54
Gluckman, Max, 7, 8, 33
Gordon, 80
Goring, B., 165
Gramsci, A., 38
Guibernau, M., 54

Hacker, Helen, 111
Haider, Jörg, 106
Hall, Stuart, 4, 11, 37, 130, 142
Halsey, A.H., 47
Hamilton, Charles, 114
Hammar, T., 104, 106
Handsworth, 9, 20, 136, 138–140, 148,
      149, 152, 154, 155, 157,
      159–163, 172
      education, 167, 168, 171
      King Edwards school, 171
      New Commonwealth immigrants,
        137
Harvard University, 18
Harvey, David, 43
hermeneutics, 66
Hill, John, 174
Hindus, 84, 172

Hitler, Adolf, 50
Hobsbawm, Eric, 9
Hollis, Martin, 62–64, 66, 71, 73
Horowitz, David, 112
House of Commons, 75
'housing classes', 145–147
    criticism of, 128–130
Howells, Tony, 169
Huddleston, Father Trevor, 15
human agency, 63, 64, 66–68, 72, 73, 76,
    130
Hume, David, 66, 68, 70
Hutt, Sir Dexter, 170

IMD, see Index of Multiple Deprivation
IMER, see International Migration and
    Ethnic Relations
immigration, 19, 91, 99–108, 131, 138,
    149
imperialism, 124
Index of Multiple Deprivation (IMD),
    81, 82, 84, 94
Indian Workers Association, 21, 143
individualism, 6, 8, 32, 62
Inner London Education Authority,
    164, 169
integration, 7, 8, 10, 19, 20, 41, 66, 93,
    100–104, 106, 138–140, 149,
    151, 157, 160
International Migration and Ethnic
    Relations, 100
International Migration and Ethnic
    Relations (IMER), 100
International Sociological Association,
    39
Irving, James, 16, 35
Islam, 132
Islamic fundamentalism, 163
Islamophobia, 138, 150
Ismaelis, 172
Israel, 48, 54–59
Israeli Sociological Association, 56

James, Henry, 65
Jenkins, Roy, 26, 137

Kant, Immanuel, 50
Kaunda, Kenneth, 17, 36
Kerner Commission, 116

Kerner Report, 116
Kierkegaard, Søren, 111
King Edwards Foundation, 167
King Edwards school, 171
Kjærsgaard, Pia, 106
Kosack, G., 124, 126, 128
Kymlicka, Will, 43

Labour Movement, 19
Labour Party, 20
Laing, R.D., 38
Latin America, 38–40
Lawrence, Eric, 4, 7, 129, 130
Lawrence, Stephen, 137
Layton-Henry, Zig, 102
The Left Review, 37
Lenin, Vladimir, 35
Lessing, Doris, 37
Lewis, Oscar, 93
Liberty Party, 14
London School of Economics, 5, 17, 23,
    39, 61

Macherson, Sir William, 165
MacIntyre, Alasdair, 37
MacNamara, Sylvia, 174
Macpherson Report, 137, 166
Mahmood, Khalid, 161
Major, John, 142, 164
Malinowski, Bronislaw, 18
Mandel, Ernest, 38
Mannheim, Karl, 35, 47, 48, 50–52, 57,
    59, 60
Marshall, T.H., 159
Martins, Herminio, 3, 32, 99
Marx, Karl, 5, 7, 23, 24, 35, 41, 117
Marxism, see dependency theory, 14,
    20, 21, 23, 24, 36–39, 41–43,
    113, 114, 122–125, 128, 129
Mason, David, 33, 54, 175
Mattausch, J., 131
Mboya, Tom, 17, 36
McKenzie, R.D., 143
McLagan, Graeme, 163
mediation, 74, 75
Merton, Robert, 39
Messina, A.M., 104
Meyers, Barton, 113
Midlands, 132

migration, 33, 41, 54, 93, 99–108, 126,
131, 138, 144, 161, 176
Miles, Robert, 21, 42, 123, 125, 129, 130
Miliband, Ralph, 37
Mills, C. Wright, 39, 62
minorities, 28, 29, 55, 113, 115, 134, 152
Mirza, H.S., 164, 171
Moore, Robert, 7, 11, 18, 53, 92, 93, 122,
126, 127, 130, 134, 136, 138,
144–147, 151, 154, 155, 159,
177
morphogenesis, 63, 64
morphostasis, 63
Morris, A.J.A., 58
multiculturalism, 9–11, 25–27, 44, 54,
93, 100, 134
Muslims, *see* Birmingham, *see* Britain,
see Ismaelis, 54, 84, 93, 122,
130, 132, 134, 138, 172, 173
Myrdal, Gunnar, 18, 47, 48, 50–54, 59,
60
myth of return, 103, 131

N'komo, Joshua, 17, 36
Naicker, Dr. Gagathura Mohambry, 16
National Committee for
Commonwealth
Immigrants, 137
National Front, 138
National League of Organizations, 38
National Research Unit on Ethnic
Relations, 41
National Union of Miners, 38
National Union of Students, 14
National Urban Taskforce, 146
nationalism, 9, 33, 35, 36, 43, 44, 54,
133, 176
NCCI, *see* Britain, National Committee
for Commonwealth
Immigrants
neo-orientalism, 134
New Conservatism, 122
New Labour, 122, 143, 161, 164, 165,
168
The New Left Review, 37, 38
The New Reasoner, 37
9/11, 134, 138, 139
Nkrumah, Kwame, 36
Noden, P., 165

Norström, 107
Norway, 106
nuclear disarmament, 37

Oakes, G., 50
objectivity, 49, 51–54, 59, 63, 64, 66–68,
71, 74, 76
'occupational apartheid', 114
ODPM, 81
Ofsted, 169
Oldham, 138, 149
ontology, 64–67, 71, 75, 76
oppression, 9, 23, 113, 123, 140, 156
orientalism, 134
Ouseley, Sir Herman, 139, 150

Palestine, 48, 54
Park, Robert, 40, 53, 112, 126, 143
Parkin, F., 124
Parsons, Talcott, 7, 8, 39, 48
Parsonsian theory, 31, 139
action schema, 5, 48, 49
parthenogenesis, 67
Peach, C., 131, 132
Penrose, Jan, 55
Pettigrew, Thomas, 113
Phillips, Trevor, 143
Phizacklea, A., 123
Pickvance, Chris, 43
Platt, J., 47
pluralism, 7, 18, 25, 26, 32, 53
Popper, Karl, 65
positive neutralism, 37
positivism, 5, 39, 48, 50
postmodernism, 42
Poulantzas, Nicos, 176
Powell, Enoch, 102
pragmatism, 71
prejudice, 113, 114, 140

QCA, *see* Qualifications and
Curriculum Authority
Qualifications and Curriculum
Authority, 166
Qualifications and Curriculum
Authority (QCA), 166

race, *see* United States, 18, 21, 35, 41, 42,
60, 99, 112–116, 121, 122,
124, 126, 134, 141, 145, 160

discrimination, 43, 140, 147–148
equality, 140, 141, 151, 157, 169
inequality, 116, 135
injustice, 116
media reporting of, 162
nature of, 21
policy, 116
prejudice, 113, 140
science, 42
'race', 6, 7, 9, 12, 22, 53, 124, 126, 134,
    160, 162
Race Relations Board, 137
racial oppression model, 113
racialisation, 40
racialised groups, 126
racialism, 140
racism, 7, 21, 42, 102, 112, 115, 116, 123,
    137, 138, 140, 150, 155, 176
Ranke, Leopold von, 58
Ratcliffe, P., 130
Rational Choice Theory, 71
realism, see Social Realism, 66–69,
    71–74
Redfield, 143
reductionism
    psychological, 51
Reed, Adolph, 116
Reeves, Frank, 152
reflexivity, 68, 70–75
refugees, 102, 108, 138
relations
    class, 33
    ethnic, 23, 32–34, 42, 43, 100, 135,
        156
    race, 6, 9, 21, 23, 28, 32, 42, 51, 53,
        54, 112–117, 129, 135–143,
        145, 151, 152, 155–157, 159
      Birmingham, 141
    'race' relations, 7, 48, 54
    social, 5, 6, 32, 125, 134, 144, 155
Relf, Robert, 138
REWM, 139
Rickert, Heinrich, 47, 50
riots, 20, 134, 138, 152–154, 163
Ritchie, David, 139
Rogers, Lord, 146
Rose, A., 51
Roth, Gunther, 44
Rouharla, Nadim, 56

Rowntree, Benjamin Seebohm, 79
Runnymede Trust, 141

Sainsbury, Roy, 79
Sample of Anonymised Records (SAR),
    79, 80, 84, 95
Samuel, Herbert, 58, 59
SAR, see Sample of Anonymised
    Records
Sarre, P., 127
Saville, John, 37
Schwarzenbach, James, 102
science
    concept of race, 42
    natural, 5, 50
    'normal', 12
    social, 31, 32, 34, 43, 51, 52
Searle, John, 65
segregation, 131, 139, 144, 150
7/7, 134, 139
Shaw, A., 132
Shotte, G., 166
Sikhs, 84, 172
Simmel, Georg, 5, 7
Sivanandan, 7
Smith College, 112
Smith, Ian, 14
Smith, M.G., 18, 54
Smith, Steve, 64
Smith, Steven, 26, 32, 63, 64, 66
Smith, Z., 166
Smithers, R., 170
Smutts, General Jan Christiaan, 15
social agency, 67
Social Realism, 64, 67, 68, 72
Social Science Research Council of
    England, 41
social structure, 63, 64, 66–68, 72, 73,
    76, 130
social-conflict theory, 33
society, 25–27
sociology, 42, 115, 140–142
    Chicago school, 11, 18, 42, 115,
        143
    functionlism, 18
    interpretative, 39, 49, 63
    structural-functionalist, 31
    urban, 18, 43, 122
    values, 47–53

Solomos, J., 129, 152
South African National Union of
        Students, 4
Sparkbrook, 11, 12, 18, 19, 84, 91–93,
        122, 126, 130–134, 136, 138,
        145, 147, 150, 154, 155, 157,
        159, 161, 170
Spencer, Sarah, 107, 108
SSRC Research Unit on Ethnic
        Relations, *see* ESRC Center
        for Reasearch on Ethnic
        Relations, 54
Stavenhagen, Rodolfo, 33
Sterner, R., 51
subjectivity, 63, 64, 66–76
Sweden, 106

terrorism, 93, 134, 152
Thatcher, Margaret, 142
Thompson, E.P., 37
Thouez, C.V., 104
Tomlinson, Sally, 7, 9, 12, 136, 139–141,
        148, 149, 152, 155, 156, 159,
        160, 162, 164, 165, 167, 168,
        171–173, 178
Tonnies, 143
Toulmin, Stephen, 4
transnational, 44, 131
Treaty of Amsterdam, 137
Trevelyan, Charles, 58, 60
Tritter, Jonathan Q., 71
'twilight zones', 40, 126, 144, 145, 147,
        154, 155

UN Commission on Torture, 108
underclass, 9, 125, 128, 148, 151
UNESCO, 42, 99
        Experts Commission,
                International Experts Group,
                21, 22
        International Experts Committee
                on Racism and Race
                Prejudice, 42
United States, 103, 114, 116
        affirmative action, 116
        California Proposition 209, 116
        Civil Rights Revolution, 115
        Initiative on Race, 115, 116

President's Advisory Board on
        Race, 117
    race, 112, 116
    race relations, 51–53, 113
University of Leeds, 31, 35, 36
University of Warwick, 41
        Centre for Research in Ethnic
                Relations (CRER), 34, 99,
                121
        Department of Sociology, 33
urban theory, 53, 143–145

Wales, 133
Ward, R., 131
Warren, S., 163, 170, 171, 173
Wasserstein, B., 58, 59
Weber, Max, 5, 7, 8, 23, 24, 32, 39, 41,
        43, 47–51, 53, 57, 59, 61–64,
        66, 76, 117, 122, 125–128,
        140–142, 153–155, 177
Weizmann, Chaim, 59
West Midlands, 133
West, A., 170
Westin, C., 105
Whimster, Sam, 44
'white flight', 132
'white racism', 115
Whitehand, J.W.R., 131
Williams, Raymond, 37
Wilson, D., 166
Wirth, Louis, 113, 143
Wittgenstein, Ludwig, 66
Wolverhampton, 138
Workers Educational Association, 35

xenophobia, 102, 138